COMMERCIAL LAW AND PRACTICE

COMMERCIAL LAW AND PRACTICE

Trevor Adams BSc, PhD, Solicitor

Alexis Longshaw BA (Oxon), Solicitor

JORDANS

2004

Published by
Jordan Publishing Limited
21 St Thomas Street
Bristol BS1 6JS

British Library Cataloguing-in-Publication Data
A catalogue record for this book is available from the British Library.

ISSN 1353–3568
ISBN 0 85308 906 X

Printed in Great Britain by Hobbs The Printers Ltd of Southampton

PREFACE TO THIS EDITION

This edition builds on the extensive revisions to the previous version. Alexis Longshaw remains responsible for Chapters 3 and 5 in Part I on Commercial Agreements, for Chapters 18 and 19 on Competition Law, and for Appendix 1 on Consumer Credit. I am extremely thankful that she continues to do so.

I would also like to express my gratitude to my colleagues on the Commercial Law team at the College for material they have contributed, most especially Nick Hancock who kindly provided the material for Chapter 4 and has made many helpful suggestions about the book.

The content of Parts I and II, Commercial Agreements and International Sale Agreements have been fleshed out and some new cases added. Part III on Intellectual Property has had a considerable number of new cases added, and existing accounts expanded and, hopefully, clarified for the reader. This edition is therefore more a matter of evolution rather than revolution.

As ever, I am grateful to the forbearance of the director at the Chester branch, Andrew Chadwick, especially when I have been preoccupied with this book.

As ever, my thanks to Martin West and Robbie Carnegie at Jordans for their help and patience.

TREVOR ADAMS
The College of Law
Chester

FURTHER STUDY

The following books may be of interest to readers wishing to pursue a particular topic further. In addition, there are some references to internet sources in the text, as well as the obvious ones such as the European Commission sites and the UK legislation ones.

Sale of Goods

Atiyah, Adams and MacQueen *The Sale of Goods* 10th edn (Longman, 2001)

Encyclopedia of Forms and Precedents 5th edn (Butterworths), vol 34 on Sale of Goods (1991) and Service Volume D (1995)

Rosenberg *Practical Commercial Precedents* (Sweet & Maxwell), section on Sale of Goods: Precedent L1.

(The above works have useful sections on exclusion of liability.)

Drafting

Berg *Drafting Commercial Agreements* (Butterworths, 1991)

Christou *Boilerplate: Practical Clauses* 2nd edn (Sweet & Maxwell, 1995)

Guest *Chitty on Contracts* 27th edn (Sweet & Maxwell, 1994)

Marketing Agreements

Practical Commercial Precedents and the *Encyclopedia of Forms and Precedents* have useful sections on agency distribution and other types of marketing agreement. See also:

Christou *International Agency, Distribution and Licensing Agreements* (Longmans, 1996)

Kenyon-Slade and Thornton *Schmittner's Commercial Agency and Distribution Agreements* (Sweet & Maxwell, 1992)

Commercial Law

Bradgate *Commercial Law* 3rd edn (Butterworths, 2000)

D'Arcy, Murray and Cleave *Schmitthoff's Export Trade* 10th edn (Sweet & Maxwell, 2000)

Goode *Commercial Law* 2nd edn (Penguin, 1995)

International Chambers of Commerce *Incoterms 2000* (ICC Publishing, 2000)

Sealey and Hooly *Commercial Law* 2nd edn (Butterworths, 1999)

Competition Law

Lindrup *Butterworths Competition Law Handbook* 6th edn (Butterworths, 2001)

Whish *Competition Law* 4th edn (Butterworths, 2001)

Goyder *EC Competition Law* (Oxford University Press, 1998)

Bellamy and Child *EC Law of Competition* (Sweet & Maxwell, 2001)

A number of works have been written specifically on the Competition Act 1998, including:

Coleman and Grenfell *The Competition Act 1998: Law and Practice* (Oxford University Press, 1999)

Frazer and Hornsby *The Competition Act 1998: A Practical Guide* (Jordans, 1999)

Intellectual Property

Cornish *Intellectual Property* 4th edn (Sweet & Maxwell, 1999)

CIPA Guide to the Patents Acts (Sweet & Maxwell, 1996)

Phillips and Firth *Introduction to Intellectual Property Law* 4th edn (Butterworths, 2001)

(For works which consider the relationship of competition law and intellectual property, in particular in relation to licensing, see the list under Marketing Agreements above.)

Consumer Credit

Goode *Consumer Credit Law and Practice* (Butterworths, 2000)

Guest and Lloyd *Encyclopaedia of Consumer Credit Law* (Sweet & Maxwell, 2000)

Information Technology

Reed and Angel *Computer Law* 4th edn (Blackstone, 2000)

Susskind *Transforming the Law* (Oxford University Press, 2000)

CONTENTS

TABLE OF CASES

References in the right-hand column are to paragraph and Appendix numbers.

TABLE OF STATUTES

References are to paragraph and Appendix numbers.

TABLE OF STATUTORY INSTRUMENTS

References in the right-hand column are to paragraph and Appendix numbers.

TABLE OF EC LEGISLATION AND OTHER MATERIALS

References in the right-hand column are to paragraph and Appendix numbers.

Conventions and Agreements

TABLE OF ABBREVIATIONS

ADR	Alternative Dispute Resolution
ALCS	Authors' Licensing and Collecting Society
BEA 1882	Bills of Exchange Act 1882
CA 1957	Cheques Act 1957
CA 1998	Competition Act 1998
CDPA 1988	Copyright, Designs and Patents Act 1988
CFR	Cost and Freight
CIF	Cost, Insurance and Freight
CIP	Carriage and Insurance Paid To
CJJA 1982	Civil Jurisdiction and Judgments Act 1982
CLA	Copyright Licensing Agency Ltd
CPT	Carriage Paid To
CTM	Community Trade Mark
DAF	Delivered at Frontier
DC	debtor-creditor
DCS	debtor-creditor-supplier
DDP	Delivered Duty Paid
DDU	Delivered Duty Unpaid
DEQ	Delivered Ex Quay Duty Paid
DES	Delivered Ex Ship
DGFT	Director-General of Fair Trading
DTI	Department of Trade and Industry
ECB	extortionate credit bargain
EDI	Electronic Data Interchange
EEA	European Economic Area
EFTA	European Free Trade Area
EPC 1973	European Patent Convention 1973
EXW	Ex Works
FAS	Free Alongside
FCA	Free Carrier
FOB	Free On Board
FSR	*Fleet Street Reports*
ICANN	Internet Corporation for Assigned Names and Numbers
ICC	International Chamber of Commerce
IP	intellectual property
MCPS	Mechanical Copyright Protection Society
NLA	Newspaper Licensing Agency Ltd
OFT	Office of Fair Trading
PA 1977	Patents Act 1977
PCP	Rosenberg *Practical Commercial Precedents* (Sweet & Maxwell)
PCT	Patent Co-operation Treaty
PLS	Publishers Licensing Society
PPL	Phonographic Performance Ltd
RDA 1949	Registered Designs Act 1949
RPA 1976	Resale Prices Act 1976
RPC	*Reports of Patent, Design and Trade Mark Cases*
RTPA 1976	Restrictive Trade Practices Act 1976
RUC	restricted-use credit
SGA 1979	Sale of Goods Act 1979
SGSA 1982	Supply of Goods and Services Act 1982
UCP 500	Uniform Customs and Practice for Documentary Credits
UCTA 1977	Unfair Contract Terms Act 1977

ULIS	Uniform Law on the International Sale of Goods
UNCITRAL	UN Commission on International Trade Law
URDG	Uniform Rules for Demand Guarantees (ICC)
UUC	unrestricted-use credit
VPL	Video Performance Ltd
WIPO	World Intellectual Property Organisation

PART I

COMMERCIAL AGREEMENTS

Chapter 1

INTRODUCTION TO COMMERCIAL CONTRACTS

1.1 DOES COMMERCIAL LAW EXIST?

If the answer to this were in the negative, then this would be a very short book. Commercial transactions permeate business in all countries which engage in trade. In this book, we have brought some typical kinds of commercial contract together, though consumer contracts are not dealt with here.

You will see that the topics include:

*   sale of goods, both domestic and international;
*   carriage arrangements;
*   payment and security for international transactions, agency;
*   distribution and the effects of competition law both UK and EU; and
*   the use of conventions such as Incoterms and Uniform Customs and Practice for documentary credits.

These are just an arbitrary collection of topics, though there are others which could have been added. They have been chosen to illustrate the main areas of commercial contract law that a solicitor could reasonably expect to come across in practice. We now need to see what ties these disparate areas together.

1.2 THE PRINCIPLES OF COMMERCIAL LAW

Professor Roy Goode is a leading expert on commercial law. In 'The codification of commercial law' [1988] 14 Mon LR 135, he describes eight principles of commercial law:

*   party autonomy (freedom to contract as the parties wish);
*   predictability;
*   flexibility to accommodate new practices;
*   good faith (although English law is ambivalent);
*   the encouragement of self-help;
*   the facilitation of security (over assets);
*   the protection of vested rights; and
*   the protection of innocent third parties.

Businesses need certainty in order to flourish. However, a recurrent problem for lawyers is that the law always lags behind new developments. In recent years, for example, e-commerce has sprung up without specific legislation to solve its problems, though the legislation is now appearing. Judges often have to deal with commercial disputes where the statute law is inadequate and the behaviour of the parties is framed by the practices of the trade in which they are engaged. They have to produce a decision that fits with commercial practice and they may have to adapt the law or interpret it in a new way to do so.

Professor Goode also expounds five concepts of commercial law:

- the concept of the market (often, the international market);
- the importance of customs or usage of a trade or locality (as a court will recognise them and give effect to them);
- the importance of a course of dealing (as not all terms are spelled out in a written contract);
- the concept of negotiability (as a holder of a negotiable instrument gets good title); and
- the enforceability of abstract payment undertakings (even without consideration, eg in the case of a documentary credit).

These five concepts indicate the importance of trade practice and the need to give legal effect to commercial arrangements even if they do not always sit comfortably with some legal concepts. It would be a brave, or foolhardy, judge who sought to construe a written contract in the absence of these factors.

Where do you look to find the legal principles on which commercial law is based? The sources of commercial law which are typically quoted are:

- the law of contract;
- custom and usage of the trade;
- national legislation;
- European Community law; and
- international Conventions.

If you are dealing with a commercial contract matter in practice, the sources which are likely to cause you trouble are custom and usage of the trade, and international Conventions. Legal databases are great for legislation but the 'soft' material can be harder to track down. Indeed, half the problem is knowing that it exists in the first place. As regards the custom and usage of the trade, you will be often be reliant on your client for information on this aspect.

1.3 DRAFTING A COMMERCIAL CONTRACT

The basic principles of the structure of agreements are set out in the LPC Resource Book *Skills for Lawyers* (Jordans). You may also wish to look at Berg *Drafting Commercial Agreements* (Butterworths, 1991).

As ever, the basics of the law of contract have to be kept in mind. If you are hazy on these you may want to look at the CD-ROM on black-letter law produced by The College of Law or a basic text book.

The key factor in drafting a commercial agreement is not to lose sight of your client's commercial aims. In other words, adapt precedents to fit your client's deal, do not adapt your client's deal to fit the precedents. It is easier to say this than to do it in practice.

Commercial agreements have a fairly typical running order:

- the parties;
- the recitals, if any;

- definitions;
- conditions precedent, if any;
- agreements (eg to sell the goods or to pay the price);
- representations and warranties;
- 'boiler-plate' clauses;
- execution clause and signature; and
- schedules.

Schedules are a way of removing unnecessary detail from the body of an agreement and thereby improving its readability. In a large agreement, representations and warranties would also be removed to the schedules.

1.3.1 The parties

It is not as easy to get this right as you might think. For example, is the seller Longshaw Holdings plc, or Longshaw (Chemicals) Ltd? In other words, which company in the group is the relevant one?

1.3.2 Definitions clause

All defined terms start with a capital letter. If the same word or phrase is used in the agreement without being capitalised then the inference is that something different from the defined term is intended.

It is important that the definitions meet the requirements of the agreement. For example, should the definition of 'Vegetables' include tomatoes? It is important to keep an eye on the definitions as the agreement progresses through a number of drafts and negotiation with the other side (ie do the definitions still work satisfactorily?).

All the definitions in this section should also occur in the body of the agreement. Likewise, all defined terms in the agreement should be defined in the definitions section. (In some complex agreements, the entry in the definitions section will merely be a cross-reference, possibly to an appendix or other part of the agreement.)

1.3.3 Interpretation clause

This section should be non-controversial. It covers the basics of interpretation, for example by providing that the headings do not form part of the agreement (as if they did, lawyers would feel the need to draft them more comprehensively, which would detract from their usefulness).

We will look later at some key operative provisions, especially in the context of the sale of goods. For now, we will look at so-called 'boiler-plate' clauses.

1.4 INTRODUCTION TO BOILER-PLATE CLAUSES

In all commercial contracts there are run of the mill clauses that will occur in all agreements to a greater or lesser extent. They are commonly called 'boiler-plate' clauses (or simply referred to as 'the boiler-plate'). They often remain as drafted in the precedent which is being used. They are not usually individually negotiated, as they are relatively uncontroversial. Nevertheless, you must of course check that they are not contrary to your client's interests when negotiating an agreement. It can be a bad mistake to assume that boiler-plate clauses can just be copied out of a precedent.

There is no precise definition of 'boiler-plate clauses', nor do they have to appear at a given point in the agreement. However, it is common to have a group of boiler-plate clauses at or towards the end of an agreement. Typical boiler-plate clauses are as follows.

1.4.1 The 'prevail' clause

This clause provides in effect that if there is a battle of the forms (ie both parties seek to impose their own terms on the other), then the seller's terms will prevail. Legally, this clause is ineffective – it is the 'offer and counter-offer' point. However, the prevail clause is often included for bluff value.

1.4.2 The 'whole agreement' clause

The parties to an agreement will normally want to ensure that, for convenience, all of their obligations are recorded in one document. They will also want to avoid the evidential difficulties associated with oral representations and discussions.

The parol evidence rule supports this, as it provides that outside evidence cannot be adduced to vary the written contract. This clause avoids an exception to the rule, which states that a contract can be partly written and partly oral if the parties intend it to be. The clause will not operate to avoid the battle of the forms, however. It can also be seen as an exclusion clause if it attempts to exclude liability for misrepresentation.

The danger of a whole agreement clause is that it might exclude other documents which the parties do wish to have taken into account, for example a price list.

Another danger of a whole agreement clause occurred in *Thomas Witter v TBP Industries Ltd* [1996] 2 All ER 573 where such a clause was held to have excluded liability for fraudulent misrepresentation. It therefore ran foul of Misrepresentation Act 1967, s 3.

In *Inntrepreneur Pub Co (CPC) Ltd v Sweeney* [2002] EWHC 1060 (Ch), [2003] ECC 17, the court held that an entire agreement clause prevented a pre-contractual statement becoming a collateral contract or warranty. The court also held there had been no misrepresentation.

1.4.3 The 'no authority' clause

This is an attempt by the seller:

(a) to put a limit on the extent to which its sales reps are permitted to negotiate individual terms with the buyer; and

(b) to exclude any extravagant claims made by the sales reps to induce the buyer to enter the contract.

To some extent, there is overlap with the whole agreement clause, and it is subject to the same difficulties.

Sometimes, a seller will want to give the sales reps limited discretion (eg to agree discounts) and, if so, the clause will need to be amended appropriately.

1.4.4 Buyer becoming insolvent

It is a standard provision relating to the operation of the agreement. You will recognise the various events described from the insolvency law chapters in the LPC Resource Book *Business Law and Practice* (Jordans). This clause is often linked to the retention of title clause in a sale of goods agreement, as the typical use for a retention of title clause is when the buyer is going insolvent (see **2.2**).

1.4.5 Law and jurisdiction

This would normally be the law of England and Wales and the jurisdiction of the English courts. If for any reason this clause had been omitted, then the Rome Convention on the Law Applicable to Contracts and Regulation 44/2001 ('Brussels II') would be applied (see Chapter 7). If the contract were expressed to be subject to any law other than law of England and Wales, then you would not be qualified to advise on it!

1.4.6 Service of notices

A notice clause has to provide for the places where notice is to be served, the method of service and the time at which the notice is deemed to be served. Such clauses have become more complex with the increase in the number of ways in which notice could be given (eg fax and email). Most notice clauses will not permit oral notice but rather will require it to be in writing.

The notice clause will specify the address(es) to which notice is to be sent. If one party is located overseas, then it may be best to specify an address for service in the UK (eg their solicitors or accountants).

Notice clauses will typically require notice to be served during business hours if served in person. If notice is permitted to be sent by fax or email, then it could be deemed served when received. If sent by post, then it could be deemed served two days after posting. It will all depend on the wording agreed by the parties.

The person to whom notice is sent may also be specified (eg the company secretary for a corporate party to the contract).

1.4.7 Force majeure

A force majeure clause is intended to suspend or terminate the contractual obligations in the event of an occurrence outside the control of the parties (eg bad weather). A force majeure clause is usually for the benefit of the seller, as they are the party obliged to supply and/or deliver the goods.

If one or more of the specified events occurs, then contractual performance will be suspended for a specified period. If the event is still continuing at the end of that period then the contract will be considered to be terminated.

The list of events can cause some discussion. The usual ones are so-called acts of God, adverse weather such as floods or snow, war, riot, government action, and embargoes or strikes by third parties.

1.4.8 The 'no partnership' clause

This type of clause seeks to ensure that the agreement cannot be construed as a partnership between the parties to the agreement. There are obvious disadvantages to partnership law, such as being liable for a partner's debts. However, the factor that determines whether or not a partnership is in existence is the definition of partnership in Partnership Act 1890, s 1, not the wording of a 'no partnership' clause.

1.4.9 The 'no assignment, no subcontracting' clause

If a buyer has selected a specific supplier, they will not want that supplier to subcontract the work to an unknown third party. Similarly, the buyer may not want the contract to be assigned to another supplier. Thus, a clause to cover both these possibilities is often included in commercial contracts.

1.5 LIMITATION OF LIABILITY IN CONTRACTS

This is an important area of commercial contracts and is dealt with in Chapter 3.

Chapter 2

FURTHER ASPECTS OF THE SALE OF GOODS

2.1 PRICE, PAYMENT AND DELIVERY

Before reading this Chapter, you may want to refresh your mind on the overall picture on sale of goods, as described in Chapter 32 of the LPC Resource Book *Business Law and Practice* (Jordans). The present chapter deals with price, payment and delivery terms in greater detail than is done in Chapter 32.

Although the right to reject goods under Sale of Goods Act 1979 (SGA 1979), s 35(4) is not expressly dealt with here, it is worth recording that the Court of Appeal has overruled the landmark case of *Bernstein v Pamson Motors (Golders Green) Ltd* [1987] 2 All ER 220. In *Clegg v Olle Andersson (t/a Nordic Marine)* [2003] EWCA Civ 320, [2003] 1 All ER (Comm) 721, it was held that the Sale and Supply of Goods Act 1994 allowed the buyer to have time to ascertain the actions needed to modify or repair the goods. The case concerned an ocean-going yacht. The buyer took 3 weeks to assess the situation before rejecting the goods. This was in fact many months after delivery, as the seller was slow to respond to requests for information.

2.1.1 Price

The Sale of Goods Act 1979 (SGA 1979), s 8 provides that:

'(1) The price in a contract of sale may be fixed by the contract, or may be left to be fixed in a manner agreed by the contract, or may be determined by the course of dealing between the parties.

(2) Where the price is not determined as mentioned in subsection (1) above, the buyer must pay a reasonable price.

(3) What is a reasonable price is a question of fact dependent on the circumstances of each particular case.'

The basic position is that the parties are free to fix their own price. The fall-back position is that if they fail to do so, the price will be a reasonable one.

One problem with s 8 is whether or not the parties have concluded a contract at all. If they have not, then the price has not been fixed by the contract.

The parties may conclude the contract but agree that the price will be fixed at some point in the future. There is an argument that the parties have not fully concluded their contract (ie there is an 'agreement to agree' which is usually taken to be unenforceable in English law – eg *Courtney & Fairbairn Ltd v Tolaini Bros (Hotels) Ltd* [1975] 1 WLR 297). Contrast this with the older case of *Foley v Classique Coaches Ltd* [1934] 2 KB 1, where there was an arbitration clause if the parties could not agree on the price. The contract was upheld. (In *Beer v Bowden* [1981] 1 All ER 1070, the Court of Appeal followed *Foley*, though this was on a rent review clause in a lease. In *Cable & Wireless plc v IBM United Kingdom Ltd* [2002] EWHC 2059 (Comm), [2002] 2 All ER (Comm) 1041, it was held that although the law did not generally recognise agreements to agree, the situation here was different. The fact that the agreement prescribed the means by which dispute negotiation should take place, by the identification of a specific recognised procedure, meant that the requirement for contractual certainty was fulfilled and the agreement was thus enforceable.)

2.1.2 Agreeing the price

In most circumstances, the parties will agree the price. It could be by use of a price list or it could be by quotation, or by negotiation. The contract should provide that the price is fixed, or if not, how price changes between signing and delivery are to be dealt with.

If the parties leave the price to be fixed by the valuation of a third party and he does not do so, then the contract is void (see SGA 1979, s 9).

2.1.3 VAT

A price in a contract is taken as including VAT unless otherwise specified (Value Added Tax Act 1983, s 10(2)). If the prices are to be exclusive of VAT, then that must be expressly stated. Failure to do this will result in the seller receiving 17.5% less for his goods than he wanted.

2.1.4 Payment

SGA 1979, s 28 provides:

> 'Unless otherwise agreed, delivery of the goods and payment of the price are concurrent conditions, that is to say, the seller must be ready and willing to give possession of the goods to the buyer in exchange for the price, and the buyer must be ready and willing to pay the price in exchange for possession of the goods.'

This would be the normal scenario of buying goods in a shop. The customer gives the shopkeeper the money, and the customer takes the goods away.

2.1.5 Time for payment

If no time for payment is mentioned in the contract, then the price is due on the completion of the contract, if the seller is willing to deliver the goods.

The seller is not obliged to accept payment by any means other than cash. However, if the seller accepts a cheque or other negotiable instrument, this is treated as a conditional payment. If the cheque is not honoured then the seller may sue for the price either as breach of the sale of goods contract or on the cheque as being a contract in itself. Payment by credit card will usually be treated as an absolute payment. Therefore, failure by the credit card company to pay the retailer does not allow the retailer to sue the customer (see *Re Charge Card Services Ltd* [1988] 3 All ER 702). The customer's liability is to pay the credit card company when the bill from them arrives in the post.

SGA 1979, s 10(1) provides that:

> 'Unless a different intention appears from the terms of the contract, stipulations as to time of payment are not of the essence of a contract of sale ...'

This has been interpreted as meaning that failure to pay is not a breach of condition entitling the seller to treat the contract as repudiated and to sell the goods elsewhere. Rather, it limits the seller's right to the price, and to damages, if any.

If the seller is anxious about time for payment, he can of course provide that the contract does make time for payment of the essence. It would also be sensible to provide for interest on late payments.

2.1.6 Late payment

Damages for late payment can be awarded by the court for additional costs caused to the seller (eg *Wadsworth v Lydall* [1981] 1 WLR 598). Interest can be awarded under the Law Reform (Miscellaneous Provisions) Act 1934 and more particularly, the Late Payment of Commercial Debts (Interest) Act 1998. The 1998 Act restricts the parties' freedom to contract somewhat in that it provides that the parties may provide another substantial contractual remedy for the right to statutory interest but may not provide that late payment will not carry any remedy at all (see **2.5.4**).

Section 49 provides that the unpaid seller has a right to sue for the price of the goods, even when the title to the goods has not passed.

The unpaid seller has other statutory rights. SGA 1979, s 39 states that the unpaid seller has:

(1) a lien on the goods or right to retain them for the price;
(2) a right to stop the goods in transit if the buyer becomes insolvent; and
(3) a right of re-sale of the goods.

These rights are detailed in ss 41–48. These assume that the seller has possession of, or control over, the goods. If that is not the case, then the seller can only rely on a retention of title clause, if one has been included in the contract (see **2.2**).

2.1.7 What is delivery?

Delivery is defined in SGA 1979, s 61(1) as:

> 'voluntary transfer of possession from one person to another'.

It is not confined to transfer of physical possession of the goods. In other words, it does not mean the seller taking the goods round to the buyer's premises.

Section 32(1) provides that transfer of possession to a carrier who will take the goods to the buyer constitutes delivery.

Prima facie, the risk in the goods passes with the property in the goods (s 20(1)).

2.1.8 When to deliver

Section 10(2) provides that the parties can agree whether or not a stipulation as to time is of the essence or not (see also **2.1.5** on s 10(1)).

The courts have ruled on various aspects on time of delivery. In *Hartley v Hymans* [1920] 3 KB 475, it was held that in ordinary commercial contracts for the sale of goods the rule is that time is prima facie of the essence with respect to delivery.

If the buyer waives the delivery date before the goods are delivered, the buyer is entitled to give the seller reasonable notice that he will not accept the goods after a certain date. See the case of *Charles Rickards Ltd v Oppenheim* [1950] 1 KB 616 where the buyer waived the original delivery date but then gave the seller reasonable notice of a revised date. The seller failed to meet even the revised date and the buyer was held to be entitled to refuse to accept the goods. See also *Toprak Mahsulleri Ofisi v Finagrain Compagnie Commerciale Agricole et Financiere SA* [1979] 2 Lloyd's Rep 98 where the Court of Appeal applied *Rickards* to extensions of time in the context of shipping.

Even if there is an agreed delivery date, the duty could be suspended or extinguished. This is typically dealt with in a force majeure clause in the contract.

2.1.9 What to deliver

The seller is required to deliver goods of the right quantity, as under s 30(1) the buyer may reject the goods if the quantity is less than the contract quantity.

The seller is also required to deliver goods of the right quality: s 13 compliance with description, s 14(2) and (3) goods to be of satisfactory quality and/or fit for a special purpose, and s 15 compliance with a sample. Also, s 14 states that an implied condition or warranty about quality or fitness for a particular purpose may be annexed to a contract of sale by usage in the course of a particular trade. Section 15A removes the right to reject the goods if the breach of ss 13–15 is so slight that it would be unreasonable to reject, provided the buyer is not a consumer.

2.1.10 How to deliver

There are various methods of delivery. The most obvious is actual delivery, that is physically handing over the goods, as would happen when a consumer is buying goods in a shop. Other methods of delivery include:

- transfer of a document (eg a bill of lading, see **8.2.1**);
- delivery of an object giving control (eg giving the keys to premise where the goods are stored, or even the keys to a motor car);
- the buyer's continuance of possession (eg where the buyer already holds the goods as bailee of the seller, and then on the sale there is a notional delivery of the goods to the buyer);
- 'attornment', where a seller or a third party acknowledges that goods which were held by the seller or on their behalf are now held on behalf of the buyer; and
- delivery to a carrier.

2.1.11 Where to deliver and who pays

The place of delivery depends on the contract. It would commonly be the seller's premises, or it could be at the buyer's premises on being transported there by the seller. SGA 1979, s 29 provides for rules on deciding where delivery takes place if the contract is silent on the matter.

The expenses of delivery will be borne by the seller and the expenses of taking delivery by the buyer, unless the contract provides otherwise.

2.2 INTRODUCTION TO RETENTION OF TITLE

A difficult situation is where the goods are in the possession or control of the buyer but the seller has still not been paid. This is a major concern for the seller especially where the buyer is going insolvent. The danger is that the goods will be sold by a liquidator or receiver. The seller would be only an unsecured creditor and would be unlikely to be paid much, if anything, by the liquidator.

There is a right under SGA 1979, ss 17 and 19 to reserve title to the goods. This can be done in a contract of sale by inserting a retention of title clause (also called a *Romalpa* clause after *Aluminium Industrie Vaassen BV v Romalpa Aluminium* [1976] 1 WLR 676).

The validity of retention of title clauses has been upheld where the goods remain identifiable (eg *Clough Mill Ltd v Martin* [1985] 1 WLR 111). This case concerned the yarn which had been sold to a manufacturer of fabrics. The seller was held to have title to the unused yarn.

Retention of title clauses are generally not registerable as they are considered to operate by preventing the property in the goods from passing to the buyer in the first place (see *Clough Mill Ltd v Martin* and also *Armour and Another v Thyssen Edelstahlwerke AG* [1990] 2 AC 339).

There are a number of potential complications which could occur, for example, where:

- the original goods have been used in a manufacturing process and have lost their original identity (*Borden (UK) Ltd v Scottish Timber Products Ltd* [1981] Ch 25);
- the goods have been mixed with other goods and are no longer identifiable (*Re Andrabell Ltd (In Liquidation); Airborne Accessories Ltd v Goodman* [1984] 3 All ER 407);
- the goods have been attached to other goods (*Hendy Lennox (Industrial Engines) Ltd v Graham Puttick Ltd* [1984] 1 WLR 485); and
- the goods have been sold on to an innocent third party.

A problem area is where the goods have been incorporated into other products. Generally, the original goods are considered to have been subsumed into the new products and the seller has no right to the new products. In *Borden (UK) Ltd v Scottish Timber Products Ltd*, the sellers sold resin to manufacturers of chipboard. It was held that they did not have title to the chipboard or the proceeds of its sale (see **2.3.5**).

In *Re Andrabell Ltd*, the seller sold travel bags in a number of consignments. The contracts did not have an 'all moneys' clause (see **2.3.1**) so any rights only attached to the consignment for which the seller had not been paid. The seller was not able to identify those bags from all the other bags, so could not recover any bags. They were also not allowed to trace the proceeds of sale through the buyer's general bank account.

However, where the goods are readily detachable then it is appropriate to have a clause reserving the right of the seller to detach his goods and remove them. For example, in *Hendy Lennox (Industrial Engines) Ltd v Graham Puttick Ltd*, it was held that the sellers were entitled to detach their diesel engines from electrical generating sets.

Under SGA 1979, s 25 an innocent third party will get good title to the goods.

2.3 DRAFTING A RETENTION OF TITLE CLAUSE: A BASIC CHECKLIST

You should appreciate by this stage that no clause can always be guaranteed to be appropriate in all situations. You must always remember to check when using a precedent that it fits in with their client's needs and instructions. The following suggested provisions aim to cover the basic situation of retaining title to the goods but also to go further and cover the problems mentioned above.

2.3.1 Reserving title

The seller should make it clear that the seller will remain the owner of the goods, and that (legal) ownership will not pass to the buyer until one of the two events described takes place.

These events are:

(a) the buyer has paid all amounts owing to the seller in respect of all goods which the seller has supplied to the buyer (ie paid for not just this consignment of goods, but any others which the buyer has bought previously); or
(b) the buyer sells the goods on in accordance with the agreement.

Point (a) is called an 'all moneys' clause. It aims to retain ownership of the goods until all outstanding sums have been paid. Many precedents are likely to include an 'all moneys' provision. It is not necessary for a retention of title clause to include this provision, but it is potentially a very useful protection for the seller.

Point (b) acknowledges SGA 1979, s 25, which states that an innocent third party gets good title to the goods when the goods are sold on to them by the original buyer.

As mentioned in the LPC Resource Book *Business Law and Practice* (Jordans), to be effective a retention of title clause must retain legal title to the goods. It is not sufficient to retain 'equitable and beneficial ownership' (see *In re Bond Worth* [1980] Ch 228). In this case the seller was held to have passed title to the goods, and then the buyer created an equitable charge which was then void for lack of registration under Companies Act 1985, ss 395, 396. Although this explanation has been criticised, it has been followed in *Stroud Architectural Systems Ltd v John Laing Construction Ltd* [1994] BCC 18.

2.3.2 Rights of entry, seizure and sale

The seller must make sure that the clause specifically provides for the right to go on to the buyer's premises (or the seller will commit trespass in doing so) and recover the goods (and also to re-sell them). This right would often be expressed as arising when the buyer is overdue in paying for the goods (ie the consignment actually sold under *this* agreement, or any other goods which the seller has supplied to the buyer). This could be linked through to a clause in the agreement making the price become due immediately on the buyer becoming insolvent.

2.3.3 Storage of the seller's goods while in the buyer's possession

The seller needs to decide whether anything can or should be done to maximise the chances of being able to recover the goods (or at least getting some money back if something happens to them while in the buyer's possession).

So, a clause could be included to provide for separate storage in order to maximise the chances that the seller can identify its own goods when trying to recover them.

Likewise, if the goods were destroyed, the seller would want recompense. So, a clause should be included to require the buyer to insure the seller's goods and to hold the proceeds on trust for the seller.

A further possibility for protection of the goods is the seller marking its goods to make them easily identifiable. Obviously this won't always work – for example, 100 tons of gravel is impossible to mark! Where practicable, this can be a useful back-up to a separate storage clause (which the buyer may disobey). Note that the seller will sometimes reserve the right to inspect the buyer's premises to check if separate storage provisions are being complied with. Although this may be a useful power to have, the reality is often that separate storage provisions are impossible to police. If the buyer does disobey it will obviously be in breach of contract but this may be of no use to the seller (eg if the buyer has become insolvent).

2.3.4 Passing of risk

It is important for sale of goods agreements to provide expressly for the passing of the risk of accidental loss of, or damage to, the goods. This may be done in a separate clause, but is often found in a retention of title clause.

Under SGA 1979, s 20, goods remain at the seller's risk until the property in them (ie ownership) is transferred to the buyer unless the parties agree otherwise. This is not the desired situation in a contract with a retention of title, so a clause is added which displaces s 20 by contrary agreement. The seller will often stipulate that risk passes on delivery.

2.3.5 Tracing into the proceeds of sale

Tracing has only been done successfully once, in *Romalpa* itself. The sellers there tried to claim the proceeds of sale of the goods once the goods themselves had been sold on. The Court of Appeal allowed this on the grounds that there was an express fiduciary relationship between the sellers and the buyers (with the buyers selling the goods on to a third party as agents for the sellers rather than in their own right). Subsequently, the courts have been unwilling to recognise this fiduciary relationship.

Over the years, there have been many attempts to draft retention of title clauses to permit the seller to claim sale proceeds. Very simple clauses entitling the seller to the proceeds are almost certain to be construed as charges over the goods (see **2.3.1**). It seems from the cases that the courts will take exactly the same view of more complex attempts (eg elaborate clauses describing the existence of a fiduciary relationship between the parties).

In *Compaq Computer Ltd v Abercorn Group Ltd (t/a Osiris) and Others* [1991] BCC 484, Abercorn were appointed as an authorised dealer of Compaq's computers. The agreement contained a clause that the goods were held by Abercorn as 'bailee and agent' and proceeds of sub-sales were to be accounted for to Compaq. The arrangement was held to be a charge over the proceeds of the sub-sales which was void for want of registration. Thus, it seems that even a very carefully worded clause will only create a charge. This does not stop such clauses being included, if only in the hope that they might serve to exert commercial pressure.

A typical clause would also require the buyer to pay the proceeds into a separate bank account, where the buyer will hold them on trust for the seller. The idea is to stop the money generated by the sale of the seller's goods from becoming mixed up with other money the buyer may have which is nothing to do with the seller. Such a clause facilitates tracing if it were to be allowed by the court. (Do not forget that under SGA 1979, s 25, an innocent third party will get good title to the goods. So, once the goods have been sold on the original seller's title to the goods themselves no longer exists.)

2.3.6 Claiming ownership of 'mixed' goods

The typical commercial situation where a retention of title clause is used is in manufacturing or construction or reselling. In manufacturing and construction, it is likely that the goods supplied will have been incorporated into other products (eg *In re Peachdart Ltd* [1984] Ch 131, where the leather hides had been made into handbags). The resulting goods are referred to variously as 'mixed' or 'manufactured' or 'altered' goods.

The seller may try to extend a retention of title clause to cover these 'mixed' goods. In *Clough Mill Ltd v Martin* [1985] 1 WLR 111, the seller supplied yarn to a manufacturer of fabrics. They were held not to have title to the finished fabric, only to the unused yarn. See also the cases of *Glencore International AG v Metro Trading Inc and Others* [2001] 1 All ER Comm 103; *Glencore International AG v Metro Trading International Inc (1)* (2001) unreported, 8 November, *Glencore International AG v Exeter Shipping Ltd and Others (2)* [2002] EWCA Civ 528, [2002] 2 All ER (Comm) 1, where the subject matter was oil from different suppliers which the buyer stored co-mingled in bulk containers. It was held that the onus of proof as to which unpaid supplier was entitled to a specific quantity of oil was on the defendant as they had caused the problem in the first place. It was also held that upon commingling in storage of oil owned by Glencore with oil owned by MTI or other persons, Glencore would become an owner of the whole of the commingled bulk in common with MTI and any other persons whose oil had contributed to the bulk. This would be in proportion to the quantity of oil contributed by each of them. This illustrates the problems that such cases throw up.

Mixed goods clauses are usually interpreted as charges over the buyer company's assets, which are usually void for want of registration. (The charge will still be valid against the buyer, but the typical situation we are concerned about here is an insolvency.) However, you will still see mixed goods clauses included in a retention of title clause.

2.3.7 Detachable goods

If the goods supplied to the buyer are readily detachable without damage to the buyer's products, then the seller's goods can be recovered. We have already mentioned *Hendy Lennox (Industrial Engines) Ltd v Graham Puttick Ltd* [1984] 1 WLR 485, where the seller had sold diesel engines to the buyer. The buyer had bolted the engines to electrical generators. It was therefore feasible to detach the engines without damaging the generators.

A clause allowing the seller to separate and remove detachable goods is likely to be upheld by the court.

2.4 RETENTION OF TITLE CLAUSES AND THE CREATION OF CHARGES

Some of the tactics used by sellers are not going to work in court because they create a charge which is void for want of registration. Is it feasible to register a charge in such circumstances? In practice, it is not going to be practical. A new charge would come into existence each time the buyer resold the goods, for a proceeds of sale clause, or mixed them with others for a mixed/manufactured goods clause. The seller would find it very hard to police this. It would also be onerous to complete the necessary Form 395 each time, identifying the property over which the charge had been created. Registering all these charges could also lead to adverse credit ratings for the buyer if it is a company because the buyer's file at Companies House would show numerous charges registered against it. This would discourage anyone thinking of lending money to the buyer. The effect of such actions by the seller would be to put off the buyer from contracting with the seller in the first place. In practice, therefore, the seller will not usually attempt to register any charge which a retention of title clause might create.

2.5 'BACKING UP' A RETENTION OF TITLE CLAUSE

It is worth encouraging a seller to back up any retention of title clause by taking practical steps either to minimise the chances of dealing with buyers who may not pay, or to provide an incentive for the buyer to pay up, or both. The possibilities include the following.

2.5.1 Checks on the buyer/controlling the credit the buyer is given

This is likely to be a useful practical back-up to retention of title. In an ideal world, it would include the following measures.

- Encourage the seller to run a tight system of credit control, with frequent checks on buyers' creditworthiness. The seller should take steps to ensure that buyers always pay by the due date, send out invoices on time and chase debts before they start to become a problem. Ensure that all relevant staff know precisely the limit of the credit that the buyer is allowed.
- If buyers start to fall behind in paying for the goods, the seller may want to consider reducing any credit period allowed, or even move on to demanding cash on delivery or 'up front'. Obviously, whether this is a practical solution will vary from case to case (eg will the buyer agree to the new terms?).
- If the contract permits, the seller should consider removing its goods from the buyer's premises at the first hint of trouble rather than waiting for a receiver or liquidator to be appointed. Once creditors become twitchy things can happen very quickly indeed.

- If a buyer persistently pays late, consider not dealing with him in future!

2.5.2 Debt factoring

Factoring is where the debts are sold to someone else who will then collect them. This is an alternative to retention of title rather than a supplement to it. Obviously, the debts cannot be sold for 100% of their value, as the factor has to make a profit. The discount could be as much as 15%.

2.5.3 Credit risk insurance

A seller may also be able to insure against the risk of the buyer not paying. Credit risk insurance may sometimes be too expensive to be worthwhile but in the last few years, it has become cheaper and more widely available. Sellers are able to obtain policies tailored to their precise needs rather than on an 'all debts' basis, which would be very expensive for the seller.

2.5.4 Providing for interest

The seller may charge interest on sums which become overdue. This may act as an incentive to the buyer to pay on time and will give the seller some recompense if the payment is late. Normally, the best way to deal with interest is to provide for it expressly in the contract. The seller must not go over the top when providing for the amount of interest, as a provision which claimed excessive interest could be struck down as a penalty.

The Late Payment of Commercial Debts (Interest) Act 1998 provides specifically for the payment of interest in certain commercial situations. It is now fully implemented so that all businesses and the public sector can claim interest on late payments. The Directive on Combating Late Payment in Commercial Transactions (Dir 2000/35/EC) required Member States to deal with combating late payments in commercial transactions.

The Act works in the following way:

- it implies into applicable contracts a term relating to interest (basically commercial contracts for the supply of goods or services);
- the term is to the effect that any 'qualifying debt' created by the contract carries simple interest in accordance with the Act, known as 'statutory interest'; and
- in certain circumstances, this right to interest can be ousted by contract terms if there is another 'substantial contractual remedy' for late payment, but may not provide that late payment carries no remedy at all.

Many businesses which might benefit under the Act are completely unaware of its existence and there is little evidence that it has had much impact in practice so far.

Even if there is no express provision in the contract and the Act does not apply there are statutory provisions for claiming interest in both the High Court and county court. These have the disadvantages that technically any award of interest is in the discretion of the court (although this is rarely a problem). Also, to be certain of its entitlement to interest the seller must incur the cost of proceedings and wait for judgment. Debtors routinely rely on this loophole and refuse to pay interest unless proceedings are commenced.

2.6 THE RIGHTS OF AN UNPAID SELLER UNDER THE SALE OF GOODS ACT 1979

Under SGA 1979, an unpaid seller who is still in possession of the goods or has control over them has rights which are laid down in ss 38–48 (see LPC Resource Book *Business Law and Practice* (Jordans), para **32.8**). This is a much less complex scenario than the one we have dealt with above, that is the unpaid seller who has lost possession or control of the goods.

2.7 UNFAIR TERMS IN CONSUMER CONTRACTS

See Chapter 3 for a brief account of the Unfair Terms in Consumer Contracts Regulations 1999, SI 1999/2083.

2.8 SALE OF GOODS TO CONSUMERS

Directive 1999/44/EC on Certain Aspects of the Sale of Consumer Goods and Associated Guarantees was implemented in the UK on 31 March 2003 by the Sale and Supply of Goods to Consumers Regulations 2002, SI 2002/3045.

Provisions implied into consumer contracts include the following:

- for the first 6 months after delivery, the burden of proof when reporting faulty goods is reversed in the consumer's favour;
- the Directive requires guarantees offered by manufacturers or retailers to be legally binding, to be written in plain language with clear detail on how to claim and to be available on request; and
- there is a right to have goods repaired or replaced or have a price reduction.

These remedies are already widely used in the UK but they have not had status in law. The existing right to reject unsatisfactory goods within a reasonable time will be maintained.

Section 12(2) of the Unfair Contract Terms Act 1977 has been amended by the Regulations to provide that in some limited circumstances a buyer of goods at an auction or by competitive tender will be dealing as a consumer.

Consumer contracts are beyond the scope of this book, but you may well come across these issues when you are in practice.

Chapter 3

EFFECTIVE DRAFTING OF EXCLUSION CLAUSES

3.1 INTRODUCTION

Commercial clients will always be concerned about the liability which they may incur in performing their contracts, and in most cases, their instinct will be to try to reduce their exposure as much as possible. The solicitor is likely to be approached for advice in two respects:

(1) drafting an agreement to minimise the client's liability if things should go wrong;
(2) advising on the protection given by exclusions in an agreement once problems have arisen.

Most of this chapter deals with the first point; it looks at the various matters which the solicitor should bear in mind when drafting (or reviewing) an agreement.

This chapter also considers exclusion of liability largely from the point of view of a solicitor drafting on behalf of a commercial client which is entering into agreements with other commercial parties.

3.2 BASIC RULES FOR SUCCESSFUL DRAFTING OF EXCLUSION CLAUSES

Three points are particularly important.

3.2.1 Know the commercial background

Although this may at first seem obvious, the solicitor needs to know how a client's business operates before it is possible to draft effectively for exclusion of liability on behalf of the client. Exclusion clauses in commercial contracts are in many cases only subject to the reasonableness test under the Unfair Contract Terms Act 1977 (UCTA 1977), and many of the factors which are relevant in deciding whether or not a clause passes the reasonableness test are specific to the circumstances of each contract. The solicitor should, therefore, obtain full instructions before drafting, learning as much as possible about the circumstances in which a client makes its commercial contracts, as well as about the client's business methods generally. Although it will not be possible to cover every eventuality, the likely effectiveness of an exclusion clause can be greatly enhanced if the person drafting it is familiar with the commercial background against which it will operate.

3.2.2 Know the law

Three areas are relevant:

(1) the principles relating to incorporation and construction;
(2) the rules in UCTA 1977; and
(3) the factors which determine whether a clause will pass the reasonableness test or not.

All these points, and (3) in particular, are considered in more detail at **3.4–3.10**.

3.2.3 Know the drafting principles

The way in which an exclusion clause has been drafted may have a profound influence on its effectiveness. Although the client's instructions or the circumstances in which the clause is to operate may in practice limit how a clause can be put together, the solicitor should always bear in mind the principles of good commercial drafting. This topic is not, however, considered further in detail in this chapter; for a full discussion of the principles of drafting, see the relevant chapter in the LPC Resource Book *Skills for Lawyers* (Jordans).

3.3 PREPARING TO DRAFT

Before putting pen to paper, there are several general considerations which the solicitor should have in mind, as they will relate to the likely effectiveness of the finished clauses.

3.3.1 What is an 'exclusion clause'?

There is no really comprehensive definition of what constitutes an 'exclusion' or 'exemption' clause. The closest approach to a full definition is probably s 13 of UCTA 1977, which defines very widely the type of clause to which UCTA 1977 applies. In addition, all the relevant sections of UCTA 1977 refer to 'exclusion or restriction of liability', so UCTA 1977 clearly covers limitation clauses as well as strict exclusion clauses. However, bear in mind that UCTA 1977 does not cover every case of exclusion or limitation of liability (see **3.7**). For the sake of simplicity, this chapter uses the expression 'exclusion clause' to cover all the possibilities, unless the context requires otherwise.

3.3.2 Ways of eliminating liability

Although it may be tempting to draft the 'exclusions' after the 'substantive' parts of the contract (so that, broadly speaking, the contract takes away something which it has already given), this may not always be the right approach. A 'duty-defining' clause may sometimes work better. For example, instead of one party agreeing to do something under the contract, and then excluding or limiting its liability should things go wrong, it may be more appropriate to draft the contract so that the party never agrees to do that thing in the first place. This type of clause is still, however, likely to fall within the scope of UCTA 1977, and care needs to be taken that the 'contract' does not become a mere declaration of intent.

3.3.3 Background knowledge

An exclusion clause will be of little use to a client unless it has been drafted to suit the client's business. For example, a long, elaborate clause may look impressive on paper, but turn out to be unworkable in practice because it does not fit the way in which the client does business. When drafting, therefore, the solicitor must be realistic, and, as previously noted, this involves finding out as much as possible about how the client's business works (in particular, how the client actually makes contracts with customers). Basic questions to ask would include:

- with what sort of customers does the client normally deal?
- which of the client's employees actually make the contracts (and therefore 'operate' the exclusion clauses)?
- how, if at all, are any exclusions introduced to the customers?

This background knowledge is particularly important in the light of the reasonableness test under UCTA 1977 (see **3.10**).

3.3.4 Instructions and advice

A particular problem arises when drafting exclusion clauses, since there are frequently several different and conflicting factors governing the effectiveness of the clause (see generally **3.10**). Although the solicitor must try to achieve what the client has requested, the client must also be advised (as constructively as possible) that no exclusion clause can be guaranteed to work in all circumstances.

3.3.5 Precedents

Because the effectiveness of an exclusion clause will depend to a large extent on its own individual context, precedents for exclusion clauses need to be used with some caution. The solicitor should always consider how a clause might work in a particular business context, and think carefully before simply copying a precedent which appears to be suitable on paper. Having said that, precedents can be very useful in this context as a source of inspiration, or a guide as to how the layout of the exclusions within the contract might be organised (see **3.10.7**).

3.3.6 Testing the clause

Although this chapter deals almost entirely with the drafting of exclusion clauses, rather than the more general contractual background against which they will operate, it is often helpful at the drafting stage to consider that contractual background; this can be an extremely useful way of assessing a draft clause's potential strength. The solicitor should try to anticipate what problems may arise, and consider:

(1) identifying the terms of the contract which are likely to be relevant;
(2) deciding whether those terms have actually been breached by what has happened;
(3) anticipating what remedy the injured party will be seeking.

These points will form an integral part of the process of applying the clause if problems occur, and will often provide important information at the drafting stage as to how well the clause is likely to work in those circumstances.

3.4 THREE STAGES FOR EFFECTIVENESS

A party who wishes to claim the protection of an exclusion clause must prove three things:

(1) incorporation: that the clause forms part of the contract;
(2) construction: that the clause covers the breach which has occurred;
(3) UCTA 1977: that the clause is not invalidated by UCTA 1977 (if applicable).

This 'exclusion clause checklist' can be used just as much in drafting clauses as in assessing their validity once problems have arisen.

3.5 INCORPORATION

3.5.1 Clause must be incorporated

To be effective, a clause must form part of the contract. Whether it does or not is assessed by reference to the normal contractual principles of incorporation. It is, therefore, important to consider exclusion of liability when starting to draft, rather than when the rest of the contract is finished. The solicitor must consider what practical problems of incorporation may arise in relation to the contract, and whether anything can be done about them.

3.5.2 Signed or unsigned documents?

If a clause is contained in a contractual document which the client's customers will sign, the chances of incorporation are very good (the normal contractual rules on signature will apply). If, however, the clause is in an unsigned document, it will only form part of the contract if reasonable steps are taken to bring it to the customer's attention before the contract is made. Putting the clause into a document which is to be signed should, therefore, be less risky as far as incorporation is concerned. However, this may not be the best solution if it does not fit in with the client's normal business practices. There may also be problems over signature itself. What if the clause is in a document which should be signed, but which the customer does not sign? What if a regular customer normally signs a contractual document, but fails to sign on one or more occasions? Is it possible to draft and locate the clause so that it will be incorporated even if the document is not signed? There can be no general answers to these questions; in each case, the solicitor must obtain full instructions and then draft to meet the needs of the client's particular business.

3.5.3 Timing

If the clause is contained in a document which is not intended to be signed, problems may arise if there is normally an interval between drawing the buyer's attention to the clause and the contract being made. Again, it will help to find out how the client's business operates, but the solicitor may in practice be unable to resolve this problem.

3.5.4 Course of dealings

If the clause is in an unsigned document, it may be incorporated into the contract by way of regular and consistent course of dealings. Once again, the solicitor needs to know how the client's business works in order to decide whether this is likely. Does the client do a lot of business with regular customers, is it involved mainly in 'one-off' transactions or (perhaps most likely) is there a variety of different dealings? Note that incorporation by course of dealings is far more likely to happen with contracts made between commercial parties than with contracts between a commercial party and a consumer.

3.5.5 Preventing incorporation problems

If the solicitor has acquired a background knowledge of how the client actually makes contracts, it should be possible to spot potential incorporation problems and take action before they arise. This could, for example, take the form of advice to the client (eg about staff training in relation to how contracts should be entered into), or building in safeguards when drafting (eg paying particular attention to the layout of the contract and the location of the clause). Whatever method is chosen, the client should always be made aware of the dangers; in particular, that its employees' actions when making contracts on the client's behalf could actually prevent exclusions in the contract from working.

3.6 CONSTRUCTION

3.6.1 Does the clause cover the breach?

Even if the clause is incorporated into the contract, it will be effective only if it covers the breach which actually occurs. As with incorporation, this poses problems when drafting; how far can the solicitor foresee the circumstances in which the clause will eventually operate, or the breaches which might occur? Once again, knowing the client's business as thoroughly as possible and taking full instructions will help; an awareness of the basic contractual principles of construction is also important.

3.6.2 Contra proferentem

An exclusion clause will be construed strictly contra proferentem (ie against the person attempting to rely on it). One important aspect of this principle relates to exclusion of liability for negligence, for which clear and unambiguous words are required. From this point of view, it is therefore desirable for a clause excluding liability for negligence to refer clearly to 'negligence' (or an appropriate synonym). However, a client may be extremely reluctant to state in the contract that it is excluding liability for negligence. The solicitor may use expressions such as 'howsoever caused', but whether this (or similar wording) will be effective is uncertain; it will depend on the circumstances. Whether or not to take the risk is a matter which the solicitor must discuss fully with the client.

3.6.3 Other principles of construction

In construing an exclusion clause, the court may apply various other principles to decide whether or not the clause covers the breach, for example:

(1) *Expressio unius est exclusio alterius*: by this principle, if a contract expressly mentions one or more matters, those not mentioned are automatically excluded. For example, if a clause lists claims which are to be barred, it will not apply to claims not mentioned.

(2) *Ejusdem generis*: this is a general aid to construction, which is sometimes seen as being more appropriate to property documents than to commercial contracts. The principle is that general words which follow two or more specific words are restricted to the same type of item or situation as the preceding specific words. (Note that this principle does not apply to a force majeure clause; see further **3.14.1**.)

3.6.4 Avoiding loose terminology

If words or phrases are used inappropriately, this may mean that a clause does not cover the breach which it was intended to cover. In particular, jargon may be misused (even by lawyers). For example, the words 'rescission', 'condition' and 'warranty' are all often used in commercial contracts in ways which pervert their strict legal meaning. A similar problem arises from the use of words which may mean different things to different readers of the contract (eg 'consequential loss'). When drafting, therefore, the solicitor should either try to avoid expressions which may cause problems, or define clearly what a particular expression means in context (for further discussion of this point in relation to the expression 'consequential loss', see **3.10.8**). Note that even if loose terminology does not prevent the clause from covering the breach, it may make the clause less likely to pass the reasonableness test if, for example, the effect is to make it difficult to understand (see further **3.10.7**).

3.7 THE UNFAIR CONTRACT TERMS ACT 1977

The solicitor will obviously need to be aware of statutory controls on the drafting of exclusion clauses. By far the most important of these is UCTA 1977.

3.7.1 Scope of UCTA 1977

UCTA 1977, s 13 gives the Act a wide scope, but it will by no means apply in every case.

(1) *Contracts to which UCTA 1977 does not apply*
    The most important examples of this are:
    (a) contracts listed in UCTA 1977, Sch 1. By this Schedule, ss 2–4 and 7 do not apply to certain types of contract, including contracts relating to land and contracts relating to intellectual property rights;
    (b) international supply contracts (UCTA 1977, s 26). By s 26(2), the reasonableness test under ss 3 and 4 of UCTA 1977 does not apply to an international supply contract.

Note also that, by s 27 of UCTA 1977, if the applicable law of the contract is that of some part of the UK only because of the choice of parties (and would, apart from that choice, be the law of a country outside the UK), then ss 2–7 and 16–21 of UCTA 1977 do not operate as part of the law applicable to the contract.

(2)　*Clauses to which UCTA 1977 does not apply*

Even if UCTA 1977 can apply generally to a particular type of contract, it may not apply to certain individual clauses within that contract. For example, assume that two businesses are entering into a tailor-made (ie not standard-form) contract for the sale of goods. The seller inserts a clause into the contract excluding liability for late delivery of the goods. UCTA 1977, s 3 will not apply to this clause because the buyer neither deals as consumer nor on the other party's written standard terms of business: no other section of UCTA 1977 is relevant to the clause either.

3.7.2 Continuing relevance of common law principles

Where UCTA 1977 does not apply, it is worth remembering that certain common law principles may apply. Before the advent of UCTA 1977, the courts developed numerous principles to control the use of exclusion clauses, which have survived the Act. Discussion of the principles is outside the scope of this chapter, and admittedly they have lost much of their importance as a result of UCTA 1977, but the solicitor should be aware that even if UCTA 1977 does not apply, he may not have a completely free hand in drafting.

3.7.3 A reminder of the effect of UCTA 1977 on contractual terms

The following is a brief reminder of the main points.

Void clauses

Note that although the word 'void' is used here to describe the effect of the relevant sections of UCTA 1977 on exclusion clauses, and is a convenient shorthand description, none of the sections of the Act actually uses this word. Instead, each section provides that the relevant liability cannot be excluded or restricted.

SECTION 2(1)

By s 2(1) of UCTA 1977, a person cannot, either by reference to a contract term or a notice, exclude or restrict his liability for personal injury or death resulting from negligence.

SECTION 6(1)

By s 6(1) of UCTA 1977, liability for breach of the implied condition of title under either s 12 of SGA 1979 or s 8 of the Supply of Goods (Implied Terms) Act 1973 cannot be excluded or restricted by reference to any contract term.

SECTION 6(2)

By s 6(2) of UCTA 1977, as against a person who deals as consumer, liability for breach of the implied conditions in ss 13–15 of SGA 1979 or ss 9–11 of the Supply of Goods (Implied Terms) Act 1973 cannot be excluded or restricted by reference to any contract term. The expression 'deals as consumer' is defined in UCTA 1977, s 12; perhaps surprisingly, the Court of Appeal has held that in certain circumstances, a company can deal as consumer *(R & B Customs Brokers Co Ltd v United Dominions Trust Ltd* [1988] 1 All ER 847). The point arises when a company enters into a transaction which is not in the regular course of its business. (Note that s 7 of UCTA 1977, which applies to miscellaneous contracts under which goods pass (eg work and materials contracts), contains provisions similar to those in s 6.)

Clauses subject to the reasonableness test

The two ways in which the contractual reasonableness test (see **3.8.1**) is most likely to apply are as follows.

SECTION 3

Section 3 of UCTA 1977 applies either where one party deals as consumer, or, significantly for commercial contracts, where one party deals on the other party's written standard terms of business. It imposes the reasonableness test on a wide variety of clauses.

SECTION 6(3)

An attempt to exclude the liability mentioned in UCTA 1977, s 6(2) (see above) against a person who does not deal as consumer is subject to the reasonableness test.

3.8 THE UNFAIR TERMS IN CONSUMER CONTRACTS REGULATIONS 1999

These Regulations provide (in certain circumstances) a further important statutory control on drafting exclusion clauses.

3.8.1 Introduction

The original version of these Regulations (the Unfair Terms in Consumer Contracts Regulations 1994, SI 1994/3159) came into force on 1 July 1995, and implemented Directive 93/13/EEC on unfair terms in consumer contracts. However, it subsequently proved necessary to make a number of changes to the Regulations, and as a result, the 1994 Regulations were revoked and replaced (with effect from 1 October 1999) by the Unfair Terms in Consumer Contracts Regulations 1999, SI 1999/2083.

Note that the Regulations do not apply to a contract between two commercial parties; however, for the commercial client which enters into standard-form contracts for the supply of goods and/or services to consumers, their impact is likely to be significant.

3.8.2 The Regulations in outline

Regulations 1 and 2 deal with commencement of the 1999 Regulations and revocation of the old; the definitions are found in reg 3. The definitions of 'consumer' and 'seller or supplier' require that a consumer must be a natural person who is not acting for business purposes, and that a seller or supplier must be acting for business purposes. Regulation 4 provides that the Regulations apply 'in relation to unfair terms in contracts concluded between a seller or supplier and a consumer', and also indicates a number of terms to which the Regulations do not apply.

'Unfair term' is then defined by reg 5(1):

> 'a contractual term which has not been individually negotiated shall be regarded as
> unfair if, contrary to the requirement of good faith, it causes a significant imbalance
> in the parties' rights and obligations arising under the contract to the detriment of
> the consumer.'

(An 'illustrative and non-exhaustive list of terms which may be regarded as unfair'
can be found in Sch 2.) Regulation 6 describes how unfair terms are to be assessed.
The effect of an unfair term (found in reg 8) is that it 'shall not be binding on the
consumer'.

Regulations 10–15 give power to the Director General of Fair Trading (DGFT) and
'qualifying bodies' (specified in Sch 1) to consider complaints that contract terms
drawn up for general use are unfair, and to take action. Under the old regulations,
these powers were reserved to the DGFT, but this was an obvious defect in
implementation of the Directive, and the 1999 Regulations also give these powers to
bodies such as the Consumers' Association.

3.8.3 Relationship with UCTA 1977

The Regulations apply in addition to rather than instead of UCTA 1977. Thus, a
solicitor will have to advise on situations where a term is subject not only to the
UCTA 1977 reasonableness test, but also the test of fairness under the Regulations.

3.8.4 The requirement of 'plain, intelligible language'

By reg 7, a seller or supplier 'shall ensure that any written term of a contract [to
which the Regulations apply] is expressed in plain, intelligible language'. This
concept is not further defined in the Regulations, nor is it clear from the Regulations
what will happen if a term is not expressed in plain, intelligible language. Perhaps
the most appropriate conclusion is that it is one of the factors which may render a
term unfair (compare the relationship of UCTA 1977 and 'plain English'; see **3.6.4**
and **3.10.7**). Regulation 7 also provides that 'if there is doubt about the meaning of a
written term, the interpretation most favourable to the consumer shall prevail';
compare the normal contra proferentem rule (see **3.6.2**).

3.9 DRAFTING FOR REASONABLENESS: GENERAL PRINCIPLES

3.9.1 The contractual reasonableness test

In practice, when UCTA 1977 applies to a commercial agreement, most (if not all) of
the agreement's exclusion clauses will be subject to the reasonableness test, so it is
usually against this test that the solicitor will need to assess a clause.

Section 11(1) of UCTA 1977 states that:

> 'In relation to a contract term, the requirement of reasonableness ... is that the term
> shall have been a fair and reasonable one to be included having regard to the
> circumstances which were, or ought reasonably to have been, known to or in the
> contemplation of the parties when the contract was made.'

It is, therefore, a test of reasonableness of incorporation, not reasonableness of reliance. If (in the light of the actual and constructive knowledge of the parties at the time) it is reasonable to include a particular clause when the contract is made, it should pass the reasonableness test: the court should not look at whether it was reasonable for the 'guilty' party to rely on the clause in the light of the events which actually happened (although it has to be said that it is not uncommon in practice for courts to do this). It is for the party claiming that a term satisfies the reasonableness test to show that it does (s 11(5)).

3.9.2 The Schedule 2 guidelines

The guidelines include: the relative bargaining power of the parties; whether the buyer was offered any inducement to accept the clause; whether any choice was available (could the buyer have acquired the goods elsewhere without the clause?); and the extent of the parties' knowledge of the existence and effect of the terms. The list is not intended to be exhaustive and, strictly speaking, only applies when the court is assessing reasonableness under ss 6(3) and 7(3) of UCTA 1977. However, the courts often apply the guidelines when considering the reasonableness test in relation to other sections (notably s 3; see, for example, *Flamar Interocean Ltd v Denmac Ltd (formerly Denholm Maclay Co Ltd) (The 'Flamar Pride' and 'Flamar Progress')* [1990] 1 Lloyd's Rep 434). This approach was confirmed as appropriate by the Court of Appeal in *Overseas Medical Supplies Ltd v Orient Transport Services Ltd* [1999] 2 Lloyd's Rep 273. This case also contains a useful discussion and summary of the factors which are generally relevant to assessing the reasonableness of a clause.

3.9.3 Is the contract a consumer or a commercial contract?

In determining whether a clause will survive the application of UCTA 1977, the crucial factor is often whether the contract is a consumer or a commercial contract. For example, a clause which excludes liability for breach of s 14(2) or (3) of SGA 1979 is only subject to the reasonableness test against a commercial buyer, but is void against a buyer who deals as consumer. Even if a clause is subject to the reasonableness test whatever the status of the 'victim' (eg under s 3), the courts are often prepared to be stricter in applying the test where that person is a consumer. The clause may in fact be less likely to pass the test for that reason alone. If the client deals with both commercial and consumer buyers, it is important for the solicitor to recognise this when drafting. There may be several different ways of dealing with the problem, depending on how the client does business and the other relevant circumstances. For example, the solicitor may decide to draft two different forms of contract, with the 'consumer' version either omitting certain exclusion clauses, or containing only modified versions. However, this may be risky; it would then be necessary to ensure that those operating the contract are able to distinguish between the two versions (perhaps print them on different coloured paper). A simpler solution (where possible) is to have one contract for all customers, but to draft any exclusion so that it will apply only to commercial customers.

3.9.4 No guarantee of success

Because of the way in which the contractual reasonableness test is worded, the factors which are relevant when drafting for reasonableness (see **3.10**) are often specific to the circumstances of each individual contract. The solicitor must therefore advise the client that even the best-drafted clause cannot be guaranteed to work in all circumstances. However, careful drafting can often significantly increase the likelihood of the clause passing the reasonableness test.

3.10 DRAFTING FOR REASONABLENESS: RELEVANT FACTORS

3.10.1 Introduction

Looking at the cases in which the courts have applied the contractual reasonableness test, it is possible to identify a number of factors which have been held to have a bearing on reasonableness. These must be treated with some caution when used as an aid to drafting; each contract and the exclusions it contains must be considered in its own particular context. Even if a clause has been interpreted in a particular way or held to be reasonable on one occasion, this is no guarantee that a court will react in the same way when faced with the same clause in a different case. As a result, it is not possible to produce an exhaustive list of relevant factors on reasonableness. In addition, it is unusual for one factor alone to be conclusive on reasonableness; in drafting, the solicitor must take into account all the factors (often conflicting) which could apply, and try to assess on balance whether the clause is likely to be held reasonable. However, if all this is taken into account, the following list should provide a useful guide when drafting. The Court of Appeal's decision in *Overseas Medical Supplies Ltd v Orient Transport Services Ltd* [1999] 2 Lloyd's Rep 273 (noted at **3.9.2**) provides a good summary of the relevant factors. Other interesting recent cases on the application of the reasonableness test in a commercial situation include *Watford Electronics Ltd v Sanderson CFL Ltd* [2001] 1 All ER (Comm) 696 and *Britvic Soft Drinks Ltd v Messer UK Ltd* [2002] EWCA Civ 548, [2002] 1 Lloyd's Rep 20.

3.10.2 Relationship between the parties

In deciding whether a clause is reasonable, the courts will often be influenced by the relationship between the parties and the strength of their bargaining positions (this is a Schedule 2 guideline). For example, in a consumer case, the fact that bargaining power is normally on the side of the supplier may be a vital factor in the court's decision; the court may be more likely for this reason alone to declare the supplier's attempts at exclusion to be unreasonable. Relevant factors connected with the relationship between the parties may include those set out below.

Negotiated or standard-form contract?

If the contract was individually negotiated, so that both sides were able to influence its contents, the courts may be more likely to decide that exclusions are reasonable than they would if one party had simply imposed terms on the other (as in a standard-form contract). Note, however, that a contract may not necessarily fall neatly into one particular category. An example of this is where the original 'framework' of the contract is negotiated between the trade associations of the parties, but by the time it goes into operation, the contract is in effect standard-form.

Market in which the parties operate

This raises a number of issues on reasonableness and bargaining power. The courts tend to hold that commercial parties which are operating in the same market may be taken to know exactly how that market works: if they have provided for this accordingly in their contracts, the courts are likely to assume that those provisions are reasonable. (This may relate to the previous point; in some cases, the courts have suggested that a distinction can be drawn between types of standard-form contract which have been settled over the years to reflect the realities of a particular business operation, such as bills of lading and charterparties, and standard-form contracts which are simply imposed by the strong on the weak.) However, if there is a very considerable imbalance of bargaining power, the courts may still be prepared to hold that a clause imposed by the stronger party is unreasonable, even if both parties operate in the same market.

Nature of the goods

In *Watford Electronics Ltd v Sanderson CFL Ltd* (a case which is discussed in more detail at **3.10.8**), the court, in finding the clauses to be reasonable, was clearly influenced by the nature of the product (computer software) as being liable to give rise to problems. In *Britvic Soft Drinks Ltd v Messer UK Ltd*, the court found the exclusions unreasonable and noted that the goods in question (carbon dioxide for soft drinks) were not ones where the end-user of the goods would reasonably expect to have to test them for compliance with the contract.

Financial pressure

One party may have been forced to accept an exclusion because its financial situation at the time of the contract means that it cannot afford to turn down the deal which the other side is offering, despite the presence of an exclusion. This may make the exclusion unreasonable.

Age and experience of the buyer

The courts may hold that an experienced buyer (whether individual or commercial) should know what it is doing when it enters into contracts, and, therefore, be more likely to decide that an exclusion clause against such a buyer is reasonable. Compare, for example, two cases on property surveys: in *Stevenson v Nationwide Building Society* [1984] 272 EG 663, the buyer was an estate agent, and an exclusion in the contract relating to the negligent performance of a survey was held to be reasonable. In *Smith v Bush (Eric S) (a firm); Harris v Wyre Forest District Council* [1989] 2 All ER 514, however, the buyer was inexperienced in buying property, and a similar exclusion was held to be unreasonable against him.

Effect of legal advice

If the 'victim' of the clause received legal advice, any exclusion stands a better chance of being held reasonable. However, in *Walker v Boyle* [1982] 1 All ER 634, the 'victim', the buyer in a conveyancing transaction, was legally advised (as was the seller) and the clause was a standard term in the then edition of the National Conditions of Sale. Nevertheless, it was still held to be unreasonable.

Drafting techniques

In a tailor-made (ie fully negotiated) contract, it may be useful to include a preamble to the exclusion, referring to as many of the above factors as are relevant, and stating whether and, if so, how those factors have been taken into account in drafting the exclusion. If the court appreciates the background, it may be more likely to hold that the exclusion is reasonable.

Attitude of the courts

To sum up, as a general proposition, it seems that if the buyer is a consumer, any exclusion clause is more likely to fail the reasonableness test; if the contract is between commercial parties, it is more likely to pass. In a commercial contract where there is no great inequality of bargaining power, and particularly where the parties have had the opportunity to identify the risks under the contract and cover them by insurance (see **3.10.5**), the courts have often taken the view that they should not interfere with what the parties have done (see, for example, the remarks of Lord Wilberforce in *Photo Production Ltd v Securicor Transport Ltd* [1980] 1 All ER 556 and, more recently, the views of the Court of Appeal in *Watford Electronics Ltd v Sanderson CFL Ltd* [2001] 1 All ER (Comm) 696, a case which is discussed in more detail at **3.10.8**). However, it must be stressed that there is no guarantee that a court will always take this view; each case must turn on its own facts.

3.10.3 Choice

Do other suppliers use the clause?

Could the buyer have obtained the goods or services from another supplier which does not impose the exclusion clause in question? This factor (a Schedule 2 guideline) may point in either direction. If the buyer could have gone elsewhere without having the clause imposed, and yet chose to make this particular contract, this may mean that the clause is more likely to be reasonable. Note that the buyer's knowledge of the existence and extent of the clause (see **3.10.7**) is likely to be relevant. On the other hand, if the supplier is the only one in a particular line of business using a particular exclusion clause, and is, therefore, out of step with its competitors, this may be evidence that it is unreasonable to use the clause at all.

Two-tier pricing

In a clause of this type, the supplier of the goods or services charges a lower price if the buyer accepts the exclusion clause, and a higher price if the contract contains either a modified version of the clause or no clause at all. Using two-tier pricing can help the clause to pass the reasonableness test. For example, in *Woodman v Photo Trade Processing* (1981) unreported, 3 April, Exeter County Court, it was held that a clause limiting the liability of a film processor to the cost of the film was unreasonable because (inter alia) the processor had failed to use a two-tier pricing system recommended by its own trade association. However, the use of two-tier pricing is not an automatic guarantee of success. In *Warren v Truprint* [1986] BTLC 344, Luton County Court, it was held that an exclusion clause based on two-tier pricing was unreasonable because its wording was too vague.

Note that two-tier pricing can work in both consumer and commercial cases. For example, in *RW Green Ltd v Cade Brothers Farm* [1987] Lloyd's Rep 602, the seller in a commercial sale of goods contract used an exclusion with two-tier pricing, and the clause passed the reasonableness test.

3.10.4 Price

If the loss which may result from breach of contract is wholly disproportionate to the contract price, it may be reasonable for the contract to contain an exclusion (or limitation) clause. If both parties are aware of this from the outset, the chances of the clause being reasonable may be enhanced. In a tailor-made contract, a preamble can be used to set out the basis on which the parties are contracting.

3.10.5 Allocation of risk and insurance

The parties to a commercial contract will usually be in the best position to decide what the risks under the contract are, and how to deal with them. If they decide to use an exclusion or limitation clause which has the effect of passing the risk of loss or damage from one party to the other, and the contract then clearly requires the party with the risk to take out appropriate insurance, this should improve the chances that the clause will be held reasonable. Even where there is no specific obligation to insure, the court may attach considerable significance to how the parties have identified and dealt with the risks under the contract (eg by reflecting them in the contract prices, then backing this up with a limitation clause).

It may be worthwhile obtaining expert evidence on insurance before drafting the contract and its exclusions. Without such evidence, the parties may be left at the mercy of judicial assumptions about which party should have insured, and against what. For example, in *George Mitchell (Chesterhall) Ltd v Finney Lock Seeds Ltd* [1983] 2 AC 803, the contract provided that the seller's liability for supplying defective seed was limited to the price of the seed. The House of Lords accepted that a supplier of seed could insure against liability for delivering the wrong seed, without significantly increasing its prices, and assumed that this would be more appropriate than for a farmer buying the seed to insure against loss of crop. The clause failed the reasonableness test for a number of reasons, but the House of Lords was obviously impressed by evidence that it would have been easy and inexpensive for the supplier to cover itself by insurance against extra loss caused. However, the courts will not always be in the best position to assess what the risks and the most suitable insurance arrangements are, and may, therefore, in the absence of suitable evidence, make an inappropriate decision on the reasonableness of any exclusion.

If the circumstances allow (eg in a tailor-made contract), it may be useful to preface an insurance clause with a preamble explaining how the insurance arrangements and the exclusions have been arrived at. There will, of course, be many different arrangements which can be made, and ways in which they can be expressed. The main requirement, however, is that the position should be clear. Each party should be fully aware of its rights and responsibilities.

Note that where a limitation clause is concerned, UCTA 1977, s 11(4)(b) specifically mentions the availability of insurance as a factor in assessing reasonableness (see further **3.10.8**).

3.10.6 Trade associations

Approval by a trade association (or similar body) may help an exclusion clause to pass the reasonableness test. For example, in *RW Green Ltd v Cade Brothers Farm* (see **3.10.3**), the parties used a standard-form contract which had originally been negotiated between the National Farmers' Union and the National Association of

Seed Potato Merchants. The exclusion was found to be reasonable. Equally, ignoring a trade association's recommendations may cause problems, as in *Woodman v Photo Trade Processing* (see **3.10.3**).

3.10.7 Buyer's knowledge and understanding of the clause

This factor (a Schedule 2 guideline) is particularly important where the buyer is a consumer, but is by no means confined to that situation. Consider, for example, the following comments of Staughton J in the commercial case of *Stag Line v Tyne Ship Repair Group: The Zinnia* [1984] 2 Lloyd's Rep 211: 'I would have been tempted to hold that all of the conditions are unfair and unreasonable for two reasons; first, they are in such small print that one can barely read them; secondly, the draftsmanship is so convoluted and prolix that one almost needs an LLB to understand them'.

Short and simple drafting

This can be difficult to achieve, but is worth aiming for. The solicitor should, in particular, consider the likely reading abilities of those involved with the contract. For a more detailed discussion of this topic, see the chapter on writing and drafting in the LPC Resource Book *Skills for Lawyers* (Jordans).

Size of print, layout and appearance

Wherever possible, the solicitor should advise the client to use easily readable print, and to set documents out in a way which assists reading (if this can be done without wasting space). Devices such as different typefaces, bold type, underlining and boxes are all useful for drawing attention to significant parts of a contract.

The solicitor will also need to consider where and how the exclusion should appear in the contract. There is no single correct way of doing this; it is often helpful to look at several sets of precedents to get a feel for the different methods. For example, some contracts will place each exclusion immediately after the clause to which it relates; some will have a separate section for the exclusions, cross-referring to other relevant clauses where necessary. The main thing to remember is that the way in which the exclusions are presented may have a bearing on the victim's knowledge and understanding of them, and therefore affect their reasonableness.

Practical problems

Following these guidelines should increase the chances of a clause being held reasonable, but may also create difficulties. For example, will a clause which is well laid out and clearly expressed fit onto the back of an order form? Sometimes 'wall-to-wall' layout (where the print covers virtually the entire surface of the paper, without margins or adequate space between lines) is essential because space is limited. It is worth, however, trying to achieve the best of both worlds. For example, consider whether space can be increased by getting rid of redundant clauses, or deleting clauses which cover contingencies so remote that they are not worth providing for (or which would cause few problems if they did occur). It is also possible that a document written in 'plain' English may turn out to be shorter than the same thing expressed in traditional 'legal' English. The solicitor should at least try to see what can be done.

Tactics

The solicitor must, however, also be aware of tactical considerations. The client may not want the finished document to be too clear. It may be valid to obscure the meaning of a clause for tactical reasons (and some clients may be uncomfortable with a document which is not written in what they perceive to be 'legal' English). There are no clear-cut solutions to the problems which this raises: solicitor and client must discuss the pros and cons of each approach in each individual case.

Incorporation by reference

Incorporation by reference is a common practice in both consumer and business contracts. For example, the supplier under a sale of goods agreement may wish to use standard terms laid down by its trade association as the basis of any contracts it makes. To save space, the agreement can state that the goods are sold subject to the relevant trade association's standard terms, and that the supplier will provide the buyer with a copy of the terms.

Bear in mind, however, that this practice involves some risk. It may be a useful space-saving device, but there can be problems on both incorporation and reasonableness.

Conclusion

Because of its numerous different aspects, this factor will often be difficult to weigh up; solicitor and client will have to decide what the priority is in each particular case. On the one hand, if a contract is drafted and set out clearly, clauses which are subject to the reasonableness test are more likely to pass the test. On the other hand, fitting a contract into a set amount of space (eg the back of the client's order form) may be seen as more important, even though this may require a compression of drafting and layout which could render a clause unreasonable. However, there may be some room for compromise; just because a contract must fit on to an order form, it does not necessarily also have to be drafted 'wall-to-wall', difficult to read and full of jargon.

3.10.8 Exclusion or limitation?

General principle

The House of Lords has held on a number of occasions (eg *Ailsa Craig Fishing Co Ltd v Malvern Fishing Co Ltd* [1983] 1 WLR 964) that a clause which limits liability is more likely to pass the reasonableness test than one which excludes it altogether. However, this principle should be treated with care; arguably, what is important is the difference in degree of exclusion, not simply in type of clause. A clause which limits the supplier's liability to the contract price, where the damage likely to be caused is far in excess of this, may be little different in effect from a strict exclusion, especially if the contract price is low (for an important case on limitation of liability and assessing the reasonableness of limitation clauses, see *St Albans City and District Council v ICL* [1996] 4 All ER 480).

The Court of Appeal recently considered the reasonableness of a limitation clause in the case of *Watford Electronics Ltd v Sanderson CFL Ltd* [2001] 1 All ER (Comm) 696, a case which makes a number of important points about reasonableness in relation to limitation and exclusion in commercial contracts generally.

In this case, the seller had supplied the buyer with computer hardware and software; the supply was on the seller's standard terms, which contained the following provisions:

- a clause limiting the seller's liability to the contract price and excluding liability for consequential or indirect losses;
- a clause providing that neither party relied on any representation by the other party in entering the contract; and
- an addendum to the contract in which the seller agreed to use its best endeavours to allocate appropriate resources to the contract to minimise any losses which might arise from its performance of the contract.

The software did not perform to the buyer's satisfaction, and the buyer sued for damages for breach of contract. The Court of Appeal held that the limitation clause passed the reasonableness test, noting generally that the parties were both experienced commercial parties and of roughly equal bargaining power; this clearly influenced the court's decision. In addition, the parties would (or should) have taken the risk of the software failing to perform into account when settling the contract price. As a matter of construction, the limitation clause did not deprive the buyer of the chance to recover damages for breach of contract in all situations, and the seller's ability to rely on it was further qualified by the addendum to the contract.

In the circumstances, and having regard to the Schedule 2 guidelines, the clause satisfied the reasonableness test.

Note that UCTA 1977, s 11(4) contains two guidelines which apply only where a term is designed to limit liability to a specified sum of money, rather than to exclude it altogether. By s 11(4)(a), the court should take account of the resources available to the person relying on the limitation to meet liability, should it arise; and, as previously noted, by s 11(4)(b), the court should have regard to how far it was open to that person to cover himself by insurance.

Drafting techniques

A common drafting technique with limitation clauses is, to limit liability to 'direct loss', and exclude liability for 'consequential loss'. However, since neither of these terms has any precise, agreed meaning, the solicitor should either avoid using them, or try to make as clear as possible what they cover in each particular contract.

3.11 DRAFTING FOR SEVERANCE

Instead of drafting one clause to cover all the exclusions under the contract (which carries the risk that the clause may then be struck down in its entirety as unreasonable), it is usually more appropriate to draft a series of clauses or sub-clauses, so that if one is found to be unreasonable, the others may still survive because the court is able to apply the normal principles of severance. To reinforce the point, the series can end with a statement that each clause or sub-clause is to be treated as separate and independent.

3.12 DRAFTING TO LITIGATE OR TO NEGOTIATE?

3.12.1 Tactics

In most cases, a solicitor will be drafting to negotiate, rather than to litigate, should problems arise with the agreement in the future. It is, therefore, often valid to draft a clause which a court might hold unreasonable if litigation is in fact unlikely, and the clause achieves the right result for the client (eg the client's opponent makes no claim or agrees to settle any claim on suitable terms). Obviously, the client should be informed of what the solicitor is doing (and why) and warned that it is impossible to guarantee that the clause will achieve this result. It is also important when using this technique to distinguish between clauses which are void and clauses which are subject to the reasonableness test.

3.12.2 Void clauses

The solicitor should not use any clause which is void under UCTA 1977. A clause of this nature should be easy to spot, especially if the 'victim' takes legal advice, and so is unlikely to prevent a claim being made anyway. At best, the clause will create a bad impression; at worst, it may not only be ineffective, but its use may be a criminal offence. For example, under the Consumer Transactions (Restrictions on Statements) Order 1976, SI 1976/1813, a supplier commits a criminal offence if, in a consumer sale of goods contract, he uses a clause which is void under s 6(2) of UCTA 1977 (see **3.7.1**).

3.12.3 Clauses subject to the reasonableness test

Where a clause is subject to the reasonableness test, the position is quite different. It may be possible to achieve good results for the client by using a clause which might be of doubtful reasonableness if it were ever litigated, as long as the client understands and approves of the tactic.

3.12.4 Drafting for good public relations

In some circumstances, it is worth drafting positively rather than (as is traditional with exclusion clauses) negatively. This could be worthwhile, for example in a contract for the performance of services, where the supplier promises to exercise reasonable care and skill in carrying out the work under the contract, and to accept full liability for any personal injury or death caused by breach of his promise. This gives the other party no more than its legal rights, but creates the impression that the supplier is being generous.

3.13 TRYING TO EXCLUDE EVERYTHING

Sometimes, the client may want the solicitor to exclude all liability which could arise from breach of any contractual obligation. This cannot be done. Obviously, some liability is non-excludable because of UCTA 1977. In addition, a contract which purports to exclude one party's liability for breach in respect of all its contractual obligations would not be a contract at all. That party would not be binding itself to do anything, and the 'contract' would be no more than a declaration of intent. A court faced with this situation would probably assume that the parties had made a mistake, and attempt to construe the contract in such a way that it does not exclude liability for everything. The solicitor will have to judge carefully how far it is possible to go if the client requests as much exclusion as possible.

3.14 DRAFTING SPECIFIC CLAUSES IN A COMMERCIAL CONTRACT

This chapter ends with a closer look at three types of exclusion clause commonly found in commercial contracts: force majeure, non-rejection and time bar clauses. It considers their use and their relationship with UCTA 1977; for suggestions as to how the clauses could be drafted, see for example the appropriate sections of *Practical Commercial Precedents* or the *Encyclopaedia of Forms and Precedents* (for references, see the section on Further Study at p vii).

3.14.1 Force majeure clauses

A force majeure clause is designed to apply where contractual performance has become impossible because of circumstances unforeseen by the parties and outside their control. In a sale of goods contract, it will normally seek to excuse the seller for failure to deliver the goods on time (or even at all) in these circumstances. A force majeure clause is normally classified as part of the boiler-plate of an agreement (see **1.4.7**).

Meaning of 'force majeure'

The expression 'force majeure' has been interpreted by the courts to cover act of God, war, strikes, embargoes, refusal to grant licences and abnormal weather conditions. The common factor in each case is that the event is outside the contracting parties' control. However, it is usual for a force majeure clause to do more than simply state that the supplier will not be liable for non-performance caused by 'force majeure'. Instead, it will normally set out a (non-exhaustive) list of specific events which the clause is intended to cover and the consequences of any of those events arising, so that both parties know exactly where they stand. (As previously noted, the ejusdem generis rule does not apply to force majeure clauses; specifying events does not cut down the meaning of any general words which follow.)

Frustration of the contract

Before considering further how the contract can best provide for this situation, it is worth briefly looking at what will happen if nothing is mentioned in the contract: namely frustration of the contract.

FRUSTRATION DEFINED

A contract will be frustrated when a supervening event unforeseen by the parties and not due to their fault renders performance of the contract either impossible or radically different from that envisaged *(Davis Contractors v Fareham Urban DC* [1956] AC 696). Thus, for example, a contract for supply of goods will be frustrated if it becomes clear that any delivery of the goods will be so late that performance of the contract will be radically different from that envisaged by the parties.

EFFECT OF FRUSTRATION

If the contract is frustrated, the provisions of the Law Reform (Frustrated Contracts) Act 1943 will come into operation. Prima facie, the buyer can recover any payments he made before frustration (s 1(2)) and any sums which are due before the frustration date will cease to be payable. The court, however, has the discretion to allow the seller to keep all or some of any advance payment if it considers that this will be just, having regard to any expenses which the seller may have incurred in preparing to perform the contract. If one party has conferred a valuable benefit on the other, the court may allow the first party to claim a just sum in respect of that benefit (s 1(3)), although this is less likely to be relevant in a supply of goods case. It might be more relevant in a services contract, where the supplier has done some of the work but has been unable to finish it due to a frustrating event.

Note that the above discussion assumes that the seller is unable to deliver because of some problem of transporting the goods, such as industrial disputes at the port of shipment or unloading. If the problem is that the goods themselves have perished (eg if they have been destroyed in an accident), then special rules apply and the Law Reform (Frustrated Contracts) Act 1943 will not generally apply (s 2(5)). For further discussion of these and other rules relating to frustration and its effects, reference should be made to the standard textbooks on contract.

ADVANTAGES OF A SPECIFIC PROVISION IN THE CONTRACT

The problem about frustration is that it is rather uncertain (how long must the buyer wait before the performance of the contract will become radically different from that which the parties envisaged?) and its effects are rather arbitrary. It is generally preferable to have a specific provision (ie a force majeure clause) in the contract dealing with this situation. The parties can then agree that when the disrupting circumstances have been in existence for a specific time, either party may cancel the agreement by giving the other a certain period of written notice. The contract can also make specific provision for the financial consequences of such a cancellation.

Application of UCTA 1977

So long as one party deals as consumer, or on the other party's written standard terms of business, a force majeure clause will be subject to the reasonableness test under s 3 of UCTA 1977, as an attempt by the party relying on the clause to render no contractual performance at all (s 3(2)(b)(ii)).

Drafting points to consider

If a force majeure event occurs, what should happen to the contract? Possibilities include suspension or cancellation of the contract (or suspension for a certain period followed by cancellation). Which is appropriate will depend on the client's instructions and the circumstances.

If cancellation is chosen, is it more appropriate to have automatic cancellation of the contract if a force majeure event occurs, or should the party relying on the force majeure give notice of cancellation to the other? The latter will usually be preferable. (Note that the party relying on force majeure will have to prove that the event in question has arisen.)

Should the party relying on force majeure refund any payments which the other party has already made to it? If UCTA 1977, s 3 applies (see above), the clause will be valid only if it passes the reasonableness test. Providing for a refund should help to ensure that the clause is reasonable. It need not always be a full refund; a partial refund may be appropriate, especially if the supplier has already incurred expense.

3.14.2 Time bar clauses

A client who is involved in the supply of goods or services may wish to reduce the limitation period which would normally apply to claims arising from breach of the contract (the basic contractual limitation period is 6 years). This may be justifiable; long before the statutory limitation period expires, evidence of a breach of contract may become hard to pin down, and perishable goods will have lost any market value they may have had. In addition, a supplier will probably want to close its books on a particular contract reasonably soon after performance. In a commercial contract, therefore, it may be appropriate to include a 'time bar' clause (eg in a sale of goods contract, stating that the buyer cannot claim in respect of defects in the goods unless it notifies those defects to the supplier within a certain period of time).

Application of UCTA 1977

If (as will usually be the case) the effect of the time bar clause is to exclude liability for breach of the implied conditions under SGA 1979 or the Supply of Goods (Implied Terms) Act 1973 (see **3.7.1** and **3.7.2**) then UCTA 1977, s 6 will apply, and the clause will either be void or subject to the reasonableness test, depending on whether the buyer deals as consumer or not. Otherwise, UCTA 1977, s 3 will apply (as long as one party deals as consumer or on the other party's written standard terms of business); the clause is an attempt by one party to exclude or restrict its liability when in breach of contract (s 3(2)(a)).

Drafting points to consider

Does the party relying on the clause want to be notified of defects (ie of the possible existence of a claim) or of the claim itself within a specified period, or to impose a time-limit for bringing proceedings, or all of these? A clause which raises too many barriers or is too complex may fail the reasonableness test.

It is, however, often sensible to distinguish between patent and latent defects, giving a longer time period for notification in respect of defects which are not immediately apparent on delivery. This is more likely to be reasonable than having the same time period for notification of both types of defect.

The clause should state whether it is a particular remedy (eg rejection, damages) or the claim itself which is to be barred. If only the remedy is barred, the buyer might be able to use the claim as a defence to an action for the price by the seller.

If the contract is between members of the same trade association, a time bar clause probably has a better chance of passing the reasonableness test. Parties operating in the same market should know and accept the problems likely to arise in that market, and it may then be possible to make the clause stricter (eg cut down the notification period) than if the other contracting party is unfamiliar with the problems of the trade.

3.14.3 Non-rejection clauses

For his own convenience, a seller may want to prevent SGA 1979, s 36 from applying to the contract. Broadly speaking, this provides that if the buyer rejects goods, it is not obliged to return them; the seller must collect them. This can cause problems if the goods are distant from the seller, both in checking that rejection is justified (eg that the goods really are defective) and in arranging collection. In addition, a seller may want to stop its buyer from taking advantage of a fall in the price of the contract goods by finding a technical breach of contract, rejecting the goods (with a view to getting its money back from the seller or not having to pay at all) and then buying replacement goods more cheaply at the new, lower market price. In both cases, the seller should consider using a non-rejection clause.

Application of UCTA 1977

Like a time bar clause (see **3.14.2**), a non-rejection clause may, depending on the circumstances, be subject to either s 6 or s 3 of UCTA 1977.

Drafting points to consider

As there may be different reasons for including a non-rejection clause (see above), different types of clause will be necessary according to the client's needs and so no specific example is included here. For an idea of what can be achieved, see clause 8 of *Practical Commercial Precedents,* Precedent L1. Note that it may be worth using a preamble to explain why the clause has been included.

Sometimes, a simple reversal of s 36 of SGA 1979 will meet the seller's needs (eg allowing the buyer to reject but making it clear that following rejection, the buyer must return the goods to the seller).

However, the seller may wish to go further, and state that the buyer cannot reject at all. This will also prevent the buyer claiming restitution of the purchase price, but not from suing for damages for breach of contract.

Chapter 4

OTHER CONTRACTS UNDER WHICH GOODS PASS

4.1 INTRODUCTION

The archetypal commercial agreement which the solicitor is most likely to encounter in practice is the sale of goods agreement. In addition to the sale of goods agreement, the solicitor needs to be aware of a number of other types of agreement. Many of these agreements, like the sale of goods agreement, are agreements under which goods pass. They also include contracts for services and work and materials contracts.

There is, of course, the possibility that the parties have deliberately not entered into an express written contract 'to preserve maximum flexibility in their trading arrangements' (*Baird Textile Holdings Ltd v Marks & Spencer plc* [2001] EWCA Civ 274, [2002] 1 All ER (Comm) 737).

4.2 EXCHANGE AND BARTER

Contracts of exchange and barter are found relatively rarely in practice. In the past, they have been most frequently encountered in dealings with businesses in developing countries, where foreign currency may not be available to pay cash. There is evidence that they are now also being used in some forms of online trading (see **A2.10**).

4.3 HIRE PURCHASE

In a hire purchase agreement, the buyer obtains immediate possession of the goods, in return for making regular payments. However, ownership remains with the other party to the agreement. The buyer has an option to obtain ownership by paying a final instalment. Frequently, a hire purchase arrangement will involve three parties: the buyer will agree to buy the goods from a 'seller' (for example, a motor dealer), who will introduce the buyer to a finance house. Once the financial terms have been agreed with the finance house, the 'seller' will then sell the goods to the finance house, which will in turn enter into the hire purchase agreement with the buyer. The result is that the buyer 'buys' the goods not from the 'seller' but from the finance house, pursuant to the hire purchase agreement.

Hire purchase agreements are regulated under the Consumer Credit Act 1974, see Appendix 1 for more details. However, the 1974 Act does not deal with implied terms relating to title to the goods or quality. These are governed by Supply of Goods (Implied Terms) Act 1973, which implies terms similar to those implied into sale of goods agreements by ss 12–15 of SGA 1979.

4.4 CONDITIONAL SALE

A conditional sale agreement achieves a very similar result to a hire purchase agreement. Again, the buyer obtains immediate possession and makes regular payments in return. Again, ownership remains with the other party, although the buyer can obtain ownership by making a final payment. However, the agreement is structured rather differently in that there is no option to purchase. Instead, it is a sale of goods agreement under which ownership does not pass until the final payment is made.

Conditional sale is often used to finance consumer purchases in exactly the same way as a hire purchase agreement. When used in this way it is regulated by the Consumer Credit Act 1994, see Appendix 1.

Because they are sale of goods agreements, SGA 1979 applies to conditional sale agreements in the normal way and so, for example, ss 12–15 imply terms regarding title to the goods, quality, etc.

4.5 HIRE AGREEMENTS

A hire agreement differs from a sale of goods agreement in that ownership of the goods does not pass as the hirer obtains only possession.

In some situations, hire agreements with consumers are regulated by the Consumer Credit Act 1974, see Appendix 1 for more details.

SGA 1979 does not apply to hire agreements. Instead, terms relating to title and quality are implied by Supply of Goods and Services Act 1982 (SGSA 1982), ss 3–5 and 7. The terms are very similar to those implied in sale of goods agreements by SGA 1979, ss 12–15. Exceptions are that s 7 (which deals with title) implies a term that the owner (referred to as the 'bailor') has the right to transfer possession rather than a right to sell the goods.

4.6 CONTRACTS FOR SERVICES

They are governed by SGSA 1982. The main terms implied by this Act are:

- s 4, where the supplier is acting in the course of a business, an implied term that the supplier will carry out the service within a reasonable time but this term is implied only if the time agreed for performance cannot be determined in some other way;
- s 13, where the supplier is acting in the course of a business, an implied term that the service will be carried out with reasonable care and skill; and
- s 15, an implied term that the party contracting with the supplier will pay a reasonable charge but again, this is implied only if there is no other way to decide what the parties agreed about consideration.

The terms implied by ss 13–14 are referred to in the Act as 'terms', not as 'conditions' or 'warranties'. The effect of this is that breach of one of the terms will entitle the innocent party to terminate the contract only if the breach 'goes to the root of the contract' or deprives the innocent party of substantially the whole benefit of it.

4.7 WORK AND MATERIALS CONTRACTS

These are often referred to as contracts for the supply of goods and services. A good example is a contract for repair, where the repairer supplies not only his own labour but also the necessary parts.

These contracts are governed by SGSA 1982. Sections 13–15 imply terms relating to the 'work' element of the contract in exactly the same way as a pure 'services' contract. Sections 2–5 imply terms similar to those implied into sale of goods contracts by SGA 1979, ss 12–15. It is important to remember, however, that it is not SGA 1979 itself which applies in such cases.

It can sometimes be difficult to decide whether a contract should be categorised as a sale of goods contract or a contract for work and materials. Suppose, for example, that a customer engages a designer to design and build a chair. Is this a sale of goods contract (for the sale and purchase of the chair?) or is it a work and materials contract? In *Samuels v Davis* [1943] KB 526 the Court of Appeal suggested that it did not matter too much how the agreement was categorised, as long as the correct terms were implied.

Chapter 5

MARKETING AGREEMENTS

5.1 INTRODUCTION

The topic of agreements for the marketing of goods and services is introduced in Chapter 34 of the LPC Resource Book *Business Law and Practice* (Jordans). This chapter concentrates on two of the most commonly encountered marketing agreements: agency and distribution. It begins with a brief reminder of the nature of each type of agreement and its advantages and disadvantages as a marketing vehicle, and then goes on to consider how each type of agreement might be put together. There is a short concluding section on other types of marketing agreement (including franchising and licensing); note that licensing will be covered in more detail in Chapter 19.

5.1.1 Agency

The term 'agency' is often used very loosely in relation to commercial activities to cover a number of different types of business relationship, and it is extremely important not to take at face value the label which the parties have put on their arrangement; always check carefully the actual nature of the relationship. A true sales agency agreement is one where the agent makes contracts with customers on behalf of its principal; in other words, the agent binds the principal, so there is a contract between the principal and the customer (but none between the agent and the customer). Other types of agency agreement are possible; for example, marketing or 'introducing' agency. This term normally covers the situation where the agent simply finds customers and introduces them to the principal, but is also used where the agent finds customers and negotiates terms on the principal's behalf, without having the authority to make the contract on the principal's behalf. Again, it is important not to be influenced by the terminology, but always to check the true nature of the relationship between the parties.

5.1.2 Distribution

In a distribution (also known as distributorship) agreement, the supplier sells goods to the distributor, which buys them in order to re-sell on its own behalf (a common example of a distribution agreement is where a manufacturer sells its products to a wholesaler, which buys them to sell to its own customers; the relationship between manufacturer and wholesaler is a distribution agreement). The supplier has no contractual relationship with the distributor's customers.

5.1.3 Advantages and disadvantages of each type of agreement

An agency agreement (particularly a sales agency) may require close supervision by the principal, and may, therefore, not be suitable as a marketing vehicle if agent and principal are based in different countries, or the principal cannot spare the time to supervise the agent's activities. On the other hand, an agency agreement may be essential if the principal needs to be in contact with the ultimate buyers of its products (eg because the products are tailor-made for each buyer). In addition, agency agreements normally cause few competition law problems. Genuine agency agreements are likely to be unaffected by English competition law, and are also unlikely to infringe EC competition law (see **5.2.1**). Note that an agency agreement can also be used as a vehicle for marketing services, unlike a standard distribution agreement, which is really only appropriate for marketing goods.

A normal distribution agreement requires little supervision by the supplier; once the supplier has sold the goods to the distributor, it is the distributor's responsibility to decide how best to market them. If problems arise in relation to the goods which the distributor supplies, the distributor's customers have a contractual claim against the distributor, and not against the supplier, with whom they have no contract. (Note, however, that this does not mean that the ultimate customer can never have a claim against the original supplier. Where, for example, the supplier is a manufacturer, claims in tort or for product liability may arise.) It may, therefore, be easier and cheaper for a supplier to operate a distribution agreement. However, a distribution agreement (in particular an agreement which gives the distributor some form of territorial protection; see **5.4.1**) is more likely than an agency agreement to be at risk from competition law problems. An exclusive distribution agreement can easily infringe EC competition law, in particular Article 81 EC (Article 85 of the EC Treaty, prior to the coming into force of the Treaty of Amsterdam in May 1999). This aspect of distribution agreements is covered in more detail at **18.3**.

5.2 AGENCY AGREEMENTS

5.2.1 Introduction

To help in considering how to approach an agency agreement, this section will refer to an expanded version of the agency example described in **34.6** of the LPC Resource Book *Business Law and Practice* (Jordans).

Example

Wood Magic Ltd is a medium-sized company in Chester. It has been established for about 20 years, and has built up a thriving business making custom-designed furniture in luxury woods such as yew and cherry. Its sales have been largely confined to the North of England, where it has built up an excellent reputation. However, following a recent change of management and an injection of new capital, the directors plan to expand the business. In particular, they want to target London and the South-East, but have not yet decided how best to do this. Up to now, Wood Magic has carried out its own marketing, and there are no plans to change the set-up for the existing Northern operations. However, the directors feel that Wood Magic needs to find a 'trading partner' with a presence in the target market to help the furniture become established in that market. They are prepared to commit at least one director to be permanently engaged on developing this side of the business and establishing good relations with the trading partner. This commitment will be a long-term one, and despite having the trading partner to find customers for it, Wood Magic needs to maintain customer contact itself to ensure that customers get the products they need. The directors would like to know how the involvement of a trading partner might affect Wood Magic's liability to customers, but see no problem in being liable to customers if things go wrong, as they are proud of the company's reputation.

5.2.2 Initial advice

At this stage of the proposed transaction, the solicitor is likely to be asked to advise in two related areas.

(1) What sort of marketing arrangement is most suitable for Wood Magic?
(2) What factors should it take into account when looking for a trading partner?

The facts indicate that some form of agency agreement would be most appropriate.

- Wood Magic needs to be able to supervise its trading partner quite closely, and is prepared to commit resources to this supervision.
- Wood Magic needs to have some sort of contact with the buyers of its furniture to give them the products they need.
- Wood Magic is not concerned about being liable to its ultimate customers.
- The target market is in the UK, so supervision of the trading partner should be easier.

In addition, it is unlikely that Wood Magic would need to be concerned about competition law problems: see **5.3.1**.

Either marketing or sales agency may be suitable, depending on whether the directors simply want the agent to find customers or whether they want to give the agent authority to make contracts on Wood Magic's behalf. In both cases (but particularly the second), Wood Magic should be looking for a reliable, well organised and credit-worthy business, preferably with an established reputation.

5.3 DRAFTING AN AGENCY AGREEMENT

5.3.1 Preliminary considerations

Assume now that Wood Magic's directors have found a suitable trading partner, a company called Lynwood Ltd, which is based in Kingston upon Thames. They have checked Lynwood's business credentials and are satisfied that it will make a suitable trading partner. In particular, Wood Magic is satisfied that using Lynwood will give Wood Magic an appropriate level of customer contact. The prospective parties are now negotiating the agency agreement, and have provisionally agreed certain terms, including:

- Lynwood will have authority to find customers and make contracts on Wood Magic's behalf.
- Wood Magic will deliver the finished furniture direct to customers.
- Wood Magic will pay Lynwood a monthly commission.
- Wood Magic will set the prices for the furniture (as it is custom-made, Wood Magic will supply Lynwood with a detailed 'pricing menu' which will allow Lynwood to work out the price for each order).
- Lynwood will keep certain display items of Wood Magic's furniture at its premises to show potential customers what can be achieved. Wood Magic will supply Lynwood with these items free of charge and will remain the owner of the items.

The solicitor is ready to begin drafting the agreement: what preliminary considerations should be taken into account?

How far will the agreement be affected by competition law?

If the proper law of the contract is to be English law (for choice of law, see **7.3**), English competition law is potentially applicable.

The Competition Act 1998 contains a basic prohibition (the *Chapter I Prohibition*) on anti-competitive agreements which is almost identical to Article 81(1) EC; as Article 81(1) EC generally does not apply to genuine agency agreements (see next paragraph) the position will be the same in English law.

In practice, genuine agency agreements will fall outside the scope of Article 81 EC as a result of paragraphs 12–20 of the Commission Notice of May 2000 which sets out guidelines on vertical restraints (see Chapter 18 for further explanation of this Notice and the block exemption to which it relates). The Notice replaces an earlier Notice (dated 24 December 1962) which specifically related to agency agreements.

Paragraph 12 of the Notice defines an agency agreement for this purpose; broadly speaking, it is an agreement where one person (the agent) is 'vested with the power to negotiate and/or conclude contracts on behalf of another person (the principal)' for the sale or purchase of goods or services by the principal. Paragraph 13 states that in the case of 'genuine agency agreements, the obligations imposed on the agent as to the contracts negotiated and/or concluded on behalf of the principal do not fall within the scope of application of Article 81(1)'. It goes on to state that the determining factor in assessing whether Article 81(1) EC is applicable to an agency agreement is the 'financial or commercial risk borne by the agent in relation to the activities for which he has been appointed as an agent by the principal'. The paragraph concludes by stating that 'non-genuine' agency agreements may be caught by Article 81(1) EC.

Paragraphs 14–17 then indicate the types of financial or commercial risk which are material to assessing whether an agency agreement is 'genuine' or not (note that para 16 indicates that this assessment must be made on a case-by-case basis, and with regard to the economic reality of the situation rather than the legal form of the agreement). Paragraph 14 states that two types of risk are material: risks related directly to the contracts which the agent negotiates and/or concludes for the principal (eg the financing of stocks of goods), and risks related to 'market-specific investments' (investments specifically required to enable the agent to negotiate and/or conclude the contracts). The implication is that acceptance of such risks by the agent to a significant degree will stop the agreement being a genuine agency agreement.

In para 16, the Commission states that it considers that Article 81(1) EC will not generally be applicable where the property in (ie ownership of) the contract goods does not vest in the agent, or where the agent does not itself supply the contract services; it goes on to give a non-exhaustive list of indications that an agent is not accepting significant financial or commercial risks (including that the agent does not contribute to the supply of goods or services, that the agent is not required to invest in sales promotion, does not maintain at its own cost or risk stocks of the contract goods and does not create and/or operate after-sales, repair or warranty services unless it is fully reimbursed by the principal).

Paragraph 18 indicates that if an agency agreement falls outside the scope of Article 81(1) EC, all the obligations imposed on the agent in relation to contracts made fall outside Article 81(1) EC. The following obligations are specifically identified as forming an 'inherent part' of an agency agreement:

- limitations on the territory in which the agent may sell the goods/services;
- limitations on the customers to whom the agent may sell these goods/services;
- the prices and conditions at which the agent must sell or purchase these goods or services.

On the basis of the terms agreed in principle, will Wood Magic and Lynwood have the benefit of the Notice? There seems a good chance that their argument will be a 'genuine' agency agreement, as Lynwood does not appear to be accepting financial or commercial risks that would make the agreements 'non-genuine'. In particular, there is no evidence that Lynwood will ever be the owner of the contract goods, and although Lynwood keeps display items of furniture at its premises, these are not 'stocks' in the normal sense (Lynwood has not paid for them and does not own them); there is also no evidence of Lynwood providing promotional or after-sales services. On the basis that their agreement is 'genuine', neither the Competition Act 1998 nor Article 81 EC (which would, of course, only be applicable anyway if the agreement were capable of affecting trade between Member States) would apply.

How far should the agreement expressly refer to the basic principles of agency law?

Again, this discussion assumes that the proper law of the agreement is to be English law. Should the agreement, for example, refer expressly to the agent's fiduciary duties (such as acting in all good faith towards the principal)? Should it set out the other duties which will be implied into the contract in the absence of agreement between the parties? These are difficult points to resolve. Ultimately, the answer must depend upon the relationship of the parties and how familiar they are with the principles of agency law generally. If they are new to one another and have little experience of agency agreements (this would seem to apply to Wood Magic and Lynwood) setting out the principles could be beneficial; both parties will know exactly where they stand. If, however, the parties are both experienced and already have a long-standing relationship, express inclusion of basic agency principles may only offend both sides.

Statutory restrictions on drafting

For many years, there was comparatively little statutory provision in English law which could affect the contents of an agency agreement. However, many agency agreements are now subject to the Commercial Agents (Council Directive) Regulations 1993, SI 1993/3053 ('the Regulations'), which came into force on 1 January 1994, and enacted into English law the requirements of the EC Directive on the Co-ordination of Laws of Member States relating to Self-Employed Commercial Agents (Dir 86/653/EEC). The Regulations 'govern the relations between commercial agents and their principals ... in relation to the activities of commercial agents in Great Britain' (reg 1(1)). Provision is made in reg 1(3) (as amended) for agreements which are to be governed by the law of another Member State.

'Commercial agent' is defined in reg 2(1) as 'a self-employed intermediary who has continuing authority to negotiate the sale or purchase of goods on behalf of another person (the "principal") or to negotiate and conclude the sale or purchase of goods on behalf of and in the name of that principal ...'. This definition means that the type of 'marketing' agent which only has authority to find customers and is not authorised to 'negotiate' on the principal's behalf will not be a 'commercial agent'. Obviously, it will be very important for the parties to agree on the extent of the agent's authority to act on the principal's behalf.

For an interesting recent case on what constitutes an agent and on the application of the Regulations, see the Court of Appeal's decision in *Mercantile International Group plc v Chuan Soon Huant Industrial Group Ltd* [2002] EWCA Civ 288, [2002] 1 All ER (Comm) 788. Here, the arrangement between the parties was described as an 'agency agreement', and contracts with customers stated that the claimant was acting as agent for the defendant. However, the claimant was not paid by commission, but (like a distributor) was remunerated by mark-up (it charged customers for the goods and paid a smaller sum to the 'principal'). On the other hand, the claimant clearly had authority to negotiate in the principal's name; the principal delivered direct to customers and the claimant never held any stock.

The Court of Appeal decided that in the light of all the above factors, the agreement was an agency agreement; although the way in which remuneration was paid might appear to point against agency, this was outweighed by the other factors and did not determine the question in this case. The agreement was also consistent with the agent being a 'commercial agent', and the Regulations applied.

Note the situations in which the Regulations will not apply:

- where the agent does not come within the definition of 'commercial agent' (reg 2(1));
- where the agent is an agent of a type listed in reg 2(2);
- where the agent's activities as a commercial agent are to be considered secondary (regs 2(3), 2(4) and the Schedule).

In addition, the Regulations do not extend to Northern Ireland (reg 2(5)).

They lay down rules with which the parties must comply in relation to a number of important areas of an agency agreement, in particular: the rights and obligations of both parties (see **5.3.3** and **5.3.4**); the agent's remuneration (see **5.3.5**); and the conclusion and termination of the agency contract (see **5.3.6**). Note that, by reg 23(1), the Regulations apply not only to agency agreements which have been entered into on or after 1 January 1994, but also those which were already in existence on that date. Assuming that Lynwood falls within the definition of 'commercial agent' (which it will, as long as it has in practice 'continuing authority to negotiate and conclude the sale … of goods on behalf of another person …'), the Regulations will apply to its agreement with Wood Magic.

Plan of this section

This section (**5.3**) describes the likely structure and contents of a typical sales agency agreement such as might be suitable for Wood Magic and Lynwood, and falls into six distinct parts: **5.3.2** (introduction to a sales agency agreement); **5.3.3** (agent's rights and duties); **5.3.4** (principal's rights and duties); **5.3.5** (financial provisions); **5.3.6** (termination) and **5.3.7** (miscellaneous clauses).

Precedents

Obviously, no single agreement or set of clauses can ever claim to be a comprehensive guide to drafting a particular agreement; the commercial draftsman should always be ready to consult a wide range of precedents and other sources.

Sections **5.3.2–5.3.7** refer to just one of the standard agency precedents available: Precedent K1 (Sales Agency Agreement) in Rosenberg *Practical Commercial Precedents* (Sweet & Maxwell) (PCP). Further precedents and sources are listed at **5.9**.

5.3.2 Introduction to the agreement

This section of the agreement is likely to cover the following areas: a preliminary clause setting out the date of the agreement, the parties and any recitals which are felt to be necessary; a definitions and interpretation clause; and a clause dealing with the appointment of the agent.

Date, parties, recitals (PCP K1-021)

The date of the agreement should cause few problems, but the description of the parties may need some thought. The principal will often be a manufacturer (as with Wood Magic), but as agency can be created at any stage of the marketing chain, it could be, for example, a wholesaler. Recitals may be useful for setting out the basis on which the parties are making their agreement. For example, Wood Magic and Lynwood might use a recital to show that their relationship is such that the agent (Lynwood) is not acting as an independent trader, and to indicate therefore that the parties believe that the agreement will not be affected by competition law.

Definitions and interpretation

Two definitions which are likely to require some thought are 'Products' and 'Territory'.

'PRODUCTS'

It is useful for the agreement to contain a comprehensive definition of the products which the agent is marketing on the principal's behalf. In the case of the agreement under consideration, this is clearly Wood Magic's furniture, but a more precise definition is likely to be needed. For example, will the agent handle the principal's whole product range or only some of the principal's products? Will it handle all products of a particular type which the principal manufactures? This is often best dealt with by listing the relevant products in a schedule to the agreement. Often the main problem in a continuing relationship is how to handle changes which may occur (eg what will happen if the principal ceases to manufacture a particular product or begins to manufacture a new one?). To cover this, should the agreement include provision for a mutually agreed variation? Will the principal want to force the agent to take up a new product (either with or without notice), or should any changes to the product range be made only with the agent's consent? The answers will obviously depend upon the relationship between the parties, their relative needs and their bargaining strengths.

'TERRITORY'

Where will the agent market the goods? In Lynwood's case, it is to be London and the South-East of England. In many cases, defining 'territory' will be straightforward, but it should be expressed as precisely as possible.

Appointment of the agent (PCP K1-023, clause 2)

The appointment clause defines the agent's role in the agreement, and is perhaps the single most important clause in an agency agreement. In particular, it defines the extent of the agent's authority to bind the principal, which in turn will determine a number of other matters. It is likely to cover the following areas.

AGENT'S AUTHORITY

In a sales agency agreement, the agent is given authority to enter contracts on the principal's behalf for the sale of the products. As the agent binds the principal, the principal must honour any contracts which the agent has made on its behalf. As noted previously, a marketing agent's authority will be more restricted. Whatever the parties decide is best for them, the appointment clause should always make clear the extent of the agent's authority.

AGENT'S OPERATIONS

In attempting to define the geographical limits of the agent's operations and the extent to which the agent will be protected from competition by others within this territory, the clause should be as clear as possible. A particular problem arises with the use of the expressions 'sole' agency and 'exclusive' agency. Strictly speaking, 'sole' agency means that the principal will not appoint any other agents within the defined territory, but that the principal can still sell its products there itself. 'Exclusive' agency means that the principal itself cannot sell the products within the territory or appoint any other agents in the territory. However, the legal and commercial meanings of both terms have become confused, and may even mean different things in different product markets. It is, therefore, unsafe to define the scope of the agent's protection from competition in the territory simply by using the words 'sole' or 'exclusive' in the agreement. It is better to state clearly whether the principal can appoint other agents or market the products in the territory itself (and in what circumstances). It is also sensible to make clear how far (if at all) the agent can extend its operations beyond the territory. On this last point, note that forbidding the agent to accept unsolicited orders from outside the territory can cause real problems if Article 81 EC does apply to the agreement.

DURATION AND TERMINATION

The appointment clause often also deals with duration and termination of the agreement (compare the PCP precedent, which has a combined Duration and Termination clause at clause 10).

The parties may consider entering into a fixed-term agreement. It may be desirable to grant the agent a reasonably long initial fixed term, in order to give it an incentive to build up the business. However, there are, of course, other possibilities. If the parties want an indefinite term, or a fixed term followed by an indefinite term a suitable notice provision should be included. (Note that under reg 15 of the Commercial Agents (Council Directive) Regulations 1993, the agent is entitled to certain minimum periods of notice.)

DEL CREDERE AGENCY

If the agency is to be a del credere agency (ie where the agent agrees to guarantee the customer's performance of the contract in return for an additional commission), this is likely to be an appropriate part of the agreement to include the del credere provision (note the precedent given for this at Form 11 of the Agency, Distribution and Franchising section in Volume 1 of *The Encyclopaedia of Forms and Precedents* (Butterworths, 1994)).

In the proposed agreement between Wood Magic and Lynwood, the solicitor will need to take instructions on most of the preceding matters, as there is no evidence that the parties have yet considered any of them (except the matter of Lynwood's authority).

5.3.3 The agent's rights and duties (PCP K1-024, clause 3)

Introduction

The principal needs to have an appropriate amount of control over its sales agent's activities, so the section on agent's duties is likely to be the longest of the agreement. Broadly speaking, the principal will want to ensure (as far as possible) that the agent observes certain limitations (eg in a sales agency, that the agent does not make unsuitable contracts on the principal's behalf), while still encouraging the agent to exploit the agency to its full potential. It may be appropriate when drafting the agreement to have a clause relating to general duties, followed by individual clauses covering particular duties (such as advertising and promotion). Note the provisions of reg 3 of the Commercial Agents (Council Directive) Regulations 1993 on the agent's duties. By reg 3(1), a commercial agent must look after the interests of his principal and act dutifully and in good faith; reg 3(2) deals with a number of specific developments of these general duties.

General duties

The principal may want to provide that the agent uses its 'best endeavours' in promoting and marketing the products. 'Best endeavours' does, however, put a considerable burden upon the agent (it means that the agent must make every effort possible to find customers and make contracts), and the agent may consider this duty too strict.

Specific duties

LICENCES AND PERMITS

It may sometimes be necessary to obtain a licence for the sale of the products in the territory or to comply with local regulations. Clearly, this is unlikely to be a problem for Wood Magic and Lynwood. However, if this is the case, the agreement should allocate responsibility for doing so. The solicitor should consider which party is best placed to obtain any licence or comply with any regulations and draft accordingly. It is often sensible to make the agent responsible for getting permits and licences for the sale of the products and in respect of its own performance. It is also customary to provide that the agent must comply with laws and regulations concerning the sale of the products, but not those concerning the nature of the products or their packaging; this will normally be for the principal to do (see **5.3.4**).

PROMOTION AND MARKETING

The principal will want the agent to promote the principal's business and to keep up good relations with customers. It is clear, for example, in the agreement under consideration that Wood Magic and its products already enjoy an excellent reputation, and Wood Magic will obviously want this to continue. The principal may want to make this duty more specific; for example, by requiring the agent's staff to be available when needed for meetings with the principal or potential customers, or for attending trade fairs and other relevant marketing events. The principal may also require the agent to provide premises which the principal considers suitable (it may also want the right to inspect these premises from time to time), and to set up proper office facilities and a suitable organisation for the efficient operation of the agency.

The parties need to agree which of them will have the responsibility and expense of advertising. It is common to find a clause which requires the agent to pay for the advertising, but to use only material which has either been supplied or approved by the principal, thus allowing the principal to keep considerable control of the agent's activities. For example, Wood Magic may want Lynwood to use advertising and promotional tactics which Wood Magic knows to be effective from its own marketing experience.

Note that paragraphs 16–17 of the Notice of May 2000 indicate that if the agent is 'directly or indirectly obliged to invest in sales promotion' (eg by contributing to the principal's advertising budget), this may amount to incurring a 'risk' which would bring the agreement within the ambit of Article 81 EC. Caution may, therefore, be required.

STOCK

Principal and agent may agree that the agent will itself keep stocks of the principal's products in order to fulfil the contracts it makes on the principal's behalf. If the parties have agreed, however, that the principal will supply customers direct, the stock clause could be much simpler, or perhaps omitted altogether. If the agent is to keep stocks of the products, the agreement should deal with the level of stock which the agent is to carry and what is to happen to stock while it is on the agent's premises. The principal will not want the stock to be counted as part of the agent's assets, and therefore claimable by the agent's creditors if the agent becomes insolvent, so it is desirable to provide, for example, that the stock is clearly marked as being the principal's, and is stored separately from other goods while on the agent's premises. (The principal may want to add the right to inspect the agent's premises from time to time to ensure that the agent is complying with this.) Note that if it is clear that the agent bears the risk of loss while the stock is on its premises, the Notice of May 2000 would probably cease to apply, and Article 81 EC problems might arise. However, Wood Magic and Lynwood will not have problems in this respect: Wood Magic will deliver direct to customers.

DUTY TO SUPPLY INFORMATION

It may be useful (for example, in order to plan future products, or to improve existing ones) for the principal to receive feedback from the agent on how customers are reacting to the products. How much information the principal wants from the agent, and on what matters will obviously vary from case to case; for example, some principals may be satisfied with a clause which requires the agent to report 'from time to time', others may want the agent to report on a regular basis and at definite times. The principal may also wish to restrict the agent's right to get involved in disputes or proceedings concerning the products without the principal's written consent.

CONFIDENTIALITY

An agency agreement will not always require highly sophisticated confidentiality provisions; if the agent is simply finding customers and making contracts, it may not be privy to any information or process which could be described as confidential. If, however, the agent will be handling confidential material, the principal will need to consider how best to protect its interests. This is usually done by making clear what information is confidential, and what the agent is and is not entitled to do in relation to confidential information. In the agreement under consideration, Wood Magic will need to decide if Lynwood needs any confidential information (eg about how the furniture is made) to be able to fulfil its role as sales agent. (For more on the law of confidence (and, in particular, the implied duty of confidentiality), see Chapter 17.)

INTELLECTUAL PROPERTY

This section of the agreement is likely to vary considerably (it will not be necessary at all if the agent does not 'handle' any intellectual property rights under the agreement). The nature and extent of any clause will vary according to the circumstances and the type of intellectual property involved. Generally speaking, however, the clause will be designed to protect the principal's rights in the intellectual property and prevent the agent from getting any interest in it. It may be necessary to include clauses which:

(1) require the agent to inform the principal of any infringement of the principal's rights in the territory, or any claim by a third party that the principal has infringed its rights;

(2) require the agent to act on the principal's instructions and at the principal's request to institute or defend proceedings, or to do whatever else is necessary to maintain the validity and enforceability of the principal's rights;

(3) state that the agent is not to have, or seek to gain any interest in the principal's rights (eg trade marks on products, goodwill);

(4) require the agent not to damage the principal's goodwill by using confusingly similar trade names or trade marks, or behaving in any way that would invalidate the principal's rights or be inconsistent with them. A clause of this type would in most agreements need to be made subject to the rights of the agent and any third party to challenge the validity of the principal's intellectual property, or Article 81 EC problems could arise (see Chapter 19 for a fuller discussion of the relationship of intellectual property and competition law and how this may affect the drafting of commercial agreements).

The solicitor would need to take full instructions from Wood Magic about intellectual property rights which may be involved in the marketing (eg any trade mark which Wood Magic uses, and any registered or unregistered design rights relevant to the furniture).

MISCELLANEOUS CLAUSES RELATING TO THE AGENT'S DUTIES

It is quite common to find a clause in the 'Agent's Duties' section which gathers together clauses which do not fall under any other heading. Obviously, the solicitor will need to decide whether this is appropriate or necessary in the light of Wood Magic's instructions, but a 'Miscellaneous Provisions' clause could include the following terms:

• that the agent will not pledge the principal's credit;
• that the agent will not become involved in or try to settle any dispute about the products without first getting the principal's permission to do so;
• that the agent will not do anything which might prejudice the principal's business or the marketing of its products;

- that the agent will not become involved in any way with goods which compete with the products which are the subject of the agency agreement.

5.3.4 The principal's rights and duties

These are often less onerous than the agent's duties to the principal. However, note the provisions of reg 4 of the Commercial Agents (Council Directive) Regulations 1993. By reg 4(1), a principal must act dutifully and in good faith in his relations with his commercial agent; regs 4(2) and (3) deal with specific aspects of these general duties.

Again, the solicitor would need to take instructions from Wood Magic as to what it intends its rights and duties as principal to be; however, commonly encountered provisions are as follows (note how many of them complement duties which have already been imposed on the agent):

- the right for the principal to amend the listed products which are the subject of the agreement (see PCP K1-027, clause 6.2);
- the duty for the principal to pay commission to the agent (see PCP K1-028, clause 7.1). It is customary for an agent to be remunerated by commission; the duty to pay it may be stated as part of the principal's rights and duties, or it may be included as part of a complete financial provisions clause (see **5.3.5**);
- the duty of the principal to comply with all relevant laws relating to the composition, packaging and labelling of the goods (see PCP K1-027, clause 6.3.7); this is likely to make sense, as these matters will be under the principal's control;
- the duty for the principal to supply advertising and promotional material (see PCP K1-027, clause 6.3.1);
- the duty for the principal to pass on to the agent any information which might assist the agent in marketing the goods (see generally PCP K1-027, clauses 6.3.2 and 6.3.9);
- if the agreement requires the agent to hold stock, the duty for the principal to supply stock (this should also encompass how and when stock is to be supplied, ordering procedure, returns and so on);
- the duty for the principal to provide an after-sales service for the products;
- the duty for the principal to indemnify the agent against any liability which the agent incurs as a result of being held out as the principal's agent (eg costs and expenses which the agent may incur in relation to claims arising out of the agency).

5.3.5 Financial provisions (PCP K1-028, clause 7)

This section of the agreement is likely to vary considerably in content and layout. The parties are obviously free to choose the form of agreement which suits them best, and could combine the financial provisions with the principal's and the agent's duties respectively, if appropriate. However (especially where the financial provisions in the agreement are elaborate), it will often make sense to deal with them in a separate section relating to both parties. Note that where the Commercial Agents Regulations 1993 apply, the solicitor must be aware of their impact on the financial provisions of the agreement; the Regulations have provisions relating to agent's remuneration generally (regs 6–12) and compensation or remuneration on termination of the agreement (regs 17 and 18, see **5.3.6**).

Commission

Most genuine agency agreements deal expressly with matters such as how the commission is to be calculated, and when it is to be paid. All Wood Magic and Lynwood have agreed so far is that Wood Magic will pay Lynwood a monthly commission, so the solicitor will clearly need to take full instructions on the precise requirements. In practice, there may be considerable variation in the way commission can be dealt with (for a good standard precedent, see PCP K1-028, clause 7, or the remuneration clause in the sales agency agreement of the *Encyclopaedia of Forms and Precedents* (Butterworths, 1994)), but it is important to note that the parties may not always be completely free to make their own arrangements. In particular, where the Commercial Agents Regulations 1993 apply, the principal must ensure that the remuneration provisions are consistent with the 1993 Regulations (this is something which Wood Magic must bear in mind). Briefly, reg 7 provides for the agent's right to commission on transactions which are concluded during the agency agreement, and reg 8 gives the agent certain rights to commission even after the agency agreement has ended (note that the agent's right to commission can be extinguished only in the circumstances described in reg 11; broadly, that the contract arranged by the agent will not be carried out, but that this is not the principal's fault). For an interesting recent case on the application of reg 8 and, in particular, the circumstances in which transactions concluded after the termination of the agency contract will still be 'mainly attributable' to the agent's efforts during the agency (see *Tigana Ltd v Decoro Ltd* [2003] EWHC 23 (QB), (2003) unreported, 3 February). In addition, reg 10 controls when commission becomes due and when it must be paid.

Accounting arrangements for commission

The agreement should also deal with how the agent is to get the commission. A number of possibilities arise. For example, the agent may collect payment for the goods from customers, and then account to the principal after deducting its commission. (If the agent collects money, the parties may prefer the agent to pay the gross sum to the principal, which then pays commission over to the agent.) Alternatively, the principal may collect payment from customers, and then pay the agent a regular amount of commission. If the parties are based in different countries, it is also particularly important that the agreement should state the currency in which the commission is to be paid.

Deductions

If the agent does collect money from customers on behalf of the principal, it may sometimes be obliged to deduct certain sums (eg in respect of local taxes) before handing over the balance. If this is the case, the parties should deal with the deductions expressly in the agreement.

General accounting arrangements

The parties may wish to provide (where appropriate) for the payment of interest on any sums outstanding if either side fails to account to the other (the agent in respect of money collected from customers, the principal in respect of commission). The agreement should also provide for the keeping of accounts and other financial records. This should not only cover which records each party is to keep but also whether either party has the right to inspect or ask for copies of the other side's records (note that where the Commercial Agents Regulations 1993 apply, reg 12 obliges the principal to supply the agent with a statement of commission, and entitles the agent to demand the information he needs (including 'an extract from the books' to check the amount of commission due to him).

5.3.6 Termination (PCP K1-031, clause 10)

What circumstances will allow either party to terminate?

Circumstances in which either side may want the right to terminate the agreement would normally include: either side getting into financial difficulties such as receivership, winding up or making a voluntary arrangement; breach of the agreement (consider drafting a notice procedure under which the party in breach can be required to remedy the breach where possible); and change in control of the agent if the agent is a company. It is normally desirable to set out the circumstances expressly in the agreement.

What will the effects of termination be? (PCP K1-032, clause 11)

The agreement should state how termination will affect the following.

(1)   Any stocks of the product, samples and advertising material held by the agent.
(2)   Sales which the agent has already negotiated, but in respect of which no moneys have been paid over.
(3)   The agent's authority to negotiate on behalf of the principal.
(4)   The agent's duty of confidentiality.
(5)   The agent's right to compensation on termination.

Does the principal need to pay anything to the agent on termination?

This would normally be a matter for agreement between the parties. However, where the Commercial Agents Regulations 1993 apply, solicitor and principal must be aware that, in many cases, reg 17 obliges the principal to give the agent a 'pay-off' on termination of the agreement.

The position under reg 17 may be briefly summarised as follows. Broadly speaking, reg 17(1) provides that, on termination of the agency contract, the agent is entitled either to be 'indemnified' in accordance with reg 17(3)–(5) or 'compensated for damage' in accordance with reg 17(6)–(7). Regulation 17(2) states that except where the agreement provides otherwise, the agent is entitled to be compensated rather than indemnified.

The indemnity option is based on German law (it is often referred to as the 'German model'), and may seem attractive to principals because it provides a limit on the payment the agent can get (it can be no more than one year's commission, based on the agent's actual annual remuneration over the past 5 years; see reg 17(4)). There is also some evidence in practice that the actual payment will often be less than this.

The 1993 Regulations are considerably less clear about what 'compensation for damage' is. 'Compensation' in this context is based on French agency law (often referred to as the 'French model'), and often in practice, French law allows the agent on termination a sum equivalent to 2 years' commission (see below for the possible significance of this in the UK).

Regulation 17 is one of the most difficult areas of the 1993 Regulations, but there have been comparatively few reported cases so far. The first Court of Appeal case to consider reg 17 was *Graham Page v Combined Shipping and Trading Co Ltd* [1997]

3 All ER 656; however, this was in fact a case about the grant of a *Mareva* injunction (now known as a freezing injunction), and so the discussion of reg 17 was very limited. The court did, however, emphasise that because the Regulations are implementing legislation, courts must adopt a purposive approach to their interpretation. The court was in no doubt that the main purpose of the Commercial Agents Directive was to protect the agent. In a number of cases (eg *Duncan Moore v Piretta PTA* [1999] 1 All ER 174); the courts have awarded an indemnity in accordance with reg 17(3)–(5) (in the *Duncan Moore* case, the judge expressly stated that his calculation was based upon the 'German model'). Authority on 'compensation for damage' is somewhat scarce and contradictory. For example, in the Scottish case of *King v T Tunnock* [2000] IRLR 570, the Inner House of the Court of Session indicated that it was appropriate to refer to the relevant principles of French law in assessing compensation for damage. Contrast this with the decision of the High Court in *Barrett McKenzie v Escada (UK) Ltd* (2001) unreported, 1 February, where the court held that the French tariff system of calculating compensation on termination of an agency agreement was not applicable when calculating compensation for damage under the Regulations.

Note that reg 17(5) expressly provides that the grant of an indemnity 'shall not prevent the commercial agent from seeking damages'. It is generally assumed here that 'damages' refers to normal contractual damages, and that this provision would be relevant where, for example, the agreement has been unjustifiably terminated with no or insufficient notice. There is no express equivalent of this provision in relation to compensation for damage. However, in *Duffen v FRA BO SpA* [1999] ECC 58, the Court of Appeal held that following unjustified termination of an agency agreement, it was in principle open to the agent to seek not only common law damages, but also compensation under reg 17(6) to augment those common law damages.

There is still considerable debate in practice as to whether an agreement should go for indemnity or compensation, how far the agreement should deal expressly with the point (in many cases, the agent will be entitled to a pay-off regardless of what the agreement says: see next paragraph) and how any termination payment clause should be worded: for one way of approaching the problem, see PCP K1-032, clause 11.

Whatever the parties decide, the principal should be aware that there are only very limited grounds for excluding the agent's right to either indemnity or compensation. These are contained in reg 18, and include default by the agent justifying immediate termination under reg 16. In addition, reg 19 provides that the parties may not derogate from regs 17 and 18 to the detriment of the agent before the agency contract expires. This appears to mean that any provision in the agreement which removes or cuts down the agent's right to a pay-off will be of no effect.

5.3.7 Miscellaneous

An agency agreement will usually have a 'boiler-plate', containing a number of miscellaneous clauses (eg arbitration, choice of law and jurisdiction). For the 'boiler-plate' of the PCP agreement, see K1-030–K1-035.

5.3.8 Particular points to consider when drafting a marketing agency agreement

As noted above, a standard marketing agency agreement is substantially similar in content and layout to a sales agency agreement; the main differences result from the fact that a marketing agent has no authority to conclude contracts on the principal's behalf. A complete precedent for a marketing agency agreement can be found in PCP section K2.

Appointment

The agreement should define the nature of the agent's operations, with a clear statement that the agent is not authorised to enter into contracts on the principal's behalf. Normally, the agent also agrees not to describe itself as a sales agent.

Care needs to be taken about defining the exact limits of the agent's authority; is it to have authority only to find potential customers and pass them on to the principal, or is it to have authority to do at least some negotiating on the principal's behalf (without actually making any contract)? Note that an agent which does not have 'continuing authority' to negotiate on the principal's behalf is not a 'commercial agent' within the meaning of the Commercial Agents (Council Directive) Regulations 1993 (see **5.3.1**).

Introducing potential customers

The agreement should provide that the agent is to pass on all orders and enquiries promptly to the principal.

Principal's response to potential customers

Is it desirable or possible to provide that the principal should comply with all orders generated by the agent's efforts? A marketing agent does not bind its principal. If the principal refuses to accept an order from a particular customer introduced by the agent, however, this could damage the agent's reputation, and possibly make it more difficult for the agent to earn commission in future. The parties may be able to agree some sort of compromise; for example, that the principal will comply with orders from all customers, as long as it is satisfied that they are good credit risks. (Note how this point is dealt with in the PCP agreement at K2-027, clause 6.1.1; the principal is in fact entitled to reject any order for any reason.)

Agent's duties

A marketing agent is very unlikely to carry stock or collect payments on the principal's behalf.

5.4 DISTRIBUTION AGREEMENTS

5.4.1 Introduction

This section proceeds with the Wood Magic example, but in relation to a different aspect of Wood Magic's business.

Note that a distribution agreement is sometimes referred to as a 'distributorship agreement' (or simply 'distributorship'). Some commentators prefer this term, on the grounds that in practice, 'distribution agreement' is sometimes used loosely to refer to an agreement for the carriage of goods.

Example

Assume that Wood Magic has, for the past 5 years, carried on a small sideline business of manufacturing ready-made furniture (such as coffee tables, dining tables and chairs). The directors feel that this side of the business is now ready to be developed much further. Wood Magic recently rented a stand at a trade fair in Paris to show this furniture. The response was such that the directors believe that there is an important market in France consisting of wealthy customers who admire 'le style anglais' and want English furniture for their country homes. In the short term, the directors believe that Wood Magic can spare the time and commitment needed to establish relations with a 'trading partner' in France (the directors who attended the trade fair made some promising contacts, and believe that one company in particular, Bois Massif SA, could be the partner which Wood Magic is looking for). However, assuming that they do establish relations with a partner they can trust, the directors would, in the long term, seek to market Wood Magic's goods in France in a way which does not require close day-to-day supervision. They believe that if they give the right training to the French partner at the outset, it will be easy for the partner to sell the ready-made furniture, without major involvement from Wood Magic. One particular reason why the directors are keen to involve a trading partner in this part of Wood Magic's expansion is that they have little experience in the export trade, and they admit that their collective knowledge of the French language and of French business practices is negligible.

5.4.2 Initial advice

At this stage (as with an agency agreement) the solicitor is likely to be asked to advise in two related areas:

(1) What sort of marketing arrangement is most suitable for Wood Magic?
(2) What factors should it take into account when looking for a trading partner?

This time, the facts indicate that a distribution agreement would be appropriate.

(1) The goods can be marketed in France in the same form in which Wood Magic sells them (eg no customising is necessary).
(2) Wood Magic needs the help of a trading partner based in the target territory, because it is not familiar with that territory's language or business practices.
(3) The marketing of the goods does not require much supervision by Wood Magic (after initial training has been given).
(4) Wood Magic will not be liable in contract to the ultimate customers.

Note that whereas some of these factors would not necessarily make an agency agreement unsuitable, they indicate that the main advantages of that type of agreement (eg supervision of agent, contact with customers) are not really needed here. A distribution agreement is likely to be the cheapest and most efficient way to market these goods.

Wood Magic will need to be aware, however, that if it is considering giving Bois Massif some sort of territorial protection, competition law problems may arise (see **5.5.1** and Chapter 18).

As with the agency agreement, Wood Magic should check out any potential trading partner very carefully; for example, credit-worthiness is even more important here than in the agency agreement, as the distributor will actually be buying the goods from Wood Magic.

5.5 DRAFTING A DISTRIBUTION AGREEMENT

5.5.1 Preliminary

Assume now that Wood Magic's directors are satisfied that Bois Massif is the right trading partner for them in France, and have begun detailed negotiations over the terms of the distribution agreement which the parties will enter. They have still to decide how to deal with many areas of the agreement, but have agreed the following in principle.

(1) Wood Magic has agreed that (to give Bois Massif the best possible choice of getting the distributorship established) it will not appoint any other distributors (or agents) for the sale of its goods in France, and that it will not sell any of its own goods in France.

(2) In return, Bois Massif has agreed to concentrate on the French market only: it will not actively seek customers from outside France (although it will be free to fulfil unsolicited orders).

What considerations arise for the solicitor in drafting the agreement?

Agency and distribution agreements: similarities and differences

It is important to note that the relationship of distributor and supplier is created and defined by the distribution agreement. Many of the clauses already discussed in relation to agency agreements are equally relevant to distribution agreements; these include interpretation, appointment, duration and many of the 'duties' clauses (allowing for some necessary modifications; see below). However, a distribution agreement is essentially an agreement for the sale of goods from the supplier to the distributor, and so matters relevant to drafting a sale of goods agreement must be considered (see Chapter 2). A complete precedent for a distribution agreement can be found in PCP section K3.

Distribution agreements and competition law

This topic is discussed in more detail in Chapter 18. Briefly, however, a distribution agreement is more likely than an agency agreement to infringe Article 81(1) EC as its potential for affecting trade and competition is greater (particularly if it gives the distributor some form of territorial protection from competition, as Wood Magic's proposed agreement does). The agreement may, however, be ignored by the Commission if it falls within the Notice on Agreements of Minor Importance (to advise on this, it would be necessary to know the parties' market shares; see **18.3.6**). Even if this does not apply, it may be possible to draft the agreement to comply with a relevant block exemption.

In the agreement under consideration, Wood Magic is offering Bois Massif 'exclusive territory' (see **5.5.2** below) and Bois Massif will agree not to sell actively outside that territory. Both parties are therefore limiting their commercial freedom, and (in theory at least) doing so in a way which may affect trade and competition (eg French buyers will have only one authorised source of supply within France) and infringe Article 81(1) EC. However, if in practice the agreement contained only these two restrictions, the block exemption contained in Regulation 2790/99 would apply to the agreement, and therefore Article 81(1) EC would not. This block exemption is discussed in more detail at **18.3.9**.

5.5.2 Introduction

Date, parties, recitals, interpretation

This part of the agreement is likely to be very similar to the agency agreement (see **5.3.2**). In particular, similar points are likely to arise in relation to 'Products' (see PCP K3-051, Sch 1) and 'Territory'.

Appointment

The appointment clause will be vitally important; in particular, the question of exclusivity. How much protection will the distributor get against competition from others in its territory? The distributor may want protection (against the supplier appointing other distributors or agents, or against the supplier selling within the territory) in order to benefit as much as possible from its investment in the distributorship. Businesses often regard territorial exclusivity as a fundamental term in a distribution agreement, without which a potential distributor might not agree to take on the distributorship at all. To some extent, even under EC law, protection from competition is permitted (see **18.3.9** for a discussion of block exemption).

It is always desirable to define the extent of the distributor's protection from competition as clearly as possible, rather than relying on the words 'sole' or 'exclusive', which raise problems in the same way as they do in an agency agreement (see **5.3.2**). Strictly speaking, a 'sole' distribution agreement is one in which the supplier agrees not to appoint any other distributors in the territory, but reserves the right to sell in the territory itself. An 'exclusive' distribution agreement is one in which the supplier agrees not to appoint any other distributors in the territory nor to sell there itself (as with Wood Magic and Bois Massif). However, the legal and commercial meanings of these words have become too confused in practice to make it safe to rely on them alone when drafting (see how PCP K3-023, clause 2.2 deals with this). The agreement should also define the limits of the distributor's freedom to operate outside the defined territory. Note that if Article 81 EC applies, the agreement must not forbid the distributor to export the goods from the territory, as this is likely to infringe Article 81(1) EC (and will not get the benefit of Regulation 2790/99: see **18.3.9**). It is, however, possible to provide that the distributor must not actively solicit orders from outside the territory, as Wood Magic and Bois Massif have in mind.

The appointment clause may also deal with the duration of the agreement, although this can be done elsewhere in the agreement (see PCP K1-032, clause 11). Whichever method is chosen, note that an initial fixed term may be even more appropriate here than in an agency agreement, as it will give the distributor (which may have taken risks by making a large investment in the distributorship) both security and an incentive to build up the business. If this is what the parties require, the agreement must state when the fixed term is to commence. If the parties require an indefinite term, the agreement must include suitably drafted notice provisions.

5.5.3 The distributor's duties

Some of the distributor's duties will be similar to those in an agency agreement (eg in relation to confidentiality, transmission of information, training and availability of the distributor's representatives). However, other duties are likely to be significantly different because of the different nature of the agreement.

Minimum target obligations

The supplier will normally want to impose some form of minimum target obligation on the distributor to ensure that the distributor exploits the relevant market to the full. The supplier will often see this as justifiable in return for giving the distributor an initial fixed term. A minimum target obligation can be either for a minimum level of sales by the distributor to its customers, or for a minimum level of purchases by the distributor from the supplier. It is sometimes suggested that the latter may be more commercially flexible. For example, with a minimum purchase target, the distributor can buy extra goods from the supplier to meet the targets, and so perhaps cover a temporary bad patch more easily; purchase targets are also easier for the supplier to monitor. Note that although target obligations are often acceptable from a competition law point of view, care may be needed if the target is so exacting that it effectively limits the distributor's commercial freedom. (For more on the potential competition law implications of distribution agreements, see Chapter 18.)

If targets of either sort are imposed, the supplier must decide what is to happen if the distributor does not comply with them. The supplier may want either to end the distributor's freedom from competition in the territory or to terminate the agreement itself. The former may appear to be less drastic from the distributor's point of view, but could be as devastating as termination of the entire agreement in the long run. Note that ending territorial protection for failure to meet targets is not always seen as being commercially sensible; if the distributor is finding it hard to succeed with the help of sole or exclusive territory, presumably its task will be even more difficult without it, and the supplier may not benefit in any way. The supplier should therefore consider doing this only if it is certain that matters will improve if the distributor's protection from competition is ended (eg it will encourage the distributor to make greater efforts, or the supplier will benefit by being able to appoint another distributor or market the goods itself).

Advertising and promotion

The distributor is normally made responsible for advertising and promotion. It will often be better placed than the supplier to know what sort of advertising and promotional campaigns will succeed in the territory. Wood Magic may see this as a valuable contribution which Bois Massif can make to the success of Wood Magic's furniture in France. However, the supplier may wish to reserve the right to vet the distributor's activities, especially if it wants to keep a reasonably uniform brand image over several different territories. The supplier may also wish to provide that the distributor spends a minimum sum each year (or quarter, or month) on advertising and promotion.

Stock

The distributor will inevitably hold stock; it has actually bought the products from the supplier. The agreement will therefore need to provide for numerous matters relating to stock, including:

(1) How much stock should the distributor carry?
(2) What procedure should the distributor follow when it orders and pays for the goods?
(3) What procedure should the distributor follow for returning unsatisfactory goods?
(4) When are title and risk in the goods to pass to the distributor?

(5) Is it necessary to insure the products (eg while they are in transit from supplier to distributor)? If so, who should do this?

(6) What is to happen to stock if the agreement is terminated? The supplier often faces a dilemma here, especially when Article 81 could apply to the agreement. If the distributor is still holding stock after termination, it may deal with it in ways which could damage the brand's reputation (eg sell it cut-price in markets or through discount shops). However, because the stock is the distributor's own property, to deal with as it sees fit, any clause in the agreement which obliges the distributor to sell the stock back to the supplier on termination potentially restricts competition, and could infringe Article 81 EC. In most cases, the supplier will have to decide whether the risk of competition law problems is greater than that of harm to the supplier's reputation. However, note that a clause which gives the distributor the option of selling the stock back to the supplier (rather than forcing the distributor to do this) should not cause competition law problems, as the distributor is not then obliged to deal with its own property in a particular way. Subject to these points, any clause dealing with the fate of stock on termination is more likely to be an aid to negotiation than anything else.

(7) What is to happen to any advertising or promotional material on termination?

(8) What is to happen to obsolete stock? If the agreement requires the distributor to sell it back to the supplier, competition law problems may arise (in the same way as in (6) above). The parties should try to come to a workable compromise which will prevent obsolete stock affecting the market for new stock.

Confidentiality and intellectual property

The areas of confidentiality and intellectual property may be more relevant in a distribution agreement than in an agency agreement. As the distributor is actually buying the products and then selling them on, it may be necessary to supply the distributor with confidential information relating to the products, or to allow the distributor to use the supplier's intellectual property. PCP K3-029, clause 8 gives a standard precedent for a confidentiality clause; PCP K3-028, clause 7 covers intellectual property.

Competition

The supplier may want the distributor to agree not to handle products which could compete with the products which are being supplied under the agreement. However, this may cause problems if the agreement could be subject to Article 81 EC, as being potentially restrictive of competition. For more detail on how this might be handled, see Chapter 18 and PCP K3-023, clause 2.8.

5.5.4 The supplier's duties

If dealt with separately (the PCP agreement, for example, does not do this), the list of supplier's duties is likely to be comparatively small. It may be appropriate to deal with the following.

(1) Will the supplier need to supply any promotional literature, models or samples of the goods to allow the distributor to market them properly?

(2) Should the supplier be obliged to supply the distributor with information which may help the distributor to market the goods?

(3) Is the supplier prepared to offer the distributor an indemnity against defects in the products? If so, what liabilities will it cover? In addition, does the supplier wish to give limited warranties to the distributor (eg to cut down the protection given by s 14 of SGA 1979 if English law applies)? PCP K3-030, clause 9 illustrates how this may be done.

5.5.5 Sale of goods terms

Because the supplier will be selling goods to the distributor, it will be necessary to include in the agreement suitable terms to cover this sale of goods. For discussion of the basic terms in a sale of goods agreement see the LPC Resource Book *Business Law and Practice* (Jordans), and Chapter 2 of this book. Consider particularly in relation to a distribution agreement:

(1) Are the supplier's sales to the distributor to be on the supplier's standard terms (see PCP K3-024, clause 3.9)? If so, the agreement should make clear what these are. Perhaps the best way of doing this is to set them out in a schedule to the agreement, so that both parties are certain which terms apply.

(2) Which basic sale of goods terms (such as price, payment, delivery, description and quality) need to be included in the distribution agreement? Note that the term relating to price will be of particular importance to the distributor; it will make its money from the difference between the price at which it buys the goods from the supplier and the price at which it can sell them to its customers.

5.5.6 Termination

The termination of the agreement and the consequences of termination may be handled in a number of ways (see, eg, PCP K3-032, clause 11 on termination and K3-033, clause 12 on consequences of termination). One matter which will require particular care (for the reasons outlined in **5.6.3**) is disposal of stock on termination, which the solicitor may feel is better dealt with here than in the 'stock' clause. Note that it is relatively rare for distributors to be entitled by law to compensation on termination (compare the position of agents under the Commercial Agents Regulations 1993; see **5.6.3**), but this may be relevant in certain jurisdictions (not the UK). The supplier, may, however, be prepared to agree to include a term in the agreement providing for compensation.

5.5.7 Miscellaneous

Like an agency agreement, a distribution agreement usually has a 'boiler-plate'. Many of the miscellaneous clauses will be the same as those arising in an agency agreement (see, eg, PCP K3, clause 10 on force majeure, clause 14 on arbitration and proper law, and clause 15 on notices and service). However, because competition law problems are more likely to arise with a distribution agreement, the parties should review their agreement and decide whether competition law is likely to be a problem. If it is, they should agree who is to be responsible for any notification which may be necessary (see Chapter 18). Responsibility should then be set out expressly in the agreement (see PCP K3-037, clause 16).

5.6 STRUCTURE OF THE AGREEMENTS AT A GLANCE

The following summarises the likely structure of the two agreements previously considered.

Agency

- Date, parties, recitals
- Interpretation clause
- Appointment of the agent
- Agent's rights and duties
- Principal's rights and duties
- Financial provisions
- Termination (if not dealt with elsewhere)
- Boiler-plate clauses
- Signatures
- Schedules

Distribution

- Date, parties, recitals
- Interpretation clause
- Appointment of the distributor
- Standard terms of sale (may be reserved to a schedule)
- Distributor's rights and duties
- Supplier's rights and duties
- Termination (if not dealt with elsewhere)
- Boiler-plate clauses
- Signatures
- Schedules

5.7 OTHER TYPES OF MARKETING AGREEMENT

Given the nature of Wood Magic's business operations, it is unlikely for the moment to need to consider anything other than agency and distribution. However, if it continues to be successful and the business develops, other marketing situations may arise.

5.7.1 Licensing

Assume that Wood Magic comes up with a very popular new product (eg a new design of chair), but that it does not have the resources to manufacture and distribute enough of the new product to satisfy customer demand. It therefore grants a licence to a much larger furniture manufacturing business, allowing that business to make and sell the chair. Very broadly, the licence agreement will permit the licensee to do this in return for payment to Wood Magic (possibly a one-off licence fee, but more likely continuing payments of royalties on chairs manufactured and sold).

Licensing agreements (or simply 'licences') will usually involve the licensing of intellectual property rights. For example, Wood Magic may own design rights (see

Chapter 15) in relation to the chair, which it will license to the furniture manufacturer. They may also involve competition law considerations. Intellectual property rights generally are dealt with in Chapters 10–17 and the competition law aspects of licensing in Chapter 19.

5.7.2 Franchising

In the example given earlier in the chapter, Wood Magic decided to extend its custom-made furniture business by opting for an agency agreement. Another way of extending this business format would be to franchise the Wood Magic 'concept' of furniture making. This would mean that Wood Magic (the franchisor) would establish a 'Wood Magic' uniform business format, which it would then authorise other businesses (the franchisees) to use in return for payment. In the franchise agreement, Wood Magic would lay down conditions and specifications for the franchisees to meet (eg what their premises should look like, how they should offer the furniture-making service to customers). This would allow Wood Magic to extend this part of its business without having to raise capital to do so, while still retaining considerable control over what the franchisee does with the business.

A franchise agreement often involves the franchisor giving the franchisee the right to use the franchisor's intellectual property rights (eg, the 'Wood Magic' name may be a registered trade mark, and intellectual property rights and trade secrets may be involved in the design and manufacture of the furniture). There may also be competition law considerations (see Chapter 19).

5.7.3 Joint venture

This may become relevant if Wood Magic's directors come up with a project which requires input from another business with different but complementary skills. For example, assume that the directors decide to develop a range of upholstered furniture: they may seek to set up a joint venture with a company specialising in furnishing fabrics. If they did so, the two businesses would normally pool their resources to set up a separate joint venture company to carry out the project.

5.8 CONCLUSION AND FURTHER READING

This chapter can do no more than give an outline introduction to two important types of commercial agreement. Further exploration of other agency and distribution precedents (and, indeed, of precedents for other types of marketing agreement, such as franchising) is therefore recommended. The book already mentioned in this chapter (Rosenberg *Practical Commercial Precedents* (Sweet & Maxwell)) provides a wide range of precedents for commercial agreements generally.

PART II

INTERNATIONAL SALE AGREEMENTS

Chapter 6

INTRODUCTION TO INTERNATIONAL SALE AGREEMENTS

An international sale of goods contract will need to cover the same type of issues as a domestic agreement (eg price, payment, delivery). However, there are added complications. For a start, the UCTA 1977 does not apply (see s 26). On the other hand, if the contract is subject to English law, SGA 1979 will apply to an international contract.

There are various additional, or increased, risks, for example:

- physical risks to the goods associated with sea or air transport and the associated extra handling;
- the increased costs of long-distance freight carriage;
- the increased delivery period because of long journeys;
- financial risks, for example due to changes in currency exchange rates;
- increased risks of not being paid, or being paid late;
- political risks, possibly even of war or terrorist attack or blockades; and
- legal risks if the contract is subject to foreign law – are you qualified to advise on foreign law?

Some issues can be covered by insurance, if it is economically viable for the seller to purchase it. Other issues can be covered by care in drafting the contract. Many problems can be solved by the parties using a standard contract drawn up by a trade association or by an international body. For example, there are the GAFTA contract forms of the Grain and Feed Trade Association, or those of the London Metal Exchange. The ones which we shall look at in this Part are the Incoterms, produced by the International Chamber of Commerce. These are a set of standard form rules which can be used in various commercial situations. It is up to the parties to choose which one is best for them. They are produced in a variety of languages, so the use of Incoterms can avoid misunderstandings due to language problems.

International contracts for the sale of goods are thus intertwined with the contracts for carriage of the goods, contracts of insurance, and contracts with the banks to secure payment.

Chapter 7

CHOICE OF JURISDICTION AND LAW

7.1 INTRODUCTION

The whole area of jurisdiction, and of law, has been given a boost in the minds of commercial lawyers by the advent of e-commerce. Today, international contracts can be concluded at the touch of a mouse-click. The collision of opposing jurisdictions is therefore an increasingly important issue.

Jurisdiction means the courts which would hear the dispute. Normally, any contracts you deal with in practice would be subject to the jurisdiction of the English courts. Choice of law obviously means choosing which law would apply to the contract. Normally, both law and jurisdiction would be decided by a clause in the contract. If that has not been done, then the two Conventions below will apply.

The basic principle is that if the parties choose the law and jurisdiction which they wish to cover the contract, then that choice prevails. In practice, any competently drafted written contract should have a clause covering law and jurisdiction. However, there will be circumstances where the issues need to be resolved. The 1980 Rome Convention deals with choice of law. It is implemented by the Contracts (Applicable Law) Act 1990.

Choice of jurisdiction is now dealt with by EU Regulation 44/2001, also known as Brussels II. The main change from its predecessor is that it gives greater protection to the consumer, including when the consumer contracts with a business on the internet. (There is also a draft convention on jurisdiction and foreign judgments under the Hague Conference on Private International Law, but it is unclear how it will relate to Brussels II if the Hague Convention does come into existence.)

For the record, the Lugano Convention still determines jurisdiction between EU Member States and the European Free Trade Agreement (EFTA) States (of which there are now very few). We will not consider it further.

However, there are circumstances where the outcome of the Conventions would be different for law and for jurisdiction, so it is feasible to have an English court hearing a dispute under German law, for example. In such circumstances, the English court will be advised by experts in the law in question, here that of Germany. (For an example of an English court deciding a case under foreign law, see the *Glencore* litigation at 2.3.6, where the court considered the law of *Fujairah*, as well as English law.)

7.2 BRUSSELS II – REGULATION 44/2001

This deals with jurisdiction. It applies if both parties are resident in Member States. (Strictly speaking, Brussels II does not apply to Denmark which is still bound by Brussels I.)

7.2.1 The basic position under Brussels II – general jurisdiction

The basic rule is that the defendant is sued in the courts of his home country, subject to the other provisions of the Regulation (Article 2). This rule is said to give 'general jurisdiction' to those courts. There are exceptions to this rule. The major ones are contracts, torts, situations where the defendant has a local branch office, real property, companies, IP, insurance, consumer contracts, and employment matters, see **7.2.2–7.2.4**.

7.2.2 Special jurisdiction – contract, tort and local branch offices

If the dispute is a contract matter, then there is the option of suing the defendant in the Member State where the contract should have been performed (Article 5(1)(a)). If more than one obligation is in question, the Brussels II regulation gives jurisdiction to the courts of the place of performance of the principal obligation.

In the case of a sale of goods contract, it is presumed that the 'place of performance of the obligation in question' is the Member State where the goods were delivered, or should have been delivered (Article 5(1)(b)). Thus, for sale of goods contracts, there is only one 'place of performance of the obligation in question' for the whole of the contract.

In matters relating to tort, the defendant may be sued in the courts of the Member State where the harmful event occurred or may occur (Article 5(3)).

If the defendant has a branch or office in another Member State, then he may also be sued there (Article 5(5)) if the dispute arises out of the operations of that branch or office.

7.2.3 Exclusive jurisdiction

Under Article 22 of Regulation 44/2001, there are situations in which certain courts are regarded as having particular expertise and so are given exclusive jurisdiction. This overrides the normal rules on general and special jurisdiction. The main instances are:

*   proceedings concerning rights in rem in immovable property or tenancies of immovable property: the regulation normally gives exclusive jurisdiction to the courts of the Member State in which the property is situated;
*   proceedings concerning the constitution or dissolution of companies: the regulation gives exclusive jurisdiction the courts of the Member State in which the company has its 'seat' (in the UK this will usually be the registered office); and
*   proceedings concerning the registration or validity of registered intellectual property rights: the regulation gives exclusive jurisdiction to the courts of the Member State in which the right is registered or in which registration has been applied for.

7.2.4 Special rules for insurance, consumer contracts and employment contracts

These are situations in which one party is considered to have greater economic power than the other. In order to redress the balance, the rules on jurisdiction are shifted in favour of the 'weaker' party. Generally, he can be sued only in his own courts but is given the choice as to whether he sues the other party in his own courts or in the other party's courts. There are limits to the extent to which the parties can contract out of these rules.

The rules on consumer contracts are contained in Articles 15–17. They apply in various situations set out in Article 15. The most usual of these is where the consumer concludes a contract with a person 'who pursues commercial or professional activities in the Member State of the consumer's domicile'. This provision should be fairly self-explanatory. However, Article 15 also applies where the other party 'by any means, directs [his commercial or professional] activities' to the Member State in which the consumer is domiciled. This is taken to include internet selling (ie e-commerce, see **A2.10**). So, Articles 15–18 will protect the internet consumer by requiring that he be sued only in his own courts whilst giving him a choice as to where he sues the seller.

This can mean that an internet business could be sued in any jurisdiction in which its website happens to be accessible to potential customers. It might be worthwhile considering which jurisdictions the business is prepared to deal with. Most businesses that sell goods can control this by refusing orders from countries to which they are not prepared to sell, and by not sending the goods. It would be harder to exercise such control in a business involving the sale of on-line products such as plane tickets, or the downloading of software.

7.2.5 Contracting out

Article 23 allows the parties to override the rules on general and special jurisdiction by agreeing that the courts of a specified Member State are to have jurisdiction. The Article lays down the formal requirements for such an agreement. Generally, it must be in writing.

However, it is not possible to contract out of the rules on exclusive jurisdiction (in Article 22 – see **7.2.3**). There are also limits to the extent to which the parties can contract out of the rules on insurance, consumer and employment contracts.

7.2.6 First to file

The court which is first involved in the proceedings will generally have jurisdiction (Article 21). Any other court may decline jurisdiction or stay proceedings if the actions are related (Article 22).

In England, the principle of forum non conveniens means that the court could stay proceedings that have also been brought before another court.

Judgments obtained in contracting states must be recognised and enforced, but with some exceptions (Articles 27 and 28).

For a case involving Brussels I, see the *Bonnier* case at **11.9** and **A2.10.3**.

7.3 ROME CONVENTION

This applies to Member States of the EU. It deals with the choice of laws, that is, the question of which law applies to the contract.

7.3.1 The basic position under the Rome Convention

Article 1(2) specifies the matters to which the Convention does not apply, for example wills and probate, and matters governed by company law.

Article 3(1) allows the parties to choose the law of the contract, either expressly or impliedly. If they have done so, then that is the law that governs the contract.

If no such choice has been made, then the contract will be governed by the law of the country with which it is most closely connected (Article 4(1)). Article 4(2) provides that the relevant country is the one where the party who is to effect 'characteristic performance' of the contract has their habitual residence. In the case of a company, this is the place where it has its central administration. 'Characteristic performance' is the performance for which money is due (ie delivery of the goods, or the provision of a service).

For some examples of the Rome Convention in practice, see *American Motor Insurance Co v Cellstar Corporation and Another* [2003] EWCA Civ 206, [2003] All ER (D) 26 (Mar) and *Welex AG v Rosa Maritime Ltd (The 'Epsilon Rosa') (No 2)* [2002] EWHC 2035 (Comm), [2002] 2 Lloyd's Rep 701.

7.3.2 The exceptions in Article 4

There are exceptions to Article 4(2), in sub-Articles 3, 4 and 5.

Article 4(3) deals with a right in 'immovable property'. The presumption here is that the contract is most closely connected with the country where the immovable property is situated. This does not apply to contracts for repair or construction of immovable property.

Article 4(4) provides that the presumption in Article 4(1) does not apply to a contract for the carriage of goods (not *sale* of goods). In that case, it is the country where the carrier has their place of business if that is also the country of loading or discharging the goods, or if it is also the country where the consignor has their principal place of business.

Article 4(5) provides that the court may disregard the presumption in Article 4(1) if it appears that the contract is more closely connected with another country. In practice, it is likely that a court will endeavour to use this provision.

7.3.3 Local 'mandatory rules'

There are limitations on the use of the applicable law. If any provisions of the applicable law conflict with local laws relating to the contract, those conflicting provisions of the applicable law cannot validly be used. These local law provisions are the 'mandatory rules' which are referred to in the convention. These are 'rules' which cannot be derogated from (eg in the case of the UK, the Financial Services and Markets Act 2000, or the Unfair Terms in Consumer Contracts Regulations 1999). Article 3(3) provides that the choice of foreign law by the parties will not prejudice the application of the mandatory rules of the home country to the contract. So, even if the applicable law was held to be, say, Austrian law, the Financial Services and Markets Act 2000 could also apply to a relevant dispute heard by a court in England and Wales, and would override any inconsistent provisions in Austrian law.

There are four particularly important situations in which the mandatory rules will take precedence over the applicable law. The first is where the contract is connected with only one country. In that situation, the parties cannot avoid their country's mandatory rules by choosing the law of another country as the applicable law. The second situation is where the applicable law conflicts with the mandatory rules of the country whose courts are hearing the dispute. The other situations relate to consumer and employment contracts and are dealt with below.

7.3.4 Exceptions for consumer and for employment contracts

Article 5 concerns the supply to a consumer of goods or services, or credit for their supply. The choice of law shall not operate so as to deprive the consumer of his protection under the mandatory rules of his country of residence. So, a consumer in England and Wales could not be deprived of the protection of UCTA 1977, for example.

Article 6 deals with individual contracts of employment. Where there is no choice of law in the contract, then the presumption is that contained in Article 6(2). This is basically that the law is that of the country where the work takes place, or where the business is situated. However, a contractual choice of law cannot operate so as to deprive the employee of the protection of the mandatory rules which would apply under Article 6(2).

Chapter 8

INTERNATIONAL SALE OF GOODS

8.1 INTRODUCTION

The typical international sale of goods transaction is one where the goods are shipped by sea over a long distance. This means there could be a considerable time delay between the goods being supplied and the seller being paid for them. The seller would ideally like to be paid when the goods are dispatched. The buyer would ideally only want to pay when he has received the goods and had a chance to inspect them.

The seller's desire to be paid is not just wishful thinking. The seller will have to pay his own suppliers, his employees and other business expenses. This is a cash flow problem that happens in all business but the situation is exacerbated in international sale contracts because of the distances over which the goods are shipped.

In addition to the possible delay in payment, there are increased costs of insurance, to cover the sea voyage and possibly other risks.

To solve the problems of slow payment, the documents involved in an international sale have been elevated to a special status. In effect, they come to represent the goods themselves for the purposes of contract law. So, for example, delivery of the goods, in the legal sense, is performed by handing over documents.

8.2 THE DOCUMENTS

The key documents are:

* the bill of lading (or alternatives – see **8.2.2** and **8.2.3**);
* the commercial invoice; and
* the policy of marine, or air, insurance.

Other documents may also be relevant (eg export/import licences and a certificate of origin).

8.2.1 The bill of lading

The bill of lading is given by the carrier of the goods to the consignor of the goods, at the time of the goods being loaded.

The bill of lading serves three purposes:

* it is a receipt for the goods and evidences that they are in good condition at loading;
* it contains the terms of contract of carriage; and
* it is evidence of title to the goods, and a right to possess them.

Thus, at the destination the goods will be handed over to the person holding the bill of lading. The bill is given to the carrier in exchange for the goods. It will arrive before the goods as the goods travel by sea but the bill is sent by airmail. A key property of a bill of lading is that its holder has title to the goods.

The disadvantage of the bill of lading is that it is intended for the sale of bulk commodities which are shipped a considerable distance by sea. Today, air transport is used more, and ships have become faster. The cargo can reach the destination before the bill of lading does. Today, sea waybills and freight forwarders receipts are often preferred to a bill of lading, as they can be sent by fax or email. Although they give less legal protection, the buyer can collect the goods from the carrier by giving proof of his identity without having to produce a bill of lading, as such.

Only an original bill of lading will suffice. A photocopy or faxed copy is no good. For short (international) journeys, it is conceivable that the goods may arrive before the bill of lading, as noted above. It has been estimated that up to 50% of shipping documents are either late or have discrepancies. In such cases, the carrier will usually deliver the goods to the buyer in return for a buyer's indemnity. Obviously, this is a bit risky for the carrier.

An additional complication is that it is common practice to issue in bills of lading in sets of three. Only one copy needs to be presented to claim the goods from the carrier. The practice was originally devised to enable the resale of goods whilst at sea in days gone by, even though criticised then (see *Glyn Mills Currie & Co v East and West India Dock Co* (1882) 7 App Cas 591). Today, this practice can lead to fraud. The use of bills of lading has decreased dramatically as alternatives that are more amenable to electronic communication have gained acceptance, see **8.2.2**

Bills of lading are still favoured in the transport of bulk cargoes, eg grain, coal, metal ores. There are attempts to produce an e-commerce equivalent by creating a network of contracts that has the same end effect as a paper bill of lading, eg the system known as BOLERO. This would seem to be where the future lies for bills of lading. For further information on BOLERO, see www.bolero.net.

Bills of lading are governed by the Bills of Lading Act 1855.

8.2.2 An alternative to bills of lading – waybills

A waybill is an alternative to a bill of lading. A waybill is a receipt for the goods and evidence of the carriage contract but it does not constitute a document of title to the goods. It also specifies the person to whom delivery should be made. The original does not have to be sent to the buyer for them to be able to collect the goods from the carrier. Its disadvantage is that it does not enable the buyer to sell the goods on before he has possession of them, as he can with a bill of lading.

An advantage of waybills is that they can be sent electronically (or by fax). The transaction can thus by undertaken as e-commerce, with the payment being sent from the buyer to the seller by electronic means (see **A2.10**).

Waybills have traditionally been used for air freight. They have been used for sea freight with increasing frequency.

8.2.3 Road, rail or air transport

There is no equivalent to the bill of lading in air transport. An 'air waybill' is normally used. This would be made out to the buyer as consignee. Often, the basis is an 'FOB airport' contract (see **8.4.2**). The seller's duties end when the goods are delivered at the destination airport to the carrier or buyer's agent.

For road and rail transport, the contract would usually be made with a firm that undertakes the whole transport chain, normally using containerised transport for the goods. The contract document is a 'combined transport document'. There are various standard-form contracts from the International Chamber of Commerce (ICC) that deal with these arrangements (see **8.4**).

For a discussion of the problems of multi-modal transport, see *Faber* [1996] LMCLQ 503.

8.2.4 The commercial invoice

This lists and describes the contract goods (eg '20 cases of Adams Baked Beans, each comprising 30 tins of 100g size'). It will also usually constitute a demand for payment by the buyer.

8.2.5 The policy of marine (or air) insurance

This should be worded so as to cover the goods specified in the commercial invoice for the journey described in the bill of lading. The policy would be transferred from one party to another along with the bill of lading (and would obviously need to be a transferable policy).

8.3 EFFECT OF TRANSFER OF THE DOCUMENTS

The Carriage of Goods by Sea Act 1992 provides a solution to any problems of privity of contract which would occur when the bill of lading is transferred from one holder to another. The Act provides that anyone who holds the bill of lading is entitled to sue the carrier on the contract of carriage. A holder also assumes the contractual burdens. (The Act also applies to other documents such as waybills, which are mentioned at **8.2.2** and **8.2.3**.) The holder also has rights in tort in relation to the goods (eg for negligent damage).

The buyer who is in possession of the shipping documents can enforce his:

- contractual rights against the person who sold to him, under the contract of sale;
- contractual rights against the carrier under the contract of carriage; and
- rights against the insurer under the terms of the policy of which he is the assignee.

Motis Exports Ltd v Dampskibsselskabet AF 1912 (No 1), A/S and Another [2000] 1 All ER (Comm) 91, is an example of the problems of bills of lading. In that case, the defendant carrier delivered goods against a forged bill of lading. The owner of the goods successfully sued the carrier, as the Court of Appeal affirmed that a forged bill of lading was simply a worthless piece of paper. Delivery of the goods against a forged bill of lading was held to be misdelivery of the goods, and the carrier's general exclusion of liability for loss in transit did not cover the situation.

8.4 INCOTERMS

In an international sale of goods, there will be various stages in the transport chain. For example, if the goods are being exported to Korea from a factory in Manchester, they will first of all have to be taken by road or rail from Manchester to a British port, possibly Liverpool or Hull. They will then need to be loaded on to a ship and be taken by the ship from the British port to a port in Korea. Once they reach there, they will then be taken by road or rail from the Korean port to the premises of the buyer.

There are legal and practical issues to be considered. The major ones are:

• who pays for each stage of the journey; and
• which party is responsible for the goods at each stage?

So, how do you draft the contract to take care of this?

One way is to use a standard contract. The ICC publishes Incoterms, which are sets of standard terms. The obligations of each party are laid out in simple terms in a standard book, known as Incoterms 2000. As these terms are intended for consumption by commercial entities, not their lawyers, they are laid out concisely.

Incoterms are published in more than 30 languages. This means that each party to a carriage contract can look up the relevant Incoterm in their own language, and see the buyers and sellers obligations laid out in simple steps. This helps to avoid misunderstandings, especially when the parties are separated by distance and by language. It thus helps to avoid disputes and litigation, with the consequent cost and time involved.

It should be realised that the Incoterms are part of the sale of goods contract. They do not deal with the terms of the carriage contract but merely provide which party is to arrange and pay for each of the stages of carriage. In particular, they do provide for the delivery, in the legal sense of the goods, and the passing of the risk in the goods (ie the obligation to insure the goods). They also cover the obligation to obtain export or import clearance (not relevant for deals entirely within the EU), the buyer's obligation to take delivery, and the obligation to provide proof that the various obligations have been complied with. However, Incoterms do not attempt to cover all the terms of the sale of goods contract.

It is also worth adding that the Incoterms use the word 'delivery' both in the legal sense and in the commercial sense of transporting the goods to the buyer.

The use of a particular Incoterm does have implications for the other contracts between the parties. For example, if the parties choose a CIF or CFR contract (see below) the mode of transport must be sea transport for these terms to work.

There is information on the ICC site at www.iccwbo.org/index_incoterms.asp.

Some typical Incoterms are as follows.

• ex works (EXW);
• free carrier (FCA);
• free alongside (a ship) (FAS);
• free on board (a ship) (FOB);
• cost and freight (CFR);
• cost, insurance, freight (CIF);
• carriage paid to (CPT);
• carriage and insurance paid (CIP);

- delivered at frontier (DAF);
- delivered ex ship (DES);
- delivered ex quay (DEQ);
- delivered duty unpaid (DDU);
- delivered duty paid (DDP).

The burden on the seller increases as one goes down the list. Thus, the lightest burden on the seller is when the goods are delivered to the buyer 'ex works', that is at the seller's premises. The heaviest is when they have to be delivered to the buyer's premises with the relevant duty paid. These burdens on the seller are reflected in the price agreed for the deal. The less the burden, then the less the price. However, it does mean that the buyer has to arrange and pay for the other parts of the chain of transport.

Both the 'F' group and the 'C' group of Incoterms are contracts where the seller fulfils their obligations in the country of shipment, ie the country of departure of the goods. The 'D' group are different in nature from the 'F' and 'C' group, in that the seller is responsible for the arrival of the goods in the country of destination and must bear all the risks and costs of doing so.

The traditional sets of terms cannot always be adapted for modern shipping practice. For example, the typical situation today is not of the ship lying at the dockside waiting for cargo to be loaded. Rather, the aim is to minimise the time spent in port. The goods are therefore in shipping containers which are stored in the docks pending arrival of the appropriate ship. It would also be typical today for goods to be put into shipping containers at the sellers' premises or at a depot run by the carrier. They would stay in the container until they reached either the buyer or a carrier's depot in the country of destination.

Some terms which are used for the container trade are as follows:

- full container load (FCL);
- less than full container load (LCL);
- free carrier (equivalent to FOB);
- freight, carriage paid (equivalent to CFR); and
- freight carriage and insurance paid (equivalent to CIF).

8.4.1 Examples of Incoterms – ex works (EXW)

The burden is lightest on the seller and heaviest on the buyer, in that the buyer has to arrange and pay for collection at the seller's premises.

The seller delivers the goods when he places the goods at the disposal of the buyer at the seller's premises (or other named location, eg a warehouse).

The first point is that the place where the 'works' are has to be specified. So, it could be 'ex works Adams Waste Recycling, Pepper Street, Christleton', for example.

The obligations on the two parties are as follows.

    Seller is required to:

- supply goods conforming to the contract, measured and packed;
- supply the invoice and any other documents;
- deliver the goods (in the legal sense) by placing them at the buyer's disposal;
- pay for any costs incidental to placing the goods at the buyer's disposal;

and

- provide further assistance to the buyer for the buyer to obtain necessary licences or insurance.

Buyer is required to:

- accept delivery of the goods and pay for them;
- obtain appropriate licences and customs clearances; and
- pay any costs incidental to the export of the goods.

Under EXW, the seller does not arrange for export clearance (which is, of course, only relevant to sales to a buyer located outside the EU). If the buyer were unable to arrange export clearance, then the FCA set of terms should be used instead (see **8.4.2**), providing that the seller is also willing to take on the burden and risk of loading the goods.

The purchase price would always become due on delivery of the goods unless the parties agreed otherwise.

8.4.2 Examples of Incoterms – the 'F' group of terms: main carriage unpaid

These impose more responsibility on the seller than under the ex works terms. The 'F' group of terms require the seller to deliver the goods for the main carriage (usually sea or air transportation) as required by the buyer. The buyer will usually arrange and pay for the main carriage and the insurance for that journey. In the 'F' group, risk in the goods passes with delivery, in contrast to the 'C' terms. There are a variety of 'F' terms. The difference between the 'F' terms is the hand-over point for the goods (ie the point of legal delivery of the goods).

Free carrier (FCA) (named place)

The seller fulfils his obligations when he delivers the goods to the carrier chosen by the buyer at the named point. The risk of loss or damage is transferred at that point. The hand-over point could be the seller's premises, or it could be the carrier's depot, especially if the goods are to be sent by container. The term is frequently used when goods are shipped by container. It can also be used for air freight.

Free alongside ship (FAS) (named port of shipment)

Here, the seller fulfils his obligations when he delivers the goods alongside the ship (ie on the dockside) at the named port of shipment. The buyer will have arranged for the ship, and be paying for the sea carriage and insurance. The costs of loading the goods on to the ship will also be the buyer's expense.

Free on board (FOB) (named port of shipment)

These terms impose higher obligations on the seller than FAS. Here, the seller undertakes to place the goods on board a specified ship in a specified port of shipment. All charges up to and including loading the goods on to the ship are the sellers expense. The buyer has to pay the subsequent charges including sea freight, marine insurance, unloading charges and import duties.

'Free on board' means the seller delivers the goods when the goods 'pass over the ships rail' at the port of shipment. (If this is not suitable then FCA or FAS should be used.) The buyer therefore has the task of making the shipping arrangements and the insurance arrangements. FOB can only be used for sea or inland waterway transport.

The delivery point in FOB is the same as for CFR and CIF. Although consideration was given to changing this for FOB in the revisions to Incoterms, it was decided to keep it as it was for Incoterms 2000. The 'over the ships rail' provision does not always accord with modern shipping practice, that is containerised transport and roll-on, roll-off ferries. However, it was felt that FOB was adapted in practice by commercial parties to modern loading techniques and to the goods in question. It is also widely understood in the commercial world. FOB contracts were analysed in *Pyrene Co Ltd v Scindia Steam Navigation Co Ltd* [1954] 2 All ER 158 and *Ian Stach Ltd v Baker Bosley Ltd* [1958] 2 QB 130.

The risk in the goods passes with delivery, that is the goods are at the sellers risk until they cross the ship's rail.

FOB has been declining in popularity, and losing out to alternatives, especially the CIF terms.

Under FOB, the following are the obligations on the seller and buyer.

Seller is required to:

- supply goods conforming to the sale of goods contract;
- deliver the goods to the buyer by placing them on board the ship, that is 'over the rail' of the ship;
- place them on board in the position required;
- pay any costs incidental to delivery of the goods;
- obtain an export licence; and
- provide to the buyer proof of delivery to the ship.

Buyer is required to:

- give sufficient notice to the seller of the time and location of the delivery point (the buyer having contracted with a carrier for the sea journey, and insured the goods from the port of shipment);
- obtain any appropriate licences;
- pay costs incidental to the importation of the goods; and
- pay for the goods.

You should be aware that there are many varieties of FOB contract used in international trade. You have to be sure which one you are using (eg Incoterms 2000 FOB Hull). It is one of the two sets of Incoterms that you will come across frequently in practice (the other is CIF).

8.4.3 Examples of Incoterms – the 'C' terms: main carriage paid

These sets of terms have more onerous obligations on the seller than do the 'F' group of terms. In the 'C' group, the seller arranges and pays for the main carriage, usually the sea freight. Therefore, the point up to which the seller is responsible for transport costs needs to be stated after the relevant 'C' term (eg CIF Sydney). In the CIF and CIP terms, the seller is also responsible for arranging and paying for the insurance. However, the 'C' terms are still contracts where the seller fulfils the contract in the country of dispatch (ie usually the seller's own country), like the 'F' terms. Thus, the goods are only at the seller's risk under the 'C' terms until they are handed over to the carrier, that is in CIF when they pass over the ship's rail. So, under the 'C' terms the passing of risk differs from the place to which the seller arranges transport. Under the 'D' terms, the risk will not pass until the goods reach their destination (see **8.4.4**).

Documentary credits are commonly used with 'C' terms. This is in line with the nature of the 'C' terms, in that the seller is not at risk once the goods have been handed over to the carrier, so can be paid against the documents received (see **9.4**).

The most commonly used set is CIF.

Cost, insurance, freight (CIF) (named port of destination)

This is the typical contract where payment against documents would be used, usually on presentation of a bill of lading. In a CIF contract, the seller is in effect undertaking to arrange for the goods to be supplied and transported to the buyer's country.

Seller is required to:

- ship goods conforming to the description in the contract;
- clear the goods for export;
- arrange a contract for sea carriage to the port of destination;
- obtain a bill of lading or waybill when the goods are loaded;
- arrange insurance under which the buyer can claim, and provide insurance documents to the buyer;
- provide an invoice for the cost of the goods and carriage and insurance; and
- transmit to the buyer the bill of lading, insurance documents and invoice, and any other documents needed.

Buyer is required to:

- accept the documents tendered by the seller if they are in order;
- pay the contract price;
- receive the goods at the port of destination;
- pay any ancillary costs of the sea voyage, and costs of unloading and land transport to buyer's premises;
- bear all risks of the goods after their passing over the ship's rail at the port of shipment;
- pay all customs dues and taxes; and
- obtain any import licences.

Under CIF, the price quoted to the buyer for the goods includes insurance and freight to the buyer's home port. This increases the certainty of the price for the buyer. Under an FOB contract, the buyer bears the risk of fluctuations in freight and insurance rates. The use of payment against documents means the seller will be paid quickly, and that the goods can be sold on by the buyer whilst they are still on the high seas.

The property in the goods passes when the buyer pays for them and accepts the documents. However, the risk in the goods has already passed to the buyer when the goods were loaded on to the ship in the port of shipment (ie in the seller's country). Thus, CIF is an exception to SGA 1979, s 20, where prima facie risk passes with the property in the goods.

A CIF contract is always an export contract, and can only be used for sea or inland waterway transport.

As with FOB, there are many variations of CIF used in the commercial world. CIF and FOB are the two commonest sets of Incoterms in commercial use.

Cost and freight (CFR) (named port of destination)

The seller has to arrange and pay for the carriage of the goods to the foreign port. He is not obliged to take out insurance for the sea voyage, which is the buyer's responsibility both to arrange and to pay for, unlike CIF. If the seller fails to give the buyer enough notice for the buyer to be able to insure the goods, the goods could be regarded as travelling at the seller's risk, under SGA 1979, s 32(3).

The CFR terms lead to a rather artificial division between the arrangements for carriage and those for insurance. As such, they are not frequently used. They may be of use where the buyer's country requires their importers to insure at home, possibly for foreign exchange reasons.

Carriage and insurance paid to (CIP) (named place of destination)

This is on the borderline between being a CIF contract and one of the 'D' group.

These terms are suitable for any mode of transport including multimodal transport. The seller pays the freight to the place of destination (which could be a port, as with CIF) but in addition the seller arranges and pays for insurance to that place of destination for the buyer's benefit. As with CIF, the risk in the goods passes when the goods are handed over to the carrier (ie over the ship's rail if it is sea transport).

Carriage paid to (CPT) (named place of destination)

This differs from CIP in that the seller is not obliged to obtain insurance cover for the transport.

8.4.4 Examples of Incoterms – the 'D' group of terms: arrival

This group of terms imposes the highest burden on the seller.

In the 'D' group of terms, the passing of risk and delivery of the goods occurs at the same time. It is not split as it is in the 'C' terms. The goods are delivered, in the legal sense, to the buyer at the place of arrival in the buyer's country, at which point risk passes as well. This is in contrast to the 'C' group of terms where (legal) delivery takes place in the port of shipment. In the case of 'D' contracts, payment by the buyer is made against the goods arriving, not against documents. However, the seller would hand over a bill of lading or a waybill to the buyer to enable the buyer to obtain delivery of the goods from the carrier.

Delivered ex ship (DES) (named port of destination)

This set of terms is only suitable for transport of goods by sea or inland waterway. The seller is not under an obligation to the buyer to insure the goods for the sea voyage as they are at the seller's risk. Thus, if the goods are lost at sea, the buyer would have had no insurable interest in the goods.

The goods would normally be described as being delivered on a named ship on a specific day at a specified port.

Delivered ex quay (DEQ) (named port of destination)

This set of terms is only suitable for transport of goods by sea or inland waterway. The seller's obligations are similar to DES but, in addition, the seller agrees to pay for import duties and unloading charges at the port of destination. The buyer is responsible for onward carriage from the quayside to the ultimate destination. DEQ is not often used in British practice as it is necessary for the seller to have a local agent in the port of destination.

Delivered at frontier (DAF) (named place at frontier)

This set of terms may be used for any mode of transport where goods are delivered at a land frontier. No sea or air carriage is involved. The terms do not require the seller to obtain insurance for the buyer's benefit. It is up to the parties to come to an agreement. The contract would normally specify the border and the place on the border where delivery is to take place.

Delivered duty paid (DDP), delivered duty unpaid (DDU) (named place of destination in the buyer's country)

These terms on the seller place the highest burden of all the Incoterms. They would normally only be used for the supply of a small quantity of goods by air.

The goods are at the seller's risk and expense until the buyer takes delivery at the place of destination. Under DDP, the seller pays all charges including import duties and carriage in the buyer's country. Under DDU, the buyer undertakes the costs of importing the goods.

There is no obligation on the seller to insure the goods under either DDU or DDP.

Chapter 9

FINANCING OF INTERNATIONAL SALE OF GOODS

9.1 COLLECTION ARRANGEMENTS

If we assume that the goods have been sent on a CIF contract, the seller will obtain from the ship operator a bill of lading (or a waybill). He will send this with the insurance documents and the commercial invoice to his own bank in the UK (with other relevant documents, eg an export or import licence). They will send them to the foreign bank. The foreign bank will pass the documents to the buyer, at the same time asking him for payment. On payment, he receives the shipping documents. He uses these to get the goods from the carrier. The foreign bank then sends the money to the seller's bank in the UK.

Payment for the goods can be made by a bill of exchange, though this is simply one method of payment (see **9.3**). There are others. The law and practice in this area can be complex. The following account is simplified. You may wish to make reference to works on this subject if you want to know more, especially if you come across this area when you are in practice.

9.2 NEGOTIABLE INSTRUMENTS

An instrument is a document which evidences the holder's right to enforce a legal right (eg to receive a sum of money). A negotiable instrument can be freely transferred by giving it to another person, and possibly endorsing it as well. The new holder can then enforce the legal right. This is the big advantage of a negotiable instrument.

Negotiable instruments include:

- cheques;
- bills of exchange;
- bank notes; and
- bankers' drafts.

Sometimes, they can be made payable to the person in possession of them (ie to 'bearer'). This is the case with bank notes.

In other cases, they are made out to a specific payee, who can endorse the instrument and make it payable to a third party. This can be done with cheques, for example. You can endorse them to make them payable to a third party, for example your landlord.

Bills of exchange can likewise be endorsed to make them payable to a third party, perhaps a creditor of the person that the bill is made out to. Bills of exchange are defined in the Bills of Exchange Act 1882 (BEA 1882), s 3(1) as:

'A bill of exchange is an unconditional order in writing, addressed by one person to another, signed by the person giving it, requiring the person to whom it is addressed to pay on demand or at a fixed or determinable future time, a sum certain in money to or to the order of a specified person, or to a bearer.'

A cheque is defined as a 'bill of exchange drawn on a banker, payable on demand' (BEA 1882, s 73). A cheque is therefore a sub-species of a bill of exchange.

9.3 BILLS OF EXCHANGE

There are three original parties to a bill of exchange:

- drawer
- drawee; and
- payee.

Perhaps the analogy of a personal cheque is the easiest one to visualise. Here, you would be the drawer of the cheque, your bank would be the drawee (eg Barclays Bank) and the payee would be the person you are paying (eg your landlord).

With a bill of exchange the basic position would be:

- drawer – the buyer;
- drawee – the buyer's bank; and
- payee – the seller of the goods.

Typical characteristics of a bill of exchange are:

- every obligation in the bill must be expressed in writing;
- the order to pay must be unconditional;
- it is addressed by one person to another (even to himself) (see **9.3.2**);
- it is payable on demand or at a fixed time in the future (see **9.3.1**);
- it is for a specific sum of money;
- the drawer, or his agent, must have signed it;
- the obligations, typically payment, can be transferred by 'negotiation', usually at a discount (see **9.3.1**); and
- performance of the obligations (eg payment) can only be demanded by the person holding the bill.

A bill of exchange will specify the place of payment (eg 'payable in New York City at XY bank').

For a case dealing with the rights of an assignee of a bill of exchange, see *Glasscock v Balls* (1889) 24 QBD 13. A more recent example is *Credit Agricole Indosuez v Ecumet (UK) Ltd and Another* [2001] WL 482940.

9.3.1 'Term' bills and 'sight' bills

Bills of exchange must be presented to the drawer in order to become payable. Most bills of exchange are 'term bills', that is, they are expressed to be payable at some date after they have been initially presented to the bank (which is the drawee). This is usually 90 or 180 days from that date. In other words, they must be presented twice to the bank, and payment is due on the second occasion. 'Negotiation' means discounting the bill of exchange, that is, selling it on to a third party who will eventually present the bill to the bank for payment. When a bill is negotiated, the original payee will not receive 100% of the face value as it is to his advantage to have payment then rather than wait for 90 or 180 days, as the case may be.

The other type of bill is a 'sight' bill, which will be paid on the first occasion it is presented to the drawee (the bank), so the payee does not have to wait for payment. In both cases, payment of the bill depends on the conditions on the bill being met, including for example the place of payment.

9.3.2 Payment chain

If the bill of exchange were drawn up as indicated at **9.3**, by the buyer using the buyer's bank, then the seller would have to deal with the foreign bank. The bill of exchange would have to be seen twice by the foreign bank, if the bill were a term bill, that is once for 'acceptance' and once for payment.

One way to simplify all this is the slightly odd concept that the seller draws up the bill using the seller's bank, and with the seller as payee. It's a bit like writing a cheque to yourself. Obviously, the seller's bank is not going to pay money out to the seller for the sheer hell of it. Rather, the seller's bank will arrange in advance with the buyer's bank to be reimbursed by it. Once the seller's bank is happy about that, it will turn the bill of exchange into a binding document by 'accepting' the bill when it is presented. The bill will then be paid on the second occasion it is presented to the seller's bank, if it is a term bill, or immediately on acceptance if it is a sight bill. The buyer's bank will reimburse the sellers' bank. The buyer's bank will then arrange for the money to be taken from the buyer's account. The end effect is the same, in that the payment moves from the buyer's account to the seller's account but the mechanics are a little simpler.

9.3.3 The 'holder in due course'

This term is defined in s 29(1) of the BEA 1882. The 'holder in due course' gets title to the bill 'free of equities', that is, free of any defects in the title of his predecessor. In other words, he can still sue on it regardless of such defects. The only problem is if there is a forged endorsement (ie a fraudulent transfer in the chain). He is the equivalent under the BEA 1882 of a bona fide purchaser for value under the general law.

The holder has the right to sue previous endorsers if the acceptor fails to pay, including any who endorsed the bill after the forged endorsement, if applicable.

Other types of holder have less protection under the 1882 Act.

9.3.4 Claused bills

A bill of exchange is not normally set out as simply as is a personal cheque. It has 'clauses'. There could be provisions, for example, dealing with exchange rates for currencies, or stating that the bill is payable with bankers charges. If a bill does not stipulate that incidental charges are borne by the drawee (the bank), then they are borne by the drawer (buyer of the goods).

9.4 DOCUMENTARY CREDITS (OR LETTERS OF CREDIT)

This is one system of backing up payments. It can be thought of as analogous to using a cheque guarantee card to back up a personal cheque. The documentary credit is the guarantee card.

Almost all documentary credits are expressed to be drawn up under the Uniform Customs and Practice for Documentary Credits (UCP) published by the ICC. The current version is UCP 500.

The buyer is contracting with a bank. The result is that the bank gives the seller an undertaking to pay the price due, on condition that the specified terms are met. The seller can then ship the goods. He presents the documents specified in the documentary credit to the bank. If those documents are in order, the bank pays the seller. This could be in cash, or by accepting a bill of exchange (see **9.3**).

The documentary credit offers the seller the virtual certainty of being paid, but see *Mitsui & Co Ltd and Another v Flota Mercante Grancolombiana SA; The Ciudad de Pasto; The Ciudad de Neiva* [1989] 1 All ER 951. The Court of Appeal held that the seller was entitled to retain title to the goods even though the balance of the price was secured by a documentary credit because there was still a slim chance that the seller might not be paid under the documentary credit.

The bank is acting as a principal in the case of a documentary credit, not acting as a mere guarantor. There is a cost to the buyer, in terms of bank fees, but the existence of the documentary credit may enable the buyer to negotiate favourable terms in the sale of goods contract with the seller. Documentary credits offer the parties many advantages and are therefore very widely used.

The documentary credit could provide for any one of four methods of payment:

- cash on presentation of the documents by the seller – 'payment at sight';
- cash at some future time, eg after 90 days – 'deferred payment';
- a bill of exchange drawn by the seller, probably a term bill payable at a future date – 'acceptance credit'; or
- negotiating a bill of exchange drawn by the seller – 'negotiation credit'.

There are also different types of documentary credit, but that is beyond the scope of this chapter.

The definition of a documentary credit in UCP 500, Article 2 is:

> 'Any arrangement, however named or described, whereby a bank (the "issuing bank") acting at the request and on the instructions of a customer (the "Applicant") or on its own behalf,
>
> (i)   is to make a payment to or to the order of a third party (the "Beneficiary"), or is to accept and pay bills of exchange (Drafts) drawn by the Beneficiary, or
> (ii) authorises another bank to effect such payment or to accept and pay such bills of exchange (Drafts), or
> (iii) authorises another bank to negotiate
>
> against stipulated documents, provided that the terms and conditions of the Credit are complied with.'

The buyer will be the applicant for the credit. The seller will be the beneficiary.

There are two fundamental principles of documentary credits. These are:

- the autonomy of the documentary credit; and
- the doctrine of strict compliance.

9.4.1 The autonomy of the documentary credit

The bank is only concerned whether or not the documents presented by the seller correspond with the list of specified documents in the documentary credit. The bank is not concerned with the sale of goods contract, or its subject matter, be it grain or widgets.

9.4.2 The doctrine of strict compliance

Again, the bank has no knowledge about the subject matter of the sale of goods contract. The bank deals in money, not in corn. The bank is entitled to reject the documentary credit if the documents specified are not in total compliance. The reason for this is that the seller's bank (the 'advising' bank) is an agent of the buyer's bank (the 'issuing' bank) which is in turn the agent of the buyer. If an agent acts outside his limited authority, he could be unable to recover from his principal and be left with a loss.

In *Equitable Trust Company of New York v Dawson Partners Ltd* [1927] 27 Ll L Rep 49, which concerned a fraudulent seller and a contract to buy vanilla beans from Indonesia, Sumner LJ held:

> 'There is no room for documents which are almost the same or which will do just as well.'

The House of Lords held that the claimant bank could not recover from the buyer as it had relied on the opinion of one expert, not of two experts as specified in the documents.

An example of this doctrine is the case of *Gian Singh & Co Ltd v Banque de l'Indochine* [1974] 1 WLR 1234. The Privy Council upheld the actions of a bank that used reasonable care in complying with the prima facie requirements of a documentary credit, notwithstanding that one of the specified documents was in fact a forgery.

In *Credit Industriel et Commercial v China Merchants Bank* [2002] EWHC 973 (Comm), [2002] 2 All ER (Comm) 427, the documentary credit did not require the bills of exchange themselves to be in English, only the documents needed to negotiate the bills. The bills of exchange were from a French bank, and were in French. The defendant was held to be unjustified in rejecting the documentary credit.

An example of taking the doctrine of strict compliance to the extremes is *Krediet Antwerp v Midland Bank plc; Karaganda Ltd v Midland Bank plc and Another* [1999] 1 All ER (Comm) 801. The defendant bank had rejected documents specified in the documentary credit. The insurance policy was the original but was not marked with the words 'as original'. The survey report came from the Dutch subsidiary of the named surveyors, and therefore not from the named parent company. The Court of Appeal upheld the decision in favour of the claimant, and in effect said that the defendant was being pedantic.

9.4.3 The fraud exception to strict compliance

The only exception to the doctrine of strict compliance is fraud. The likely scenarios are that one or more of the documents is a forgery (or has been altered in a material matter) or that the beneficiary or his agent is a party to a fraudulent transaction involving the goods. Even so, the fraud has to be pretty clear cut before the bank could be restrained from making payment (*Czarnikow-Rionda Sugar Trading Inc v Standard Bank London Ltd and Others* [1999] 1 All ER (Comm) 890). That case is a good illustration of the general reluctance of judges in commercial law cases to interfere with established commercial practices, in this case reliance upon documentary credits (letters of credit). Thus, Rix J held:

> '... even if I assume for the sake of argument that Rionda [the buyer] has otherwise brought itself within the fraud exception, its claim against Standard [the bank] for a pre-trial injunction must fail on the balance of convenience alone. I would seek to put the matter in the following way.
>
> (1)   The interest in the integrity of banking contracts is so great that not even fraud can be allowed to intervene unless the fraud comes to the notice of the bank (a) in time, ie in any event before the beneficiary is paid, and (b) in such a way that it can be said that the bank had knowledge of the fraud.
>   ... Unless the banking commitment can be insulated from disputes between merchants, international trade would become impossible.
> (2)   ... Once, however, a letter of credit arrangement has been set up, the special rule that only the fraud exception permits interference comes into play.
> (3)   Thus, in the absence of the fraud exception, a buyer can no more seek to prevent his seller from drawing on the letter of credit for which the seller has stipulated, than the buyer can seek to prevent his bank from making the payment under it. The reason is that otherwise the special rule could be subverted, and the integrity and insulation of banking contracts could be overthrown, simply by the device of injuncting the beneficiary rather than the bank.'

So, Rix J would not allow an injunction to prevent the bank from paying out on the documentary credit, or an injunction to prevent the seller from drawing on the documentary credit. Instead, he suggested that the claimant could seek a freezing ('*Mareva*') order against the seller's bank accounts, so that the proceeds of the alleged fraud could not be disposed of before the dispute was resolved.

9.4.4 Factors influencing the use of documentary credits

Documentary credits give the seller security but, like all bank services, they cost money. The effect is to increase the overall price to the buyer. The creditworthiness of the buyer is a major factor. However, government controls on foreign currency payments have been a factor, at least in the past.

9.4.5 How a documentary credit works

The buyer will go to his own bank and open a documentary credit in favour of the seller. The bank will issue a letter of credit and will usually ask a bank in the seller's country to 'advise' (ie ratify) the credit. The buyer's bank is therefore the 'issuing bank' and the seller's bank is the 'advising bank'.

9.4.6 Revocable or irrevocable

Documentary credits come in different forms. The revocable documentary credit, as its name suggests, can be revoked by the buyer at any time. It is therefore more or less useless (see *Cape Asbestos v Lloyds Bank Ltd* [1921] WN 274). The 1993 version of the UCP states that all credits are presumed to be irrevocable unless specifically stated to be revocable. An irrevocable documentary credit cannot be revoked by the buyer once it has been put in place, and is therefore infinitely preferable.

9.4.7 Unconfirmed and confirmed credits

If the seller were not paid he would have to sue the buyer's bank in the buyer's country, even with an irrevocable credit. However, if the documentary credit is confirmed by the seller's own bank then that bank is adding its own guarantee of payment (so it is then referred to as the 'confirming bank'). The seller could then sue his own bank in his own country.

So, a documentary credit can be 'unconfirmed' or 'confirmed', as well as being 'irrevocable' or 'revocable'. Obviously, the best option for the seller is a documentary credit that is irrevocable and confirmed. It is also the most expensive option for the buyer.

9.4.8 Practical matters

The sale of goods contract should provide when the documentary credit is to be provided to the seller. In the absence of an express term, it would normally be implied that it would need to be sent no later than the earliest shipping date for the goods. There would also need to be enough time before then for the seller to make the shipping arrangements (eg *Ian Stach Ltd v Baker Bosley Ltd* [1958] 2 QB 130).

The expiry date of the credit will be on the face of the document. If it has been omitted, the documentary credit is taken as expiring after a reasonable time. Under the UCP, an expiry date must be stated, otherwise the seller is entitled to reject the documentary credit.

It is likely that at some stage in the future electronic submission of documents will be possible (see **8.2.1** on the BOLERO system for replacing bills of lading).

9.4.9 Payment

The seller's bank will pay the seller when he presents the documentary credit and the documents specified therein (eg a carrier's receipt, invoice, packing list, insurance certificate). Various methods of payment could be used, including a bill of exchange (see **9.4**). This would typically be used when the buyer wants a credit period but the seller wants immediate payment. By use of a bill of exchange, the seller can sell the bill immediately (ie 'negotiate' it) at a discount to a third party. He will immediately receive money, whereas the buyer does not have to part with his money until the bill is presented for payment by the third party (see **9.3.1**).

There are other mechanisms for financing exports which we do not look at in this book.

PART III

INTELLECTUAL PROPERTY

Chapter 10

INTRODUCTION TO INTELLECTUAL PROPERTY

10.1 SO WHAT IS INTELLECTUAL PROPERTY?

The basic concept is that of protecting the products of human intellect. However, it has to concentrate on the products of the intellect because no one can see into somebody else's mind.

So, the selection of a football team may involve a lot of intellect on the part of the manager, but the team is not generally regarded as being his property. The team manager does not own the players.

In order to be protected the product of the intellectual effort has to be 'owned' by someone, that is it has to be property. Ultimately, the products which society has decided are worth protecting are, first, the artistic ones, where otherwise the genuine artist could be ripped off by some third-rate imitator. The genuine artist could have difficulty making a living if his creative efforts are reproduced without him receiving any payment.

The second category for protection are those products that are used in business, for example brand names like 'Coca Cola'. Again, without the protection of intellectual property (IP) law the owner of the genuine brand could otherwise have their world-famous product ripped off by a backstreet purveyor of obnoxious sludge. This would damage the reputation of the genuine article, and ultimately the sales.

There is also a strong element of protecting the consumer. If the consumer buys goods, or services, then they want to have a genuine indication of the quality of the goods in question. The law of IP prevents the consumer being deceived about the product they are buying. This also has a bearing on the price paid. The consumer knows that Jaguar or Mercedes are high-quality cars and will be prepared to pay a higher price than they would for an Adamsmobile, which is known to be a very inferior make.

10.2 WHAT TYPES OF INTELLECTUAL PROPERTY ARE THERE?

IP rights fall into two camps, the artistic and the commercial ones. Some common law rights come under the heading of IP, mainly passing off and breach of confidence. There are also a number of lesser IP rights, some of which are mentioned at **10.2.7**.

10.2.1 Trade marks

A trade mark is a brand name, for example Coca Cola for soft drinks, BMW for cars and motorcycles, or Levi's for jeans. It is a highly commercial right. Trade marks are best protected by registration (and all well-known trade marks are registered). This gives the owner of the trade mark statutory rights, under the Trade Marks Act 1994 (TMA 1994), to defend their trade mark against infringers who are using the same mark or a similar one.

The registration of a trade mark can be renewed indefinitely provided the trade mark does not run foul of some restrictions under TMA 1994. The oldest trade mark in the UK is the Bass red triangle for beer. It was registered in the 1870s and is still valid today.

If a trade mark is not registered, then it can only be protected by the law of passing off.

10.2.2 Passing off

This is a common law right. It enables a business to defend itself from someone who is trying to rip off the trading reputation of that business, for example by using its name or selling goods in packaging that looks similar. Passing off is less important than trade mark law, and also less certain as regards the outcome. It has also been diminished by the increased scope of registered designs (see **10.2.4**).

10.2.3 Copyright

Copyright is a right to prevent copying. It is primarily an artistic right (though attempts have been made to drag it into the industrial arena). It is not a registered right.

The printing of books was a monopoly granted by the Crown up until the eighteenth century. By this means, the government could control the printed media. The Statute of Anne in 1709 granted book publishers copyright to protect them against unlicensed copyists, which the common law was unable to do. Thus, authors and their publishers were protected from copying as such. It has to be 'copying'. Copyright does not stop you writing an exciting novel on the life of lawyer just because John Grisham has produced many such books. However, it does stop you copying the works of Mr Grisham.

Copyright has also been extended to cover paintings and drawings, industrial plans, sculpture, music and films. These media are 'artistic' but also highly commercial, if you think about the money involved in a major film, such as the James Bond films.

10.2.4 Designs

Designs can be protected by registration. The first Act in 1787 protected the patterns of textiles. Since then, the period of protection has extended and the coverage has been revised. A major revision to the design regime occurred in December 2001, thanks to an EC directive. Designs are commercial rights.

Designs that relate to the appearance of the object can be registered, but ones that relate to its technical function cannot. Registration gives statutory protection for up to 25 years.

There is also an unregistered design right for functional objects, that can protect them for 10 years.

10.2.5 Patents

Patents are a commercial IP right. A patent is protection for an invention. The invention could be a better mousetrap, or a wonder drug to treat cancer. A patent is a registered right, administered by the Patents Office.

A patent gives the holder the right to a monopoly for 20 years over the technology revealed in the patent. 'Revealed' is an important concept. 'Patent' is derived from 'letters patent', meaning that the description of the invention is made public in return for the grant by the Crown of the period of protection. Thus, after the 20-year period expires, the invention is then public property. Anybody can use it because the technology is revealed in the patent document, known as a patent specification.

The philosophy is that inventors need to be able to reap the reward of their efforts. If they were not, then for example the pharmaceutical companies would not spend the vast sums of money needed to invent new drugs as they would not otherwise be able to recoup that cost.

An alternative approach for an inventor is to keep the technology secret, possibly with the aid of confidentiality agreements with employees or with businesses using the technology. This works for as long as the technology can be kept secret. This technology is often referred to as 'know-how' and can be ancillary to a patent rather than being truly distinct. Know-how can be secrets of the trade that are needed to enable the patent to be worked.

10.2.6 Confidential information

The law of confidence is not an IP right in a pure sense but is often classified with the mainstream rights as it is sometimes associated with them. For example, maintaining confidentiality before submitting a patent application is vital to avoid destruction of the invention's novelty.

Case-law rather than statute govern the law of confidence and, as you would expect, the vast majority of cases relate to circumstances where express obligations of confidence are lacking and implied duties of confidentiality have to be considered. It is, however, important to remember that express obligations can (and often should) be imposed (eg on key employees or independent contractors).

10.2.7 What else is there?

There are various other IP rights. For example:

The IP right	What does it protect against?
• Database right	• Copying of information
• Semiconductor topography	• Copying of computer 'chips'
• Plant varieties	• Anyone else selling the registered new variety of plant
• Moral rights	• Bastardisation of an artiste's work
• Performers rights	• Copying of a live performance by an artiste

10.3 SUMMARY OF IP RIGHTS

10.3.1 Trade marks

• What is protected?	• a brand name and/or a logo for goods or services
• What benefit is there?	• exclusive right to the trade mark with statutory protection
• How is it obtained?	• registration
• How long does it last?	• indefinitely

10.3.2 Passing off

• What is protected?	• goodwill (eg a logo or a name)
• What benefit is there?	• gives protection against 'rip-offs'
• How is it obtained?	• arises automatically (no registration)
• How long does it last?	• indefinitely

10.3.3 Copyright

• What is protected?	• 'artistic output'
• What benefit is there?	• prevents copying
• How is it obtained?	• arises automatically (no registration)
• How long does it last?	• 70 years from death (usually)

10.3.4 Database right

• What is protected?	• collections of information
• What benefit is there?	• protects against unauthorised copying
• How is it obtained?	• arises automatically (no registration)
• How long does it last?	• 15 years from creation of the database

10.3.5 Registered design right

• What is protected?	• new designs for consumer items
• What benefit is there?	• monopoly right
• How is it obtained?	• registration
• How long does it last?	• 25 years from registration

10.3.6 Unregistered design right

• What is protected?	• 3-dimensional shapes
• What benefit is there?	• prevents copying
• How is it obtained?	• arises automatically (no registration)
• How long does it last?	• 10 years in most cases

10.3.7 Patents

•	What is protected?	•	new invention
•	What benefit is there?	•	monopoly right
•	How is it obtained?	•	registration
•	How long does it last?	•	20 years from application

10.3.8 Confidential information

•	What is protected?	•	secret information
•	What benefit is there?	•	protects against unauthorised disclosure
•	How is it obtained?	•	arises automatically (no registration)
•	How long does it last?	•	indefinitely

Chapter 11

TRADE MARKS

11.1 FUNCTIONS OF A TRADE MARK

A trade mark is a brand name. You might think of Coca Cola, BMW or Easyjet. These are all protected as registered trade marks.

Registered trade marks have existed in the UK for 130 years. (The only way of protecting a trade mark which is not registered is by using the common law action of passing off – see **12.1**.)

Three functions of a trade mark are:

- **origin** – the trade mark serves as an indication of the trade source from which the goods come, or are otherwise connected;
- **quality** – the trade mark indicates to the consumer the quality of the goods they are buying; and
- **investment** – the trade mark is a symbol for the money spent in advertising of the product, that is in building up the brand image.

Although we have indicated above that the trade mark is used for goods, it can also be used for services.

•	What is protected?	•	a brand name and/or a logo for goods or services
•	What benefit is there?	•	exclusive right to the trade mark with statutory protection
•	How is it obtained?	•	registration at the Trade Mark Registry
•	How long does it last?	•	indefinitely

11.2 WHY REGISTER?

There are advantages to registering a trade mark which are as follows.

- **Easier to sue for infringement of a trade mark.** It is much quicker, cheaper, and less uncertain than passing-off actions. With a registered trade mark there is an initial presumption of validity and the claimant usually starts off in a quite a strong position. There is no need for the claimant to prove reputation in the mark.
- **You can register a trade mark before you start using it.** Usually the trade mark is 'bagged' by making an application before the product is launched. This is a major advantage.
- **There is a public record for trade marks.** This records both applications and registered trademarks. If somebody is intending to launch a new product (or to name a new company) then they will usually search the trade mark register to check whether anybody else has registered or applied for the same or a similar

name. If it has been registered, then they will think twice about using the name. In practice this is a very important reason for registering a mark – warning others off.

- **Danger that somebody else will register.** If you rely on building up rights in a mark through use, you run a risk that somebody else will register the same mark and even be able to stop you using it. However, a mark can be struck off for 5 years non-use in relation to the specified goods or services so a purely defensive registration can be problematic (s 46(1)(a)). If 'BMW' was registered for, say, hair dryers but not used for 5 years, it could be struck off in relation to hair dryers but not of course in relation to cars, and whatever else it is actually used on.

Theoretically, a 'spoiling' registration should not happen because s 5(4)(a) of the TMA 1994 provides that a mark should not be registered if its use could be stopped by a third party on the grounds of passing off. Section 11(3) provides that a mark is not infringed by the use of an earlier right (an earlier right being defined as a mark protected by the law of passing off).

A trade mark registration can last indefinitely, if it retains its ability to distinguish the goods or services in question. The Bass red triangle for beer has been in existence for some 130 years and is still valid today.

11.3 HOW TO REGISTER AND THE PROBLEMS THAT ARISE

Any person can apply to the Trade Mark Registry of the Patent Office to register a trade mark.

In TMA 1994, s 1(1) a trade mark is defined as:

> 'any sign capable of being represented graphically which is capable of distinguishing the goods or services of one undertaking from those of other undertakings.'

'Graphical representation' is taken as meaning that the trade mark can be described in written form. Thus, a musical jingle could be a trade mark because it could be written in musical notation. There are obvious problems, however, with registration of a smell, as you can only register a description of the smell in words (eg 'smell of roses'). There is no way to register a sample of the scent itself.

'Capacity to distinguish' is now construed widely. In particular, s 1(1) provides that a trade mark could be a shape. Under the old Act (Trade Marks Act 1938), the House of Lords held that the shape of the Coca Cola bottle was not registerable as it was not capable of distinguishing the goods (*In re Coca-Cola Co* [1986] 1 WLR 695). It is now registered under the TMA 1994.

As regards registration of colour, even under the more restrictive criteria of the now defunct Trade Marks Act 1938, a combination of colours was held to be registerable for drug capsules (*Smith Kline & French Laboratories Ltd v Sterling-Winthrop Group Ltd* [1975] 2 All ER 578) (see **11.5**).

However, even under TMA 1994 it would be impossible to register the word 'soap' as a trade mark for soap. Otherwise, the proprietor of that registration would be able to prevent any other producer from using the word 'soap' in relation to their soap (*Philips Electronics NV v Remington Consumer Products Ltd* [1998] RPC 283). In other words, it could not be a trade mark as it would not distinguish the products of one business from those of another. It would simply be an attempt to monopolise an ordinary English word.

Attempts to register in bad faith will also be refused (TMA 1994, s 3(6)). For example, attempts to:

- stockpile marks because others may want them in the future;
- misappropriate marks with a strong reputation elsewhere; and
- acquire 'merchandisable' marks such as the names of well-known people or characters.

Registration can be refused on absolute grounds, that is that it fails to meet the criteria for a trade mark under TMA 1994, s 3 (see **11.4**). It can also be refused on relative grounds, that is that it is too close to an existing registration (TMA 1994, s 5 – see **11.6**).

A trade mark has to be registered in relation to named goods or services. There will be a 'statement of goods or services' for the trade mark in each of the registration classes in which it is registered, eg one of the registrations for Coca Cola is in class 32, beers and non-alcoholic drinks. The statement for that registration is 'syrup for use in making a beverage'.

Trade marks are registered in one or more of 45 classes (see **11.15**). The main purpose of the classes is to facilitate searching for trade mark registrations. However, the more important issue is the statement of goods or services as that determines the scope of the registration. It is a central factor when looking at possible infringement. A trade mark will often be registered in more than one class. For example, the trade mark for a beer would be registered in class 32, but the same trade mark could also be registered in class 25 for clothing as the name might be used on clothing to promote the beer.

The importance of the wording in a statement of goods or services was illustrated in *Associated Newspapers Limited and another v Express Newspapers* [2003] EWHC 1322 (Ch), [2003] All ER (D) 140 (Jun). The proprietors of the *Daily Mail* and the *Mail on Sunday* newspapers were seeking to prevent the use of the registered trade marks 'Mail' or 'Mail on Sunday'. The defendants were seeking to launch free newspapers with the titles *London Evening Mail* or *Evening Mail*. The claimants failed under TMA 1994, s 10(1) for infringement by use of an identical trade mark on identical goods, as their trade marks were registered for 'newspapers for sale'. It was held that, as the defendants' newspapers would be free newspapers, the proposed use of the trade marks by the defendants did not come within the ambit of the statement of goods and services of the registered trade marks. However, the claimants did succeed under s 10(2) which provides for infringement if the use is of an identical trade mark on similar goods, and there is a risk of confusion on the part of the public (see **11.9**).

Until the legislation governing trade marks was amended in the mid 1980s, it was not possible to have a registered trade mark for services. Even under TMA 1994, an area of difficulty was the registration of a trade mark for retail services. However, since the case of *Giacomelli Sport SpA's Application* [2000] ETMR 277, it seems to be accepted that retail services can be registered (eg the name of a shop). (This was a decision in relation to a Community trade mark by the appeal board of the EU Trade Mark Office (OHIM).)

11.4 ABSOLUTE GROUNDS FOR REFUSAL

In TMA 1994, s 3 the absolute grounds for refusal are laid down. The most common ones are in s 3(1):

'The following shall not be registered—

(a) signs which do not satisfy the requirements of section 1(1)

(b) trade marks that are devoid of distinctive character

(c) trade marks which consist exclusively of signs or indications which may serve, in trade, to designate the kind, quality, quantity, intended purpose, value, geographical origin, the time of production of goods or of rendering of services, or other characteristics of goods or services,

(d) trade marks that consist exclusively of signs or indications which have become customary in the current language or in the bona fide and established practices of the trade

Provided that, a trade mark shall not be refused registration by virtue of paragraph (b), (c) or (d) above if, before the date of application for registration, it has in fact acquired a distinctive character as a result of the use made of it.'

The key to understanding these grounds is that a mark will only be registrable if it is distinctive (ie it can be understood by customers as a sign that indicates the origin of the product). Distinctiveness is the idea that lies behind all the subsections of s 3(1).

The mark will undoubtedly be distinctive if it is a made-up name. The ones usually quoted are 'Kodak' or 'Exxon'. Beware of words that are merely phonetic spellings of ordinary words so they look distinctive until pronounced (eg 'Orlwoola' for all wool (see **11.4.5**) or 'Writs' for a sandwich bar (ie potential problems with the Ritz restaurant)).

So in what situations will the mark not be distinctive? Some of the ones that come up most frequently are as follows.

11.4.1 Surname or forename (s 3(1)(b))

A registered trade mark is a monopoly use, so is it fair to grant a monopoly over a name and would it in any event be regarded by the public as a mark for merchandise? In effect, names are registered with evidence of previous use for the goods or service in question. The more unusual the name, the easier the burden of proof to show that it is distinctive of the goods or services in question.

English courts are reluctant to grant monopoly rights over the 'image' of a well-known person. 'Elvis Presley' was held not to be a trade mark protecting a monopoly over merchandise but in effect merely an indication of the style of merchandise (ie memorabilia of 'old swivel hips' – *Re Elvis Presley Enterprises' Application* [1999] RPC 567). Attempts to monopolise the name of the late Diana, Princess of Wales also failed (*Executrices of the Estate of Diana, Princess of Wales' Application* [2001] ETMR 25). See **11.9** for other aspects of this problem.

11.4.2 Characteristics of the goods – kind, quality, intended purpose, value (s 3(1)(c))

This includes where the mark is descriptive of the goods or services for which it is to be registered. 'Cornflakes' is a good example of an unregistrable name. It merely describes the goods, that is they are made from rolling corn (maize) into flakes. If they were not, then the mark should be unregistrable on the grounds that it is misleading.

In other words, the name of that type of goods is not registerable (eg 'orange juice' would not be registerable but 'Fanta' is registerable). The same philosophy applies to the smell or shape of the goods themselves, that is, they are not registerable. You can register a smell or shape that is not determined by the nature of the goods (eg the Coca Cola bottle is a registered shape, but it could have been any shape of bottle as Coca Cola is a liquid and could be sold in, say, a cube-shaped bottle) (see **11.4.4**).

'Tastee-Freez' for ice-cream and 'Weldmesh' for wire mesh were also held to be unregisterable for being descriptive.

Anything that goes toward describing the quality of the goods especially in a praising sense, that is so-called 'laudatory' words, for example 'Magic Safe' was refused for safes.

A good type of trade mark is a name that has no connection with the characteristics of the goods, for example 'Mars' or 'Galaxy' for confectionery.

The trouble is that marketing people want to use descriptive names because they want to convey something about the product. What advice can you offer them? The best type of trade mark is a mark which suggests some characteristic of the goods or services without actually describing them. Examples of trade marks that succeed in doing this are:

Walkman   for a personal stereo
Workmate   for a bench that makes it easier to saw and drill bits of wood

The case of *Proctor & Gamble Co v Office for Harmonisation in the Internal Market (Trade Marks and Designs)* [2002] RPC 17 has widened the scope for businesses that want to use trade marks which could be descriptive. This was a case before the ECJ. The applicant appealed from a decision of the OHIM. The application was for registration as a European trade mark of 'Baby-Dry' for 'disposable diapers made out of paper or cellulose and diapers made out of textile'. The application had been rejected by OHIM as being the combination of two descriptive words, that is 'baby' and 'dry'. However, the ECJ held that while each word on its own was not distinctive, the use of the two words together produced an unusual combination which was not in common English usage.

In contrast, in *DKV Deutsche Krankenversicherung AG v Office for Harmonisation in the Internal Market* [2002] ECR I-7561, the appeal against the refusal of OHIM to allow 'Companyline' to be registered as a Community trade mark for insurance and financial advice was rejected by the ECJ. The judgment of the Court of First Instance, and therefore the refusal to register, was upheld. The ECJ judgment states:

> 'The Court of First Instance found, first, in paragraph 26 of the contested judgment, that the sign for which registration had been refused was composed exclusively of the words "company" and "line", both of which are customary in English-speaking countries. The word "company" suggested that what was in point were goods or services intended for companies or firms. The word "line" had various meanings. In the insurance and financial services sector it denoted, amongst other things, a branch of insurance or a line or group of products. They were thus generic words which simply denoted a line of goods or services for undertakings. Coupling them together without any graphic or semantic modification thus did not imbue them with any additional characteristic such as to render the sign, taken as a whole,

capable of distinguishing the appellant's services from those of other undertakings. The sign "Companyline" was therefore devoid of any distinctive character.'

11.4.3 Geographical name (s 3(1)(c))

In the majority of cases, geographical names will not be acceptable.

In the leading case of *Windsurfing Chiemsee Produktions und Vertriebs GmbH v Boots und Segelzubehör Walter Huber and Another* [2000] Ch 523, the ECJ refused to allow the geographical name to be registered. They held that a geographical name had to be left available for other traders to use in the future, particularly those actually located at Chiemsee (a holiday lake in Bavaria).

A geographical name which did not indicate the origin of the goods would be unregisterable for being deceptive. For example, 'Swiss Miss' was refused as the chocolate was not produced in Switzerland. However, if it is totally fanciful it could succeed, for example 'Sahara' for ice cream.

Beware that, as an exception to the general rule, protection of a geographical name by a group of traders located there is allowed, for example 'Harris Tweed' or 'Parma' (for ham) in *Consorzio del Prosciutto di Parma v Asda Stores Ltd and others* [2001] UKHL 7, [2001] 1 CMLR 43 (see **11.12**). Passing off could be applicable as well (see *Consorzio del Prosciutto di Parma v Marks & Spencer plc* [1991] RPC 351, and also **11.12**).

11.4.4 Where the mark consists purely of the shape of the goods or their packaging (s 3(2))

The key words here are 'purely of the shape'. In other words, to be a registerable trade mark, the shape to be registered has to be one which is specially created to distinguish those goods from those of other manufacturers. The registrar accepts that a shape can be distinctive, but the Trade Marks Manual (used by Registry staff as a guide) says that it will only be registrable if it 'immediately strikes the eye as different and therefore memorable'. If the shape is functional it will not be registrable, and even a decorative shape may not succeed. The result is that few shapes will be registrable (but the Coca Cola bottle is now registered, though there is of course immense goodwill in the product – see **11.5**).

The Court of Appeal upheld the Registrar's refusal to register the shape of the shaver heads of the Philishave razor (*Philips Electronics NV v Remington Consumer Products Ltd (No 2)* [1999] RPC 809). On a reference to the ECJ on construction of Directive on the Approximation of the Laws of Member States about Trade Marks (Dir 89/104/EC) from which TMA 1994 derives, the ECJ held that a shape determined by technical function of the product was not registerable as a trade mark (*Philips Electronics NV v Remington Consumer Products Ltd* [2002] 2 CMLR 52).

In effect, the logic is that shapes of products should be protected as registered design if the shape is new and has individual character (see **15.1.1**). Registered trade mark is not the appropriate right. Since the amendment in December 2001 of the Registered Designs Act 1949 (RDA 1949), the scope of registered designs has been increased to include the possibility of even registering as a design the appearance of the packaging of a product.

Cases where registration of shapes has been sought include the following. In *Bongrain SA v Trade Mark Registry* [2003] EWHC 531 (Ch), [2003] All ER (D) 329 (Mar), it was held that a cheese in the shape of a six-lobed flower was not registerable as it was devoid of distinctive character (ie it did not indicate that this was cheese from a particular manufacturer). In *Dyson Ltd v Registrar of Trade Marks* [2003] EWHC 1062 (Ch), (2003) unreported, 15 May, trade marks which consisted of the shape of the transparent dust-collection chamber in Dyson vacuum cleaners were held to be devoid of distinctive character (and therefore prima facie unregisterable). The trade marks in question were merely the shape of the goods. An argument that the trade marks have in fact acquired distinctiveness, as there are no other goods on the market with this feature, has been referred to the ECJ. It will be interesting to see how the ECJ deals with this in light of the decision in *Philips*. In *Societé de Produits Nestlé SA v Unilever plc* [2002] EWHC 2709 (Ch), unreported, it was held that it was arguable that the shape of Vienetta ice cream resulted from the nature of the product itself, which of course would render it unregisterable as a trade mark. It was also held that there was insufficient evidence that the public recognised the shape of Vienetta as a badge of origin of the goods (ie as emanating from Unilever), which also renders it unregisterable. Various issues on the law on shapes have been referred to the ECJ.

Overall, the lesson seems to be that it is very difficult to register a shape as a trade mark, though evidence of it having acquired distinctiveness through use is immensely persuasive (eg the Coca Cola bottle).

11.4.5 Public interest (s 3(3))

An application will not succeed if the trade mark in question is likely to deceive or is contrary to public policy or morality.

(a) Likely to deceive

For example, 'Orlwoola' for clothes would be deceptive if the clothes were not made entirely of wool (and if they were, it would be descriptive). 'Instant dip' for cleaning materials was refused on the basis that some of the materials were not in fact dips (*In the matter of Application No 713,406 by Otto Seligmann for the Registration of a Trade Mark* [1954] 71 RPC 52).

An example of an existing trade mark registration being struck off as being in bad faith occurred in *Byford v Oliver and Another* [2003] EWHC 295 (Ch), [2003] All ER (D) 345 (Feb). This concerned a number of registrations obtained in 1999 by the defendants for the name 'Saxon' which was a 1980s heavy metal band that is still performing, very loudly. The membership of the band had changed over the years but the claimant had always been a member. The defendants had only been members for part of the period. The defendants were held not to own the name and goodwill of the band 'Saxon' in its various guises.

An application to strike off a mark as being deceptive was made in *Zakritoe Aktsionernoe Obchtechestvo 'Torgovy Dom Potomkov Postavechtchika Dvora Ego Imperatorskago Velitschestva PA Smirnova v Diageo North America Inc* [2003] All ER (D) 99 (Apr). The (Russian) appellant's argument was that the (American) respondent's 14 registrations of the word 'Smirnoff' implied an unjustified connection with the Russian Federation. Smirnoff vodka has been sold since 1952 and is described as the world's leading brand. The appeal failed as there was held to be no deception as to the origin of the goods. The registrations for 'Smirnoff' were upheld.

(b) Public policy or morality

For example, 'Hallelujah' for women's clothing was refused 'on account of its likely positioning' (*Hallelujah Trade Mark* [1976] RPC 605).

In *Ghazilian's Trade Mark Application* [2002] RPC 23, the applicant appealed the refusal of the Registrar of Trade Marks to register as a trade mark for clothing the words 'Tiny Penis'. Not surprisingly, the judge agreed with the Registrar and refused registration. The judge held that the hearing officer had to consider objectively how a right-thinking member of the public would view the mark in question, as in *Re Masterman's Design* [1991] RPC 89. (This concerned a Scottish doll made wearing a kilt but nothing under it. Registration of the design was allowed.) The *Hallelujah* case was disapproved of in *Ghazilian* as being over cautious.

Note that slogans can be registered under TMA 1994. The slogan 'I can't believe it's yoghurt' was registered even under the more restricted scope of the Trade Marks Act 1938.

However, more recently applications to register the slogans 'Have a break' and 'Cycling is …' have both been rejected for not being distinctive (*Societé des Produits Nestlé SA v Mars UK Ltd* [2002] EWHC 2533 (Ch), [2002] All ER (D) 05 (Dec) and *Consortium of Bicycle Retailers v Halfords Ltd* [2002] RPC 37).

11.5 EVIDENCE OF USE TO OVERCOME ABSOLUTE GROUNDS

In **11.4**, you have seen how the criteria for absolute grounds work. However, there are lots of registered trade marks which would offend these criteria. The registration system would therefore unfairly deprive the proprietors of the protection of registration when in fact the trade marks are already well known in the trade or to the public. Examples of trade marks which prima facie offend the criteria for absolute grounds but yet have been registered include:

- the 'Toblerone' triangular shape for chocolate bars;
- 'York' for lorry trailers (geographical);
- the 'Jiff' plastic lemon (formerly the subject of a well-known passing-off case); and
- 'Premier' for high-quality luggage, on evidence of use, and consequent recognition of the mark amongst trade buyers and wholesalers (as it is, of course, otherwise laudatory).

The reason is of course that lack of distinctiveness can generally be overcome by use, that is by building up goodwill in the mark. If an applicant can show that it has built up a reputation in, say, a descriptive mark by using it then it may have acquired distinctiveness in fact through use and it can be registered. The applicant will establish reputation in the mark by sending a statutory declaration to the Trade Mark Registry giving evidence of advertising spend, turnover in the goods and length of use. (Also it needs to be use as an indicator of origin of the goods or services, sometimes referred to as 'trade mark use'.)

An informal minimum number of years' use is five. If you do not have 5 years of use, it is not generally worth trying. Generally of course the client does better to choose a mark that is registrable from the outset without use.

Very few colours are registered, but the colour of Heinz tins of baked beans has now been registered on the basis of use. Usually for colour to be considered it has to be a combination of colours, not just a single shade. See *Smith Kline & French Laboratories Ltd v Sterling-Winthrop Group Ltd* [1975] 2 All ER 578, where a complex of colours for a pharmaceutical capsule was accepted on evidence of wide recognition of the complex of colours as distinguishing the goods. (Be aware that this case was under the old Trade Marks Act 1938.)

However, in *BP Amoco plc v John Kelly Ltd* [2002] FSR 5, it was held that BP's trade mark registration of a single colour was valid. The trade mark consisted of the green colour defined in colour charts as Pantone 348C which BP used as the livery for their petrol filling stations. In *Libertel Group BV v Benelux-Merkenbureau (Case C-104/01)* (2003) unreported, the ECJ held that in order to be capable of being registered as a trade mark, a colour had to be defined by reference to an international identification system. It was not sufficient to lodge a sample with the trade mark office in question. The colour also had to have distinctive character (ie to have been used in relation to the goods or services in question).

11.6 RELATIVE GROUNDS FOR REFUSAL OF AN APPLICATION (s 5)

'Relative grounds' means a conflict with an existing registered trade mark which is identical or similar to the one being applied for.

The words have to be judged by their appearance and their sound to test for any similarity. For example:

- 'Rysta' for stockings was disallowed because of its similarity to Aristoc (*Aristoc Ltd v Rysta Ltd* [1945] AC 68); and
- 'Skin Dew' for comestics was allowed in spite of objections from the owners of 'Skin Deep' as it was held that the idea of two marks was different (*In the matter of Helena Rubinstein Ltd's Application for the Registration of a Trade Mark* [1960] RPC 229).

How do you find out whether your client's proposed trade mark is going to run foul of an existing registration? The answer is to do a trade mark search. Most large firms have facilities for doing this online. Alternatively, you can get one through an agency like Compumark. If you are inexperienced in this kind of work then it is best to go for an agency because they will analyse it for you to some extent. If you really don't know what you are doing, you instruct a trade mark agent. Beware that the results of a trade mark search are never completely up to date.

Do not forget that trade marks are registered in relation to specified goods or services. So, the starting point is to look for trade marks registered for the same types of goods and services, that is, in the relevant classes (see **11.3** and **11.15**).

A trade mark application can also be refused on the grounds that it is likely to be the subject of a passing off action (TMA 1994, s 5(4) and see **12.1**). To check for earlier rights in passing off, you can do a common law search by looking in telephone directories, and journals (for example in magazines on mountain bikes for marks used in connection with push bikes), etc. This common law search cannot, of course, be comprehensive.

If the 'new' trade mark is used and it is close to an existing registration, then infringement proceedings are very likely.

Under TMA 1994, s 5 relative grounds were extended. They can now be claimed not only for an identical mark for identical goods but also in relation to dissimilar goods, or in relation to a trade mark that is not identical but only similar.

Goods or services	Trade mark Identical	Trade mark Similar
Identical	+ s 5(1)	* s 5(2)(b)
Similar	* s 5(2)(a)	* s 5(2)(b)
Dissimilar	# s 5(3)	# s 5(3)

* likelihood of confusion needed
# unfair advantage or detriment needed

For example, someone trying to register 'Coca Cola' for fizzy drinks would find it impossible on relative grounds because of the existing registrations for the real 'Coca Cola' (ie 'identical' goods). However, this could also be the case for someone trying to register 'Coca Cola' for cars, lavatory brushes or other 'dissimilar' goods. In the case of the use in relation to cars, it would be held as obtaining an unfair advantage from the reputation of the existing trade mark. In the case of goods such as lavatory brushes it would held to be detrimental to the existing mark, as well as taking unfair advantage.

In *Intel Corporation v Sihra* [2003] EWHC 17 (Ch), [2003] All ER (D) 212 (Jan), registration of 'Intel-Play' was refused as it was held that it would take unfair advantage of or be detrimental to the character and repute of the existing registered trade mark 'Intel', under s 5(3). The application was for use on constructional toys, whereas the Intel registration was for computer components. See also the *Associated Newspapers* case at **11.3**.

The situation with relative grounds is very close to that under s 10 for infringement (see **11.9**) and to all intents and purposes ss 5 and 10 can be treated as equivalent provisions.

11.7 PUBLICATION OF THE APPLICATION

Applications are published in the *Trade Marks Journal*. A third party has the right to oppose the grant of a registration. This is often where objections on relative grounds will come to light. The objections can lead to opposition proceedings in the Trade Mark Registry.

At the time of writing (August 2003), it looks as if the Trade Mark Registry will cease to examine applications on relative grounds. Instead, they will rely on third parties to object to the published application.

11.8 PROTECTING THE MARK ONCE REGISTERED

Once the client has the registration he needs advice on protecting the mark. If it is not protected it can become subject to misuse, including infringement, and ultimately to revocation. The most important grounds of revocation to be aware of are as follows.

11.8.1 Non-use

If the mark has not been used for 5 years it can be struck off for non-use in that category of goods or services. It is a matter of 'use it or lose it' (s 46(1)(a)).

11.8.2 Has become generic

A trade mark becomes generic if, as a result of action or inaction by the proprietor, it has become a common name in the trade for a product or service for which it is registered. So, under TMA 1994, s 1(1), the trade mark no longer distinguishes the goods or services of one business from those of another business.

Biro, Linoleum, Refrigerator and Launderette have become generic. These were once registered trade marks but have lost their ability to identify the goods of one business and are now simply part of the language.

How do you avoid your trade mark becoming generic? You should:

- use an adjective and not as a noun 'Gordons gin and tonic', not 'Gordons and tonic',
- distinguish it from the surrounding writing, for example by putting it in bold or in capitals or quotation marks, or
- acknowledge it as a trade mark (use R in a circle if registered but do not use R if it is not registered because this is a criminal offence – TMA 1994, s 95).

11.8.3 Has become misleading

A trade mark can be revoked if it has become misleading because of the way the proprietor has used it or allowed it to be used (s 46(1)(d)). One concern here is that if the mark is licensed to others then they may not produce goods of the same quality as the trade mark proprietor, or as each other. For this reason, it is essential to include quality control provisions in any licence to manufacture goods under a trade mark.

11.9 INFRINGEMENT OF A REGISTERED TRADE MARK (s 10)

To constitute infringement, use of the offending mark must be 'in the course of trade'. Thus, a painting by Andy Warhol of a can of soup did not infringe Campbells' trade mark as Andy Warhol was not in the business of making soup.

This issue came up in the case of *Arsenal Football Club plc v Reed* [2003] EWCA Civ 696, [2003] All ER (D) 289 (May). Mr Reed sold football merchandise outside the ground of Arsenal Football Club on match days. He had a notice on his stall to the effect that the goods were not official Arsenal regalia. However, the goods did bear the Arsenal logo. At first instance, there was some doubt as to whether this use was that of a trade mark 'in the course of trade'. Was the Arsenal badge a trade mark, or was it just an indication of loyalty to a football team? The ECJ held that the badge was a trade mark (*Arsenal Football Club plc v Reed (Case C-206/01)* [2002] All ER (EC) 1). Professional football clubs such as Arsenal are multi-million pound businesses. They register trade marks to protect their commercial rights. The ECJ held that this was use of an identical mark on identical goods. The Court of Appeal followed the reasoning in the ECJ judgment. Aldous LJ explained that the unauthorised goods sold by Mr Reed affected the ability of the trade marks to guarantee the origin of the goods.

A different problem occurred in *R v Johnstone* [2003] UKHL 28, (2003) unreported, 22 May. In this case, the defendant dealt in bootleg copies of music CDs. Various of the artists concerned had registered their names as trade marks. Was the existence of such an artist's name on a CD merely an indication of the identity of the performer, or was it use of the name in a trade mark sense? The House of Lords held that to come within the criminal offence under TMA 1994, s 92, the use of the artist's name had to be use of a trade mark as an indication of trade origin of the CDs. Whilst the use of a trade mark such as 'Sony' or 'EMI' would be such a use, this was not the case with the name of an artist. Consequently, the defendant's actions did not fall within s 92.

Prior to this case, there had been discussion as to whether artists' performing rights would be better than a trade mark registration to protect artists from having their work copied without authorisation. It now looks as if performing rights are the best bet for an artist (this book does not cover that area of IP rights).

See also the case of *Elvis Presley* at **11.4.1**.

Under the old 1938 Act, infringement could only be in relation to identical goods or services. This caused undue problems for the proprietors of trade marks. The TMA 1994 now gives four types of infringement.

(1) Use of an identical sign for identical goods or services (as determined by the statement of goods or services with which the mark was registered) (s 10(1)).

(2) Use of a similar sign for similar goods or services, if there is a likelihood of confusion (s 10(2)).

(3) Use of a similar sign for dissimilar goods or services if the use is detrimental to. or takes unfair advantage of, the distinctive character or repute of the mark (s 10(3)). In *Conroy v SmithKline Beecham plc* (Trade Marks Registry 0-085-03), (2003) unreported, the applicant had applied to register 'Nit Nurse' in class 3 for oils and shampoos for the control of head lice. The opponents objected, successfully. They held registrations in class 5 for respiratory decongestants under the trade marks 'Night Nurse'. There were arguments that a consumer could confuse the two products, with unfortunate results. In contrast, see also *Premier Brands UK Ltd v Typhoon Europe Ltd* [2000] FSR 767 where the proprietors of 'Typhoo' for tea, objected unsuccessfully to a registration of 'Typhoon' for kitchen utensils.

(4) Any use of a trade mark which is not in accordance with honest practices in industrial and commercial matters. Honest use is not infringement, so comparative advertising is not infringement (s 10(6) (which it was under the 1938 Act)) provided it does not overstep the boundaries. A case where it did go too far is *Emaco Ltd and Another v Dyson Appliances Ltd* [1999] ETMR 903, where both parties were held to have made unfair comparisons of the goods and thereby infringed each other's trade mark registrations for Electrolux and

Dyson. Beware that mere advertising puffery does not count as being dishonest. In *British Airways plc v Ryanair Ltd* [2001] FSR 210, the advertising slogan 'EXPENSIVE BA_____DS' was held not to be outside s 10(6) by reason of its offensive nature.

These grounds are much the same as the relative grounds for invalidity.

The proprietor of a registered trade mark would have to produce evidence of confusion, or unfair advantage or detriment, as the case may be. This could be in the form of survey evidence, or expert witnesses from the trade in question.

Trade marks are national rights (but see below for the international dimension) so the use has to be within the UK. Thus, on the internet, pre-emptive registration of a domain name that is similar to a registered trade mark would not necessarily be 'use in the course of trade'. However, the Court of Appeal held it was so likely to lead to infringement that an injunction was granted (*British Telecommunications plc and Another v One in a Million Ltd; Virgin Enterprises Ltd v One in a Million Ltd; J Sainsbury plc v One in a Million Ltd; Marks & Spencer plc v One in a Million Ltd; Ladbroke Group plc v One in a Million Ltd* [1999] 1 WLR 903). In that case, someone had registered as internet domain names the names of various well-known businesses, including BT and Virgin. The aim presumably was to sell the domain name to the rightful owner for large sums of money. However, a website can be accessed from anywhere in the world. This does not necessarily mean that for trade mark purposes the trade marks are being used in the course of trade in a particular jurisdiction (see *800 Flowers, Trade Mark Application; 1-800 Flowers Incorporated v Phonenames Ltd* [2001] EWCA Civ 721, [2002] FSR 288 and *Euromarket Designs Inc v Peters and Trade & Barrel Ltd* [2001] FSR 288), where the mere possibility of accessing a site from the UK did not necessarily mean that there was infringement of a UK trade mark. In the *Euromarket* case, Jonathan Parker LJ said:

> 'So I think that the mere fact that websites can be accessed anywhere in the world does not mean, for trade mark purposes, that the law should regard them as being used everywhere in the world. It all depends upon the circumstances, particularly the intention of the website owner and what the reader will understand if he accesses the site. In other fields of law, publication on a website may well amount to a universal publication, but I am not concerned with that.'

Thus, in *Bonnier Media Ltd v Greg Lloyd Smith* [2002] ETMR 86, the Scottish Court of Session held that the defendants could be sued in Scotland in regard to material accessed on the internet, even though the originating site was outside the UK. The defendants intended to set up a website with a domain name similar to Bonnier's trade mark. It was held that the defendants' activities were aimed at damaging Bonnier's business, which was based in Scotland. In other words, the defendants' intentions are a key part in deciding whether or not there is trade mark infringement (or passing off).

Another aspect of the international dimension of trade marks is the interface with competition law. A trade mark proprietor could not use national trade mark rights to prevent parallel importation of his goods from another EU Member State. However, he can use trade mark rights to prevent importation of goods he has produced and has sold for resale on to a non EU market. This was the case in *Zino Davidoff SA v A & G Imports Ltd; Levi Strauss & Co and Another v Tesco Stores Ltd and Another; Levi Strauss & Co and Another v Costco Wholesale UK (Joined Cases C-414/99, C-415/99 and C-416/99)* [2002] All ER (EC) 55. Here, the claimants succeeded in preventing Tesco from continuing to import supplies of the Levi Strauss goods from North America and Mexico. The goods were for resale in the Tesco stores in the UK at lower prices than the goods officially released on to the UK market by Levi Strauss (see also the *Silhouette* case at **11.11**).

11.10 'WELL-KNOWN' FOREIGN TRADE MARKS (s 56)

This section was introduced as part of the UK implementation of the Paris Convention. If a foreign trade mark is well known in the UK, then the foreign proprietor will be able to get an injunction to restrain the use of that mark in the UK where the use would cause confusion. This measure is to protect foreign trade marks that are not registered in the UK. The most likely instance is that of a famous shop or restaurant or hotel which has no branches in the UK.

11.11 DEFENCES TO INFRINGEMENT (ss 11, 12)

The first line of defence to a trade mark infringement action is that the trade mark is not validly registered and should be removed from the register.

Section 11 limits the scope of a registered trade mark and therefore provides some defences. For example, s 11(2)(a) allows the honest use of a person's own name or address. Section 11(2)(b) allows use for the purposes of indicating the nature of the goods or services, so for example allowing an independent business to indicate that they supplied parts for BMW cars (*Bayerische Motorenwerke AG (BMW) and Another v Deenik* (Case 63/97) [1999] All ER (EC) 235).

However, in *Aktiebolaget Volvo v Heritage (Leicester) Ltd* [2000] FSR 253, the defendant motor trader had not made it sufficiently clear that it was no longer an authorised Volvo dealer. Consequently, its use of the Volvo trade mark was held not to fall within s 11, and it had infringed the trade mark registration by using an identical mark on identical goods.

Section 12 deals with the exhaustion of rights. Goods put on to the market elsewhere in the EU by the trade mark proprietor can be legitimately sold under that trade mark in the UK. Note that this does not cover goods put on to the market elsewhere in the world (*Silhouette International Schmied GmbH and Co KG v Hartlauer Handelsgesellschaft mbH* (Case C-355/96) [1999] Ch 77 and the *Zino Davidoff* case – see **11.9**).

11.12 COLLECTIVE AND CERTIFICATION TRADE MARKS

Under TMA 1994, ss 49–50, trade marks can be registered which are not intended to distinguish the products of one business from another. Rather, they are intended to indicate that the goods come from a particular region, for example, or that they are made to a certain standard. An example of a trade mark for regional origin would be Parma for ham in class 29, see for example *Consorzio del Prosciutto di Parma v Asda Stores Ltd and others* [2001] UKHL 7, [2001] 1 CMLR 43 (though that case introduces another aspect which we will not deal with here). Other similar trade marks are 'Stilton' for cheese in class 29, 'Woolmark' for textiles in class 23, and 'Harris Tweed' for Harris tweed in class 24.

This means that, under ss 49–50, certain geographical names can be registered as collective or certification trade marks, as an exception to the general rule described in **11.4.3**.

11.13 INFRINGEMENT

Under s 15, infringement of a registered trade mark is actionable by the proprietor of the trade mark.

As well as the usual remedies of damages and an injunction, s 15 allows the court to order the offending trade mark to be erased from any offending goods, or to order the destruction of such goods (s 19).

Under s 16, infringing goods and materials can be ordered to be delivered up.

Section 21 provides a remedy for groundless threats of trade mark infringement. This is a common provision in intellectual property rights, as impending intellectual property litigation is a very potent threat to a business.

Sections 89–97 deal with the offences in relation to goods which infringe a registered trade mark. Under s 97, counterfeit goods can be seized.

11.14 INTERNATIONAL TRADE MARKS

We have been looking at the law of UK trade marks. If you apply for a UK trade mark this will only give you the right to stop infringements in the UK. If you want protection in other countries (eg US, Japan, Hong Kong), then you have to make a separate application there. So if you want to protect your mark world-wide this will be a very expensive process.

Within Europe two processes allow the applicant to get wider protection on the basis of a single application.

11.14.1 Community trade mark

This is a single trade mark, effective throughout the European Community. You apply to the OHIM at Alicante. The Community trade mark system is still quite new, but it is proving very popular. Between the start of the system in 1996 and the end of 2002, there were 184,000 applications made to OHIM. If you can get a Community trade mark then this will give you protection throughout the Community on the basis of one registration. The difficulty is that the registration can be defeated by similar prior marks anywhere in the European Community. Many well-known UK marks would not be able to achieve a Community registration for this reason. However, the Community trade mark system does not do extensive investigation of existing marks but rather leaves the proprietors of existing marks to object to published applications.

If an applicant is unsuccessful, they are then left with the possibility of applying in each of those countries where there is no problem in order to get a bundle of national registered trade marks.

11.14.2 Madrid Protocol

This is a system that allows you to make one application in one country initially. Then an application can be made for registrations in all the other countries applied for on the application form, and which are member states of the Madrid Protocol. The system is run by the World Intellectual Property Organisation (WIPO).

11.14.3 Other international aspects

International treaties such as the Paris Convention for the Protection of Intellectual Property and TRIPS (part of GATT) ensure that there are certain similarities between the intellectual property laws of many countries in the world (eg TMA 1994, s 56 arises out of an obligation under the Paris Convention).

In addition, TMA 1994 implements the European Trade Marks Directive which had as its aim the partial harmonisation of European trade mark laws. However, despite this, there are many important differences between the trade mark laws of different countries both inside and outside Europe. There are also many technical differences. One should never assume therefore that the position is the same in another country. Foreign legal advice is often necessary and most intellectual property practices have foreign lawyers whom they deal with on a regular basis.

11.15 APPENDIX TO CHAPTER 11: A PUBLICATION FROM THE TRADE MARK REGISTRY

CLASSIFICATION OF GOODS AND SERVICES

When you apply to register a trade mark you must include a list of all goods and services which you want to use the mark for. You must list the goods or services in the class or classes they fall in.

The following headings give general information about the types of goods and services which belong to each class. The list is not complete. It is there to guide you to the classes that you need. If you click on the class number you will see a full list of goods or services in that class, as provided by WIPO, the international organisation which decides trade mark classification.

Goods are in classes 1–34. Services are in classes 35–45.

If you do not know which class(es) your goods or services are in, please use our Classification search.

Goods

CLASS 1

Chemicals used in industry, science and photography, as well as in agriculture, horticulture and forestry; unprocessed artificial resins, unprocessed plastics; manures; fire extinguishing compositions; tempering and soldering preparations; chemical substances for preserving foodstuffs; tanning substances; adhesives used in industry.

Includes chemicals for the making of products belonging to other classes.

Does not include fungicides, herbicides, insecticides or preparations for destroying vermin which are in Class 5.

CLASS 2

Paints, varnishes, lacquers; preservatives against rust and against deterioration of wood; colorants; mordants; raw natural resins; metals in foil and powder form for painters, decorators, printers and artists.

Does not include paint boxes for children which are in Class 16 or insulating paints and varnishes which are in Class 17.

CLASS 3

Bleaching preparations and other substances for laundry use; cleaning, polishing, scouring and abrasive preparations; soaps; perfumery, essential oils, cosmetics, hair lotions; dentifrices.

Includes deodorants for personal use.

Does not include air deodorising preparations which are in Class 5 or scented candles which are in Class 4.

CLASS 4

Industrial oils and greases; lubricants; dust absorbing, wetting and binding compositions; fuels (including motor spirit) and illuminants; candles and wicks for lighting.

Includes combustible fuels and scented candles.

Does not include fuel for nuclear reactors or electricity which are both in Class 1.

CLASS 5

Pharmaceutical and veterinary preparations; sanitary preparations for medical purposes; dietetic substances adapted for medical use, food for babies; plasters, materials for dressings; material for stopping teeth, dental wax; disinfectants; preparations for destroying vermin; fungicides, herbicides.

Includes foods and beverages which are adapted for medical purposes.

Does not include supportive bandages which are in Class 10.

CLASS 6

Common metals and their alloys; metal building materials; transportable buildings of metal; materials of metal for railway tracks; non-electric cables and wires of common metal; ironmongery, small items of metal hardware; pipes and tubes of metal; safes; goods of common metal not included in other classes; ores.

Includes unwrought and partly wrought common metals as well as simple products made of them; metallic windows and doors and also metallic framed conservatories.

CLASS 7

Machines and machine tools; motors and engines (except for land vehicles); machine coupling and transmission components (except for land vehicles); agricultural implements other than hand-operated; incubators for eggs.

Includes parts of engines and motors; some parts for vehicles, (eg exhausts for vehicles); vacuum cleaners.

Does not include engines or motors for land vehicles which are in Class 12 or specialist machines (eg weighing machines are in Class 9).

CLASS 8

Hand tools and implements (hand operated); cutlery; side arms; razors.

Includes electric razors and hair cutters; cutlery made of precious metal.

Does not include surgical cutlery which is in Class 10 or hand held and electrically powered tools, (eg electric drills are in Class 7).

CLASS 9

Scientific, nautical, surveying, photographic, cinematographic, optical, weighing, measuring, signalling, checking (supervision), life-saving and teaching apparatus and instruments; apparatus and instruments for conducting, switching, transforming, accumulating, regulating or controlling electricity; apparatus for recording, transmission or reproduction of sound or images; magnetic data carriers, recording discs; automatic vending machines and mechanisms for coin operated apparatus; cash registers; calculating machines, data processing equipment and computers; fire-extinguishing apparatus.

Includes computer hardware and firmware; computer software (including software downloadable from the Internet); compact discs; digital music (downloadable from the Internet); telecommunications apparatus; computer games equipment adapted for use with TV receivers; mouse mats; mobile phone accessories; contact lenses, spectacles and sunglasses; clothing for protection against accident, irradiation or fire.

Does not include printed computer manuals which are in Class 16, self contained computer games equipment which is in Class 28, various electrical items (eg electric screwdrivers are in Class 7 and electric toothbrushes are in Class 21).

CLASS 10

Surgical, medical, dental and veterinary apparatus and instruments, artificial limbs, eyes and teeth; orthopaedic articles; suture materials.

Includes electro-medical or surgical apparatus; massage apparatus.

Does not include contact lenses, spectacles or sunglasses which are in Class 9 or wheelchairs which are in Class 12.

CLASS 11

Apparatus for lighting, heating, steam generating, cooking, refrigerating, drying, ventilating, water supply and sanitary purposes.

Includes air conditioning apparatus; electric kettles; gas and electric cookers; vehicle lights.

CLASS 12

Vehicles; apparatus for locomotion by land, air or water.

Includes motors and engines for land vehicles and certain other parts and fittings, (eg vehicle body parts and transmissions).

Does not include certain parts or fittings for vehicles, (eg exhausts and starters are in Class 7, lights and air conditioning units are in Class 11) or children's toy bicycles which are in Class 28.

CLASS 13

Firearms; ammunition and projectiles, explosives; fireworks.

Does not include apparatus for use in playing paint ball combat games which are in Class 28.

CLASS 14

Precious metals and their alloys and goods in precious metals or coated therewith, not included in other classes; jewellery, precious stones; horological and chronometric instruments.

Includes clocks and watches; costume jewellery.

Does not include certain precious metal items, (eg cutlery is in Class 8, pens are in Class 16).

CLASS 15

Musical instruments.

Includes stands and cases adapted for musical instruments.

CLASS 16

Paper, cardboard and goods made from these materials, not included in other classes; printed matter; book binding material; photographs; stationery; adhesives for stationery or household purposes; artists' materials; paint brushes; typewriters and office requisites (except furniture); instructional and teaching material (except apparatus); plastic materials for packaging (not included in other classes); printers' type; printing blocks.

Includes disposable nappies of paper for babies; printed publications.

Does not include adhesives for industrial purposes which are in Class 1, electronic publications (downloadable) which are in Class 9, providing electronic publications (not downloadable) which are in Class 41 or wallpaper which is in Class 27.

CLASS 17

Rubber, gutta-percha, gum, asbestos, mica and goods made from these materials and not included in other classes; plastics in extruded form for use in manufacture; packing, stopping and insulating materials; flexible pipes, not of metal.

Includes semi-finished plastics materials for use in further manufacture.

Does not include unprocessed plastics in the form of liquids, chips, granules etc which are in Class 1.

CLASS 18

Leather and imitations of leather, and goods made of these materials and not included in other classes; animal skins, hides; trunks and travelling bags; umbrellas, parasols and walking sticks; whips, harness and saddlery.

Includes handbags, rucksacks, purses; clothing for animals.

Does not include leather clothing which is in Class 9 (for protection against injury) or in Class 25 (ordinary apparel); certain specialist leather articles, (eg cheque book holders are in Class 16).

CLASS 19

Building materials (non-metallic); non-metallic rigid pipes for building; asphalt, pitch and bitumen; non-metallic transportable buildings; monuments, not of metal.

Includes non-metallic framed conservatories, doors and windows.

CLASS 20

Furniture, mirrors, picture frames; goods (not included in other classes) of wood, cork, reed, cane, wicker, horn, bone, ivory, whalebone, shell, amber, mother-of-pearl, meerschaum and substitutes for all these materials, or of plastics.

Includes both metallic and non-metallic furniture including garden furniture; pillows and cushions.

Does not include duvets or covers for pillows, cushions or duvets which are in Class 24, furniture adapted for medical use which is in Class 10 or furniture adapted for laboratory use which is in Class 9.

CLASS 21

Household or kitchen utensils and containers (not of precious metal or coated therewith); combs and sponges; brushes (except paint brushes); brush-making materials; articles for cleaning purposes; steel wool; un-worked or semi-worked glass (except glass used in building); glassware, porcelain and earthenware not included in other classes.

Includes both electric and non-electric toothbrushes.

Does not include electric kitchen appliances, (eg electric food processors are in Class 7, electric kettles are in Class 11) or kitchen and table cutlery which is in Class 8.

CLASS 22

Ropes, string, nets, tents, awnings, tarpaulins, sails, sacks and bags (not included in other classes); padding and stuffing materials (except of rubber or plastics); raw fibrous textile materials.

Includes bags and sacks for transporting bulk materials.

CLASS 23

Yarns and threads, for textile use.

CLASS 24

Textiles and textile goods, not included in other classes; bed and table covers.

Includes textile piece goods; textiles for making articles of clothing.

Does not include table linen of paper which is in Class 16 or electric blankets (not for medical use) which are in Class 11.

CLASS 25

Clothing, footwear, headgear.

Does not include clothing for the prevention of accident and injury which is in Class 9, surgeons' clothing which is in Class 10 or clothing for animals which is in Class 18.

CLASS 26

Lace and embroidery, ribbons and braid; buttons, hooks and eyes, pins and needles; artificial flowers.

Includes dressmakers' articles; badges for wear (other than precious metal badges).

CLASS 27

Carpets, rugs, mats and matting, linoleum and other materials for covering existing floors; wall hangings (non-textile).

Includes wallpaper.

Does not include mouse mats which are in Class 9, mats specifically shaped/adapted for vehicles which are in Class 12 or travellers' rugs which are in Class 24.

CLASS 28

Games and playthings; gymnastic and sporting articles not included in other classes; decorations for Christmas trees.

Includes hand-held computer games equipment which is self contained (not adapted for use with TV receivers).

Does not include computer games equipment adapted for use with TV receivers or software for all types of electronic games which are in Class 9.

CLASS 29

Meat, fish, poultry and game; meat extracts; preserved, dried and cooked fruits and vegetables; jellies, jams, fruit sauces; eggs, milk and milk products; edible oils and fats.

Includes prepared meals and snacks whose main ingredients are proper to this class, (eg soups and potato crisps).

Does not include sandwiches which are in Class 30 or foodstuffs for animals which are in Class 31.

CLASS 30

Coffee, tea, cocoa, sugar, rice, tapioca, sago, artificial coffee; flour and preparations made from cereals, bread, pastry and confectionery, ices; honey, treacle; yeast, baking-powder; salt, mustard; vinegar, sauces (condiments); spices; ice.

Includes prepared meals and snacks whose main ingredients are proper to this class, (eg pizzas, pies and pasta dishes).

Does not include foodstuffs for animals which are in Class 31.

CLASS 31

Agricultural, horticultural and forestry products and grains not included in other classes; live animals; fresh fruits and vegetables, seeds, natural plants and flowers; foodstuffs for animals; malt.

Includes all food and beverages for animals.

CLASS 32

Beers; mineral and aerated waters and other non alcoholic drinks; fruit drinks and fruit juices; syrups and other preparations for making beverages.

Includes shandy, de-alcoholised drinks, non-alcoholic beers and wines.

Does not include tea, coffee or chocolate-based beverages which are in Class 30.

CLASS 33

Alcoholic beverages (except beers).

Includes wines, spirits and liqueurs; alcopops.

Does not include beers which are in Class 32.

CLASS 34

Tobacco; smokers' articles; matches.

Includes lighters for smokers.

Services

CLASS 35

Advertising; business management; business administration; office functions.

Includes the organisation, operation and supervision of loyalty and incentive schemes; advertising services provided via the Internet; production of television and radio advertisements; accountancy; auctioneering; trade fairs; opinion polling; data processing; provision of business information; certain specific services provided by retailers.

Does not include computer programming which is in Class 42 or raising finance for business which is in Class 36.

CLASS 36

Insurance; financial affairs; monetary affairs; real estate affairs.

Includes building society services; banking (including home banking); stockbroking; financial services provided via the Internet; issuing of tokens of value in relation to bonus and loyalty schemes; provision of financial information.

Does not include accountancy which is in Class 35, lottery services which are in Class 41 or surveying and conveyancing services which are in Class 42.

CLASS 37

Building construction; repair; installation services.

Includes installation, maintenance and repair of computer hardware; painting and decorating.

Does not include installation, maintenance and repair of computer software which is in Class 42.

CLASS 38

Telecommunications.

Includes all telecommunications services, (eg e-mail services and those provided for the Internet); providing user access to the Internet (service providers); operating of search engines.

Does not include creating, maintaining or hosting web sites which are in Class 42.

CLASS 39

Transport; packaging and storage of goods; travel arrangement.

Includes distribution of electricity; travel information.

Does not include travel insurance which is in Class 36 or booking holiday accommodation which is in Class 43.

CLASS 40

Treatment of materials.

Includes the development, duplicating and printing of photographs; generation of electricity.

CLASS 41

Education; providing of training; entertainment; sporting and cultural activities.

Includes electronic games services provided by means of the Internet; the provision of on-line electronic publications and digital music (not downloadable) from the Internet.

Does not include downloadable on-line electronic publications or digital music which are in Class 9 or educational materials in printed form which are in Class 16.

CLASS 42

Scientific and technological services and research and design relating thereto; industrial analysis and research services; design and development of computer hardware and software; legal services.

Includes installation, maintenance and repair of computer software; computer consultancy services; the following Internet related services are also proper to this class: design, drawing and commissioned writing for the compilation of web sites; creating, maintaining and hosting the web sites of others; compilation, creation and maintenance of a register of domain names; leasing of access time to a computer database (the last item reflects the leasing of access time to a computer database on a dedicated line and not access provided by Internet Service Providers to databases in general which is in Class 38).

Does not include providing access to the Internet or portal services which are in Class 38.

CLASS 43

Services for providing food and drink; temporary accommodation.

Includes restaurant, bar and catering services; provision of holiday accommodation; booking/reservation services for restaurants and holiday accommodation.

Does not include provision of permanent accommodation which is in Class 36 or the arranging of travel by tourist agencies which is in Class 39.

CLASS 44

Medical services; veterinary services; hygienic and beauty care for human beings or animals; agriculture, horticulture and forestry services.

Includes dentistry services; medical analysis for the diagnosis and treatment of persons (such as x-ray examinations and taking of blood samples); pharmacy advice; garden design services.

Does not include scientific research for medical purposes (such as research into cures for terminal diseases which is in Class 42), ambulance transportation which is in Class 39, health clubs for physical exercise which are in Class 41 or retirement homes which are in Class 43.

CLASS 45

Personal and social services rendered by others to meet the needs of individuals; security services for the protection of property and individuals.

Includes dating services; funeral services and undertaking services; fire-fighting services; detective agency services.

Does not include beauty care services for human beings or animals which are in Class 44 or educational services which are in Class 41.

Chapter 12

PASSING OFF

12.1 INTRODUCTION

Passing off is about stopping the infringer from selling his goods or services off the back of the claimant's reputation. Passing off can happen in a number of different ways. Typically, passing-off cases concern the get-up of goods (ie their packaging and presentation as seen by the consumer).

The classic quote is from Lord Halsbury in *Reddaway and Frank Reddaway & Co Ltd v Banham and George Banham & Co Ltd* [1896] AC 199:

> 'nobody has any right to represent his goods as the goods of somebody else.'

Other cases have made clear that the action also applies to services.

Passing off has to be in relation to a commercial activity. In *Kean v McGivan* [1982] FSR 119, an action concerning the name of a political party (the Social Democratic Party) did not succeed.

In the classic case of passing off, the defendant adopts some mark or sign or other distinguishing feature (eg the appearance of the packaging of the goods) which customers associate with the claimant. He uses this, or something confusingly similar to it, for his own goods/services with the result that customers are confused into thinking they are buying the claimant's product. In one of the most famous passing-off cases, *Reckitt & Colman Products Ltd v Borden Inc and Others* [1990] 1 WLR 491, the claimants' distinguishing feature for their goods was that the juice was sold in a plastic lemon. The defendant also started selling lemon juice in a plastic lemon. Reckitt & Colman succeeded in stopping the defendant using the plastic lemon. Today, the claimant could use trade mark infringement as, under TMA 1994, they have been able to register the shape of their lemon as a registered trade mark.

• What is protected?	• goodwill, eg logo or name
• What benefit is there?	• gives protection against 'rip-offs'
• How do you is it obtained?	• arises automatically (no registration)
• How long does it last?	• indefinitely

12.2 THE THREE ELEMENTS OF PASSING OFF

In *Consorzio del Prosciutto di Parma v Marks & Spencer plc* [1991] RPC 351, the House of Lords judgment of Oliver LJ in *Reckitt & Colman* is quoted as a good exposition of the elements of passing off:

> 'More specifically, it may be expressed in terms of the elements which the plaintiff in such an action has to prove in order to succeed. These are three in number. First, he must establish a goodwill or reputation attached to the goods or services which he supplies in the mind of the purchasing public by association with the identifying

get-up (whether it consists simply of a brand name or a trade description, or the individual features of labelling or packaging) under which his particular goods or services are offered to the public, such that the get-up is recognised by the public as distinctive specifically of the plaintiff's goods or services. Secondly, he must demonstrate a misrepresentation by the defendant to the public (whether or not intentional) leading or likely to lead the public to believe that goods or services offered by him are the goods or services of the plaintiff ... Thirdly, he must demonstrate that he suffers or, in a quia timet action, that he is likely to suffer damage by reason of the erroneous belief engendered by the defendant's misrepresentation that the source of the defendant's goods or services is the same as the source of those offered by the plaintiff.'

12.2.1 First element: goodwill

Goodwill means business reputation. The reputation must be among customers or prospective customers (ie buyers or prospective buyers of lemon juice, for example).

The reputation also needs to be in relation to some distinguishing feature, here the lemon. What the claimant needs to show is not only that customers associate the plastic lemon with the claimant, but also that they understand the plastic lemon as an indication or sign that the lemon juice comes from the claimant. The claimant generally demonstrates his reputation to the court by showing sales figures and expenditure on advertising (using the distinguishing feature in question), by witness evidence and survey evidence.

The distinguishing feature could be:

- logos, shape or style of packaging, get up, colour (eg Heinz beans tin (colour, shape of label, name); the classic Coca-Cola bottle (shape, name); Body Shop bottle (the rounded shape and lettering); Penguin (six-pack wrapper)); or
- a name (eg 'Neutrogena' where the defendant was restrained from using the similar name 'Neutralia' (*Neutrogena Corporation and Another v Golden Ltd and Another* [1996] RPC 473) or 'Harrods' (*Harrods Ltd v Harrodian School Ltd* [1996] RPC 697) although Harrods were unsuccessful in stopping the school using the same name because they could not show this would result in damage).

The category of things that the claimant can have reputation in is not closed and is not easily defined. Partly because passing off is a common law tort, its limits are quite vague.

12.2.2 Second element: misrepresentation

There must be a misrepresentation made by the defendant in the course of trade. In the Jif lemon case the misrepresentation was the use of the plastic lemon. In most passing-off cases the misrepresentation is deliberate. In other words, there is a deliberate attempt by the defendant to 'ride on the back' of the plaintiff's success. For example, consider the 'Penguin and Puffin' case, *United Biscuits (UK) Ltd v Asda Stores Ltd* [1997] RPC 513, which concerned the similarity in packaging in the two brands of chocolate biscuit. Asda produced the Puffin biscuit. They had designed packaging that was very similar to that of the Penguin biscuit. They even ran an advertising campaign with the slogan 'pick up a Puffin'. This rather suggested deliberate reference to Penguin and did not help Asda's case in court.

However, a misrepresentation could be innocent. The defendant need not even be aware of the claimants' products.

The misrepresentation must lead to confusion of customers or potential customers and generally it must be confusion as to trade source. The customers must be confused into thinking that the defendants' products come from the claimants or that they are associated with the claimant. For example, that they are made/supplied by a company within the same group or by a licensee.

The confusion must be at the point of sale, or before it. In *Bostik Ltd v Sellotape GB Ltd* [1994] RPC 556 the makers of Blu-tack failed to obtain an injunction in passing off against a rival manufacturer of a similar looking product. The similarity in the product could only be realised when the packaging was removed. There was no possibility of confusion by the customer at the point of sale.

It is not enough that there is confusion between the claimant's and the defendant's product. Customers must believe the defendant's products are associated with the claimant. This was illustrated in the case of *HFC Bank plc v Midland Bank plc* [2000] FSR 176. When Midland was taken over by HSBC and changed its name to HSBC, HFC Bank objected. They argued that customers would confuse HSBC with HFC. However, among other things, HFC were not able to show they had achieved sufficient brand name recognition in relation to the letters HFC. Even if customers did confuse the two acronyms, they would not necessarily think HSBC was a reference to HFC.

There needs to be overlap between the alleged infringer and the proprietor in regard to three aspects.

- type of goods or services: would someone confuse a bicycle maker with a law firm?
- geographical area: a restaurant in Aberdeen is unlikely to pinch trade from one in Plymouth; and
- time: the overlap must be more or less contemporaneous.

Evidence of confusion

A passing-off case will not succeed without evidence of confusion. Confusion is a question of fact and it is always very difficult to predict the outcome of a passing off action. It is difficult to generalise about the type of thing that will lead to confusion.

The usual evidence might be survey evidence or witness evidence, preferably from people employed in the relevant trade. In effect, they become expert witnesses on the question of likely confusion.

The courts are sceptical about survey evidence, but nevertheless it is frequently presented. Often what will swing it will be placing the two products before the judge. Does he think customers are likely to be confused? If he agrees, then he is more likely to accept the survey evidence. If he does not, then he is likely to reject it.

Although the defendant may use the claimant's distinctive feature, there may not be confusion if the claimant is clearly distinguishing his product in some way.

If people merely recognise the look-alike as being a cheaper copy of the branded product then this is not going to be enough for passing off. There is then no confusion as to the trade source of the goods or services.

12.2.3 Third element: damage

The claimant must show damage or the likelihood of damage. Often we are concerned with the likelihood of damage because the plaintiff will generally be seeking an interim injunction. In the ordinary case, where the claimant and defendant are trading in the same line of business, once goodwill and misrepresentation have been established the court is usually willing to infer damage.

The main types of damage are:

- loss of profits – people buy the infringing product instead of the claimant's product; and
- loss of reputation – usually because the infringing product is of inferior quality, and customers think the infringing product is made by the claimant.

If the infringer is in a different field of activity, the claimant may not succeed because he cannot show damage. For example, in *Stringfellow and Another v McCain Foods GB Ltd and Another* [1984] RPC 501 the nightclub was not able to stop oven chips being sold under the name 'Stringfellows'. In *Wombles Ltd v Wombles Skips Ltd* [1977] RPC 99 the copyright owners of the Wombles books and television series could not stop rubbish skips being hired out under the name 'Wombles'.

However, in other cases, claimants have been able to establish damage as a result of not being able to expand into a new market. The manufacturer of 'Marigold' rubber gloves was able to stop a toilet tissue being called 'Marigold' (*LRC International Ltd and Another v Lilla Edets Sales Co Ltd* [1973] RPC 560). Also, if the infringer's product is in a field that brings disrepute on the claimant then this can be a ground of damage. In the case of *Annabel's (Berkeley Square) Ltd v Schock (t/a Annabel's Escort Agency)* [1972] RPC 838, the use in question could have created an assumption that a well-known nightclub had started an escort agency.

In *Irvine and Others v Talksport Ltd* [2003] EWCA Civ 423, [2003] 2 All ER 881, the matter concerned a well-known racing driver. A photograph of him was altered to add a radio with the words 'Talk Radio' on it, and was then used by the defendants on a promotional leaflet for their activities. The Court of Appeal held that this was passing off, and that the measure of damages for a false product endorsement was the typical fee which the claimant would usually have sought.

12.3 REMEDIES FOR PASSING OFF

Remedies for passing off can include:

- an injunction;
- damages;
- an account of profits; and
- an order for delivery up or destruction of the offending items.

12.4 INTERNATIONAL ASPECTS

Other common law countries such as Australia and New Zealand also have laws of passing off but their case-law has developed differently on some points. Civil law countries have the law of unfair competition, which sometimes overlaps with passing off, but it is definitely not the same.

Chapter 13

COPYRIGHT

13.1 WHAT IS COPYRIGHT?

Copyright is a right to prevent copying, not to give someone a monopoly right over a brand name (trade marks) or over an invention (patents). Copyright protects 'arty' things. It is not a registered right, which can make it difficult to deal with in practice. Copyright is said to arise before the ink is dry on the paper.

• What is protected?	• 'artistic output'
• What benefit is there?	• prevents copying
• How is it obtained?	• arises automatically (no registration)
• How long does it last?	• 70 years from death (usually)

The first statutory copyright in England was the Statute of Anne 1709. This was passed at the request of book publishers because they were unable to protect their rights effectively against copyists under the common law. The first items protected were therefore books. Over the years, other artistic items have been added, including music and paintings. In the twentieth century, new technology allowed the development of new aspects of artistic works such as film versions of books and plays.

The main legislation on copyright is the Copyright, Designs and Patents Act 1988 (CDPA 1988). In the period before the CDPA 1988, there were attempts to use copyright for industrial items (eg *British Leyland Motor Corp Ltd v Armstrong Patents Co Ltd* [1986] 1 AC 577 on spare parts for cars). The philosophy behind the relevant parts of the CDPA 1988 was to push industrial items in the direction of registered and unregistered design right (which the CDPA respectively strengthened and created) and to restrict copyright in the case of artistic three-dimensional items. A key aspect was that copyright would otherwise have given a period of protection of at least 70 years for an industrial item, whereas registered design right is 25 years. The copyright period for artistic items which are mass-produced is now restricted to 25 years to be in parallel with the registered design right period.

The 'classic' copyrights are literary, dramatic, musical, and artistic (LDMA) works.

The 'entrepreneurial' copyrights are films, sound recordings, published editions, broadcasts and cablecasts.

It is important to be able to distinguish between the different categories of copyright, for the following reasons.

• If you cannot find a category for the item, copyright will not subsist in it. A good example of this is the position of computer programs which are now in s 1 of CDPA 1988. Until the Berne Convention clarified the position by defining software as a literary work, there was some uncertainty about whether copyright subsisted in it at all, although there had been some cases suggesting it did.

- The rules relating to the subsistence, duration and ownership of the copyright can vary slightly for the different types of work.
- If there is more than one type of work in relation to an item, the different copyright works will often be owned by different people.

Let us look at the classic copyrights.

13.2 LITERARY, DRAMATIC, MUSICAL AND ARTISTIC ('LDMA') WORKS

These are the 'classic' copyrights, that is, the authors' and artists' rights that most people associate with copyright. These rights have many things in common, so we are going to deal with them together.

CDPA 1988 provides as follows:

'1 **Copyright and copyright works**

(1) Copyright is a property right which subsists in accordance with this Part in the following descriptions of work—

(a)   original literary, dramatic, musical or artistic works,

(b)   sound recordings, films, broadcasts or cable programmes, and

(c)   the typographical arrangement of published editions.

…

3 **Literary, dramatic and musical works**

(1) In this Part—

"literary work" means any work, other than a dramatic or musical work, which is written, spoken or sung, and accordingly includes—

(a)   a table or compilation other than a database,

(b)   a computer program,

(c)   preparatory design material for a computer program, and

(d)   a database;

"dramatic work" includes a work of dance or mime; and

"musical work" means a work consisting of music, exclusive of any words or action intended to be sung, spoken or performed with the music.

4 **Artistic works**

(1) In this Part "artistic work" means—

(a)   a graphic work, photograph, sculpture or collage, irrespective of artistic quality,

(b)   a work of architecture being a building or a model for a building, or

(c)   a work of artistic craftsmanship.

(2) In this Part

"building" includes any fixed structure, and a part of a building or fixed structure;

"graphic work" includes—

(a)   any painting, drawing, diagram, map, chart or plan, and

(b)   any engraving, etching, lithograph, woodcut or similar work;

"photograph" means a recording of light or other radiation on any medium on which an image is produced or from which an image may by any means be produced, and which is not part of a film;

"sculpture" includes a cast or model made for purposes of sculpture.'

The definition of 'literary work' in s 3(1) excludes dramatic or musical works. Thus, a play or script for a film will have dramatic copyright, not literary. Also, words of a song will have literary copyright but the music will have musical copyright. This means that usually the copyright in the words and music will be separately owned and have separate duration. For example, with most of the songs of Sir Elton John, he writes the music and Bernie Taupin writes the words. So, the musical copyright in the music will expire 70 years after the death of Sir Elton John, and the literary copyright will expire 70 years after the death of Bernie Taupin.

A 'dramatic' work could be a play but it also could be dance or mime. So, a ballet is a dramatic work, but the music is a musical work. Again, the usual situation would be that the dramatic and musical copyrights are separately owned.

13.2.1 Originality

For LDMA works, copyright will not subsist unless the work is 'original' (see s 1(1)(a)). 'Originality' here means that the work must be the author's own work, not copied from anything else.

It is originality of expression and form, not of idea or content that is required. For example, someone could not legally copy a book by John Grisham without his consent but he has no monopoly over thrillers based on the exciting lives of lawyers, so you could write your own.

13.2.2 Minimum effort

A work may be an original work, but it may be completely trivial. Does it still enjoy copyright protection? There will be no copyright unless a certain minimum amount of effort has gone into the work. The amount of effort required is generally low. But the exact amount depends on the category of work.

(a) Literary works

Generally, the level of effort required is very low. Any writing will attract copyright. For example, there is literary copyright in a junior school pupil's essay, or in an ordinary business letter. However, the writing has to be substantial enough to constitute a 'work'.

Thus, an advertising jingle, or a title will not usually be protected by copyright. The courts have been reluctant to grant copyright in single words. For example, EXXON was refused copyright protection (though it would of course get trade mark protection if validly registered) (*Exxon Corpn and Others v Exxon Insurance Consultants International Ltd* [1981] 3 All ER 241).

'Compilations', that is, collections of information, are one aspect of literary copyright. Generally the English courts have been willing in the past to grant copyright in almost any compilation, for example, television listings, a directory of solicitors' names and addresses and football pool coupons. It is likely, for example, that an ordinary, alphabetical telephone directory would have been protected by copyright under English law. However, following the adoption of the Copyrights and Rights in Database Regulations 1997, SI 1997/3032, there is now a question mark over whether courts will in the future allow copyright in such mundane compilations where there is nothing special about the selection or arrangement of the contents (see **14.2**). Commentators seem to think it is likely that the alphabetical telephone directory would now no longer be protected by copyright. This is because it would fall within the definition of a 'database' in the regulations (databases do not have to be electronic) for which the Regulations impose a slightly higher standard of originality for copyright to apply. As yet, it is unclear what the impact of this will be. It may well be, for example, that the *Yellow Pages* would still be protected by copyright. However, the key point is that the database right will apply and protect such collections of mundane information and copyright will probably be largely irrelevant (see **13.5**, **14.1**).

(b) Artistic

Artistic works divide into:

* those that under s 4, which are protected 'irrespective of artistic quality', that is, graphic works, photographs, sculptures and collages (s 4(1)(a)); and
* those for which a degree of artistic quality is required, that is, architecture and works of artistic craftsmanship (s 4(1)(b) and (c)).

For the first category, the standard of effort required is low. For example, copyright has been found to subsist in a very simple picture of a hand pointing, as used at a polling station to guide people round the corner. A straight line or circle would not normally be protected. In any event, it would not be substantial enough to constitute a 'work' and would be unlikely to be original.

Some artistic merit is required for architecture, as the words 'irrespective of artistic quality' do not appear in s 4(1)(b). Cornish, in *Intellectual Property* 4th edn (Sweet & Maxwell, 1999), suggests that the artistic merit must be 'something more than the common stock'. Perhaps a mass-produced estate of similar mundane houses might not qualify, but a small development of individual 'executive' homes might.

(c) Works of artistic craftsmanship

This is a topic much beloved by academic writers but of negligible practical relevance. A work of artistic craftsmanship is any three-dimensional item which is not a sculpture, but is 'artistic'. For works of artistic craftsmanship, it seems that a significant degree of artistic merit is required before copyright protection will be given. The policy reason behind this is that three-dimensional items that are not sculptures tend to be industrial designs and should normally be protected by the law on designs rather than by copyright.

Unfortunately, the cases on works of artistic craftsmanship do not tell us how much artistic merit is needed to qualify as a work of artistic craftsmanship. In *Hensher (George) Ltd v Restawile Upholstery (Lancs)* [1976] AC 64 it was held that a mass-produced suite of furniture did not have enough artistic merit. In *Merlet and Another v Mothercare plc* [1986] RPC 115, it was held that a rain cape made by Mrs Merlet to protect her baby from the weather in Scotland did not have enough artistic merit.

A key factor in deciding whether an item is a work of artistic craftmanship is – did the author consciously intend to create a work of art? In *Guild v Eskandar Ltd* [2001] FSR 38, the claimant alleged breach of copyright in garments which she had designed for mass-production. These were held not to be works of artistic craftsmanship, but were protected by unregistered design right as they were original and not commonplace (see **15.3.1**).

In practice, one should never rely on there being copyright in three-dimensional objects other than sculptures, but instead advise the client to register a design.

13.2.3 Recorded

For literary, dramatic and musical works, copyright will only subsist if the work is recorded. This can be in writing or otherwise. Recording can be in any medium, so recording on tape or typing into a word processor is fine.

There is no express requirement as such in CDPA 1988 that an artistic work must be recorded, but of course it is difficult to conceive of an artistic work that is not recorded. How else could you create a drawing or a sculpture, for example, and not record it?

13.2.4 Duration of copyright

(a) Literary, dramatic and musical works (CDPA 1988, s 12)

The normal duration is life of the author plus 70 years. The 70 years runs from the end of the year of the author's death. If copyright vests in the employer because the author was an employee, then the duration of the employer's copyright is the employee's life plus 70 years. The same situation applies if the rights have been assigned. For example, in the copyright in the songs of Buddy Holly (now owned by Sir Paul McCartney) the period is 70 years from the death of Buddy Holly (ie it expires in 1959 + 70 = 2029).

The basic term for copyright used to be life plus 50 years. The Directive on Copyright Duration 93/98/EC increased it to 70 years. This not only extended the life of existing copyright works but also even revived lapsed copyright if the work was still in copyright anywhere within the EU on 1 July 1995. This would have been so at that date in Germany, where the copyright term then was life plus 70 years.

If the work is of unknown authorship, the period of 70 years runs from the year of creation, or the year of first publication whichever is the later.

For a computer-generated work, the period is 50 years from creation.

(b) Exploited copyright works (CDPA 1988, s 52)

If a copyright work is exploited by making articles industrially then the term of copyright it enjoys is for most purposes cut down to 25 years. The 25 years is measured from the end of the calendar year in which the articles are first marketed. Examples would be a design that is put on wallpaper, or a work of artistic craftsmanship that is exploited by making it industrially (eg a chair by Charles Rennie Mackintosh). 'Industrial' exploitation means making more than 50 articles or making things in lengths by an industrial process (eg wallpaper).

The term is not cut down for all purposes, but only in relation to the articles. So after the 25 years are up, it will not be copyright infringement to use the wallpaper design on wallpaper or on a bread bin, but it would still be copyright infringement to copy a drawing of it.

There are exceptions to this rule limiting copyright to 25 years and these are defined by statutory instrument. Exceptions include most sculpture, wall plaques and medals and printed matter which is primarily of a literary or artistic character (a long list is given in the Copyright (Industrial Process and Excluded Articles) (No 2) Order 1989, SI 1989/1070). So, for example, putting a painting on a postcard will not result in the 25-year term applying.

The policy reason for cutting down the term for industrially exploited copyright is that governments do not consider it appropriate that industrial designs should have long copyright protection. The period of 25 years is the same as the term of protection given to registered designs.

13.2.5 Ownership of copyright in LDMA works

As copyright arises 'before the ink is dry on the page', the initial copyright is owned by the author or co-authors, CDPA 1988, s 11(1). The main exception is if the author is an employee, in which case the copyright is owned by the employer (s 11(2)). The provisos are that the work was done in the course of his employment, and that there was no contrary agreement. In *Noah v Shuba and Another* [1991] FSR 14, it was held that an employed government epidemiologist had not written a document entitled 'A Guide to Hygienic Skin Piercing' in the course of his employment. He therefore owned the copyright, not his employer.

Beware that if the work has been commissioned, then the copyright rests with the author, not the person commissioning the work. A properly drafted agreement would include a clause providing for an assignment, or licence, of the copyright to the commissioner. In the absence of such a clause, a licence would usually be implied (*Blair v Alan S Tomkins and Frank Osborne (t/a Osborne & Tomkins (A Firm)) and Another* [1971] 1 All ER 468), as otherwise the commissioner would be prevented from using the work they had paid for.

13.2.6 Moral rights

These are a continental concept brought into English law by the CDPA 1988. It is the idea that the creative author or artist should retain certain rights in relation to his creation even after he has sold the copyright to somebody else. In fact, moral rights have slightly wider implications.

The moral rights are as follows.

*   **The right to be identified** ('right of paternity') (s 77). This only applies if the right has been asserted by the author. This is usually done in the copyright assignment or licence.
*   **The right to object to derogatory treatment** (s 80), for example, a novelist might object if his novel were abridged in a way that compromised its artistic integrity. In *Morrison Leahy Music Ltd v Lightbond Ltd* [1993] EMLR 144, the claimants obtained an injunction to restrain the release of a recording consisting of the claimant's music interspersed with other music, as they felt this altered the character of their music. In the unusual German case of *Re Lenin's Monument* [1992] ECC 202, the son of the sculptor of a statue of Lenin failed in his attempt to assert the moral right akin to s 80. The City of Berlin was not planning to destroy the statue, which could have been derogatory treatment, but merely 'to

preserve it by burying it', following the demise of the former communist State of East Germany.

- **The right against false attribution of a work** (s 84). A novel use of this right was in *Clark v Associated Newspapers* [1998] RPC 261. This concerned the *London Evening Standard* which was then running a spoof political column called 'Alan Clark's Secret Election Diary'. Mr Clark succeeded on the basis that some people might believe that the views expressed in the column were his.
- **The right to privacy in private photographs and films** (s 85).

If the author still owns the copyright then he should not normally need to rely on these moral rights as he can control all copying of the work, for example he can insist on being credited as a condition of allowing the work to be used. The importance of moral rights is in a situation where the author has assigned the copyright to somebody else.

Moral rights are inalienable rights, in that they cannot be assigned (s 94). However, they can be waived. If you are acting for the assignee of copyright you should always consider whether it is appropriate to insist on a waiver. You probably would not expect somebody who has produced a real work of art to waive their moral rights. However, in many commercial situations it will be appropriate (eg for advertising copy, or designs for use on fabrics or products).

Moral rights only apply to literary, dramatic, musical and artistic works and also to films (where the director enjoys moral rights). The most important exceptions to be aware of are computer programs and employees. In most situations employees do not enjoy moral rights.

13.3 ENTREPRENEURIAL COPYRIGHTS

The descriptions 'classic' and 'entrepreneurial' copyright are not terms of art. However, the distinction is often made between:

- the classic LDMA copyrights, that is, the traditional authors' rights which protect creativity; and
- the entrepreneurial copyrights which, broadly, protect people who invest in creativity, that is, production companies, broadcasters, publishers, etc.

The entrepreneurial copyrights serve the same purpose as the classic rights. That is, they give a right to stop copying of the relevant 'work'.

13.3.1 Differences between classic and entrepreneurial copyrights

The rules are slightly different for the entrepreneurial copyrights, in particular:

- There is no general requirement of originality and minimum effort (see **13.2**). Instead there are various detailed rules for each right which have the broad aim of ensuring that there is no copyright in a mere copy. For example, if I copy somebody else's tape with or without their permission, I have no copyright in the copy I make. These rules are beyond the scope of this book. (Note that in the case of *Norowzian v Arks Ltd and Others (No 2)* [2000] FSR 363, the plaintiff failed in his assertion that copyright existed in an editing process for films. The case concerned an advert for Guinness produced by the defendant by a technique devised by the claimant, termed 'jump cutting'.)

- Of the entrepreneurial copyrights, only films have moral rights. These vest in the director. The thinking behind this is, of course, that it is the director who has given the artistic input. He is the person who might want to defend his artistic integrity. (The director is the one who sits in the canvas chair behind the camera operator and tells the actors what to do.)
- The rules about ownership of the entrepreneurial rights vary (see **13.3.3**).
- The duration of the entrepreneurial rights varies (see **13.3.4**).

13.3.2 Definitions of some entrepreneurial rights

The following definitions are extracts from the CDPA 1988:

'5A Sound recordings

(1) In this Part "sound recording" means—

(a)   a recording of sounds, from which the sounds may be reproduced, or

(b)   a recording of the whole or any part of a literary, dramatic or musical work, from which sounds reproducing the work or part may be produced,

regardless of the medium on which the recording is made or the method by which the sounds are reproduced or produced.

(2) Copyright does not subsist in a sound recording which is, or to the extent that it is, a copy taken from a previous sound recording.

5B Films

(1) In this Part "film" means a recording on any medium from which a moving image may by any means be produced.

(2) The sound track accompanying a film shall be treated as part of the film for the purposes of this Part.

6 Broadcasts

(1) In this Part a "broadcast" means a transmission by wireless telegraphy of visual images, sounds or other information which

(a)   is capable of being lawfully received by members of the public, or

(b)   is transmitted for presentation to members of the public; and references to broadcasting shall be construed accordingly.

7 Cable programmes

(1) In this Part—

"cable programme" means any item included in a cable programme service; and

"cable programme service" means a service which consists wholly or mainly in sending visual images, sounds or other information by means of a tele-communications system, otherwise than by wireless telegraphy, for reception—

(a)   at two or more places (whether for simultaneous reception or at different times in response to requests by different users), or

(c)   for presentation to members of the public,

and which is not, or so far as it is not, excepted by or under the following provisions of this section.

8 **Published editions**

(1) In this Part "published edition", in the context of copyright in the typographical arrangement of a published edition, means a published edition of the whole or any part of one or more literary, dramatic or musical works.'

You should be aware of the following points from the above definitions of the entrepreneurial copyrights.

- An attempt has been made to make the definitions of 'film', 'sound recording', etc. technology neutral so that they will cover future technological developments. So, for example, film includes any recordings on any medium from which a moving image can be produced. It will include, for example, videos, DVD and many 'multi-media' recordings like computer games and websites where you have moving images. These can be 'films' even though they may be interactive.
- A 'broadcast' is over the airwaves ('wireless telegraphy') so it includes terrestrial broadcasting like the BBC and also satellite broadcasting like Sky.
- A 'cablecast' is through a cable (eg cable television services like NTL).
- The soundtrack of a film is protected by film copyright unless it is issued as a stand-alone entity, when it would be protected as a sound recording.

13.3.3 Ownership of the entrepreneurial copyrights (s 9)

The ownership goes to the 'creator' of the copyright work. So, for example the owner of the copyright in a broadcast would be:

(a)   the person providing the programme; and
(b)   the person transmitting who has responsibility for its content.

This could mean that the independent television company and the broadcasting authority could jointly own the copyright.

Entrepreneurial Right	Ownership
• Sound recording	• Producer
• Film	• Producer and principal director
• Broadcast	• Person making the broadcast
• Cable programme	• Person providing the cable service
• Typographical arrangement	• Publisher

13.3.4 Duration of the entrepreneurial copyrights

The duration of the entrepreneurial copyrights is a bit more complex than the standard period of life of the creator plus 70 years that applies to the classic copyrights.

Entrepreneurial Right	Duration
• Sound recording	• 50 years from making or being released, if later
• Film	• 70 years from end of life of last to die of principal director, author of screenplay, author of dialogue, or composer of specially written music
• Broadcast	• 50 years from first broadcast
• Cable programme	• 50 years from first broadcast
• Typographical arrangement	• 25 years from publication

13.4 INFRINGEMENT OF COPYRIGHT

There are two types of infringement, primary infringement and secondary infringement. The primary infringer is liable regardless of his state of mind whereas the secondary infringer is only liable if he knew or had reason to believe that he was dealing with an infringing copy.

Copying need not be of the whole work. The copyright is infringed if a 'substantial part' is taken. The question of what is a substantial part is considered qualitatively. So, even if you only take one line of a poem, the copyright will be infringed if it is a significant line. Similarly, a parody of a work will infringe the copyright if it amounts to a substantial copy of it.

Copying does not have to be exact copying. You can infringe:

- a drawing by doing another drawing that looks similar;
- a novel by writing another with a very similar plot; or
- a computer program not only by copying the code but also by copying the way it is structured and organised.

Copyright in a literary or dramatic work will be infringed by translating it into another language, by making it into a play (or vice versa), or by making it into a cartoon. Copyright in a musical work will be infringed by making a different arrangement.

You do not normally infringe copyright simply by using the work. For example, you do not infringe the copyright in a book by reading it. You do not infringe a recording by playing it. This is because using it does not normally involve making copies of it. However, if you read or play it in public you do infringe. The CDPA 1988 specifically provides that performing or showing a work in public will infringe the copyright and this is primary infringement (s 19). Similarly, including a work in a broadcast or cablecast will normally be primary infringement (s 20). So the permission (ie the licence) of the copyright owner is necessary in these circumstances.

13.4.1 Special position of computer programs (software) (s 17(6))

Although the normal position is that you do not infringe by using a work, a computer program is different in this respect. When a program is run in a computer, the computer has to make at least a transient copy of it in order to run it. This transient copying will infringe the copyright if you do not have the copyright owner's permission (s 17(6)). It is not possible, therefore, to use a program without a licence. Often this licence is express. For example, you get a licence with any program you buy off the shelf. Sometimes, this licence may be implied by the circumstances. If someone is a lawful licensee then they are also entitled to make one back-up copy of the software (s 50A).

13.4.2 Primary infringement (ss 16–21)

The most usual act of primary infringement is copying. Copyright is not a monopoly right. As its name implies, it is the right not to be copied. Independently produced items cannot be objected to. It follows that you cannot infringe copyright if you have never had any access to the original. So in a copyright infringement action, if the defendant had no opportunity to copy, he will not be liable. On the other hand, if the defendant did have the opportunity to copy and the defendant's work is so similar to the claimant's that the most likely explanation is that he has copied, then there will be an inference of copying. The defendant will have to prove that he did not copy.

Having said that, copying can be indirect. Copying can occur as a result of seeing not the original work itself but a copy of it or something derived from it. For example, if a novel has been adapted to make a play, then you infringe the copyright in the novel by copying the play. (In that case the separate copyright in the play is also infringed.)

The late George Harrison was sued in the US as it was alleged that his song 'My Sweet Lord' was a subconscious copy of an earlier work. The song which was the subject of the alleged copying was 'He's So Fine', composed by Ronald Mack and sung by the Chiffons. It was a minor hit in the UK in 1963 and a major one in the US. The Harrison song was held to have infringed the earlier song. Ultimately, George Harrison is reputed to have bought the copyright to the earlier song, so solving the problem.

In *Sony Music Entertainment (UK) Ltd and Others v Easyinternetcafé Ltd* [2003] EWHC 62 (Ch), (2003) unreported, 28 January, the claimants obtained an injunction against the operators of some Internet cafés. They recorded music from the Internet on to CDs for their customers for a fee. This was held to be breach of ss 17 and 18. In *Independiente Ltd and Others v Music Trading On-line (HK) Ltd and Others* [2003] EWHC 470 (Ch), (2003) unreported, 13 March, the claimants were seeking to stop the defendants from supplying sound recordings via the Internet to the UK, when those recordings had been licensed only for use outside the EU.

13.4.3 Secondary infringement (ss 22–26)

This is all about dealing with infringing copies. These are copies made without the copyright owner's permission. So, the trader who imports copies into the UK may be liable for secondary infringement, as will the trader who sells, distributes or stores such copies.

In the typical infringement situation, you will have more than one infringer. However, the main culprit will be the person who manufactures the goods. He will be the primary infringer because he is actually copying the work in order to make the goods.

Then there will be the dealers who buy the goods. Maybe this is a wholesaler who buys from the manufacturer and the retailers who buy from the wholesaler. The wholesaler and retailers will be secondary infringers but only if they knew or had reason to believe that they were dealing with infringing copies. Usually, the copyright owner is mainly concerned with stopping the manufacture. He will normally write to the retailers and the wholesalers (if known) enclosing evidence of his copyright title and asking them to stop selling the goods. If they then carry on, they will be liable for secondary infringement because from this point on at least they will not be able to argue that they were innocent.

In *Bloomsbury Publishing Group Ltd and Another v News Group Newspapers Ltd and Others* [2003] EWHC 1205 (Ch), [2003] 3 All ER 736, the publisher and author of the 'Harry Potter' books obtained an injunction to restrain unauthorised publication of the fifth book in the series. A copy had been stolen from the printers and was being offered to some national newspapers, in advance of its official release date. CDPA 1988, s 23 concerns 'possessing or dealing with an infringing copy'.

13.4.4 Remedies

CDPA 1988, s 100 allows a copyright owner to seize offending articles. However, the right is in fact very weak. It can only be used against market or street traders as the right excludes business premises. The police also have to be informed beforehand.

Section 107 provides for criminal liability for making or dealing with infringing articles. Sections 108 and 114 allow for the delivery up or destruction of infringing copies. Section 111 allows for an order to prevent the importation of infringing copies.

13.4.5 Defences – 'fair dealing'

In certain circumstances some use of a copyright work is allowed without the permission of the copyright owner. The important ones to be aware of are as follows.

(a) Fair dealing for the purposes of research or private study (s 29)

This applies to LDMA works and to published editions. It basically allows you to take copies of pages of books in the course of studying or researching. It does not allow the librarian to take lots of copies, one for each student. In practice it must be read together with the provisions about librarians and archives and about schools, which are very complicated.

Implementation of Directive 2001/29/EEC on copyright and related rights in the information society will insert the words 'non-commercial' into this defence, thus restricting it severely.

(b) Fair dealing for the purpose of criticism and review (s 30(1))

If I want to comment in an article on, say, the quality of a textbook on intellectual property, this fair dealing provision will allow me to quote bits of the book without the author's permission. The question whether I come within the exception depends mainly on:

(a) the purpose for which I use the quote – if I am actually copying what the textbook says in order to tell people about the law rather than in order to comment on the textbook then I am just letting the textbook do my work for me and this would not be within the exception; and
(b) how much I quote.

The Publishers' Association publishes guidelines on how much you can quote.

(c) Fair dealing for the purpose of reporting current events (s 30(2))

This allows all works, other than photographs, to be used for reporting current events. If the report is in a newspaper or magazine there must be acknowledgement. If the report is on television, radio, etc then no acknowledgement is required (though in practice an acknowledgement is often given). Again, the question whether the dealing is fair depends on:

• the purpose; and
• how much is taken.

The purpose must truly be for reporting current events and not simply using something that has become of interest because of a particular current event. For example, the death of the Duchess of Windsor did not justify the publication of an exchange of letters between her and the Duke of Windsor without the permission of the copyright holder (*Associated Newspapers Group plc v News Group Newspapers Ltd* [1986] RPC 515). It also did not come under fair dealing for criticism and review (see *(b)*).

It will be very difficult to give any general rules about how much can be taken as it will depend on the circumstances in each case.

In the case of *British Broadcasting Corporation v British Satellite Broadcasting Ltd* [1991] 3 WLR 174, the court held that the showing by BSB of BBC World Cup football clips lasting from 14–37 seconds, four times in 24 hours did amount to fair dealing. The use did not have to be in a general news programme. It was appropriate to use the extracts in a sports update programme.

In *Pro Sieben Media AG v Carlton UK Television Ltd and Another* [1999] 1 WLR 605, the case concerned the use by Carlton of a 30-second clip from an interview broadcast by a German satellite channel concerning Mandy Allwood who was pregnant with eight embryos. The use was held to fall under 'the purposes of criticism or review'. The use by Carlton was in a programme looking at chequebook journalism, including the treatment of Ms Allwood by the media.

In *Newspaper Licensing Agency Ltd v Marks & Spencer plc*, it was held at first instance ([1999] RPC 536) that the copying and circulation within Marks & Spencer management of extracts from daily newspapers went beyond fair dealing for reporting current events. The making of between 80 and 120 copies of each article was held to be neither fair nor for the purpose of reporting current events. On appeal, this aspect does not seem to have been disputed. The decision was overturned in the Court of Appeal ([2001] Ch 257) on the basis that the copyright in the typographical arrangement was that of a whole page of the newspaper, not of each article on the page, as had been held at first instance. So, copying an article was not 'substantial taking' of the copyright in the page (see **13.4**). The House of Lords concurred ([2001] UKHL 38, [2003] AC 551).

In *Hyde Park Residence Ltd v Yelland and Others*, *The Sun* newspaper published photographs taken from a security video of a property which had been visited by Princess Diana and Dodi al Fayed. It was held at first instance ([1999] RPC 655) that the use was fair dealing for reporting current events. The Court of Appeal reversed this decision ([2001] Ch 143). They held that the events were still 'current events' even a year after the deaths, but that the use of the photographs was not fair. The newspaper had paid for dishonestly taken photographs, which were not essential to the story in the newspaper.

In *PCR Ltd v Dow Jones Telerate Ltd* [1998] FSR 170, an employee of the defendant wrote reports on the cocoa market. She used material from reports published by the claimant. It was held that a 'substantial part' of the claimant's material had been copied. Although the use was for reporting current events, the amount taken was too much to satisfy the test of fairness, so the claim for copyright infringement was upheld.

13.4.6 Other defences

In an action for infringement of an intellectual property right, the defendant will often argue that the right in question is not valid and/or the claimant does not have the right to sue for infringement. Another defence is that the copying has been done with the consent of the copyright holder (ie there is a licence).

13.5 DATABASES

The Copyright and Rights in Database Regulations 1997 implement the Directive on the Legal Protection of Databases (Dir 96/9/EC) ('Database Directive') and introduce a new 'database right' which is not copyright but which is similar to copyright (see Chapter 14).

The new right was introduced to protect the interests of database owners (eg news agencies), though it applies both to electronic and paper databases. Under English law, such databases would generally have qualified for copyright as compilations in the past, but in many European countries they might not have been protected by copyright (because they would not be regarded as sufficiently original – see **13.2.2(*a*)**). Even where there was copyright protection, if somebody just extracts one or two pieces of information then this might not amount to substantial copying, so might not be an infringement.

The individual items from which the database was composed could each also get copyright as a literary work, if substantial enough to constitute a 'work'.

13.6 COPYRIGHT AND IT

An enormous practical problem in respect of IT and the law is that technological advances constantly outstrip the law. For example, it was suggested at the time that the CDPA 1988 was going through Parliament that parts of it were already out-of-date.

Arguably, copyright is the most important of the 'general' intellectual property rights in relation to IT matters. It is of more direct significance than either trade marks or most certainly than patents (see also Appendix 2).

13.6.1 Computer programs

Perhaps the most important aspect of the application of copyright to IT is that computer programs are protected by literary copyright. Unauthorised copying of a program therefore amounts to breach of copyright (that is, basically, normal rules and remedies apply). So, the resulting anomaly is that something functional is protected by a literary right.

CDPA 1988, s 3(1) and the Copyright (Computer Programs) Regulations 1992, SI 1992/3233 provide that software is protected as a literary work.

13.6.2 The internet

There seems to be a strongly held view in some quarters that the law cannot apply to or control the internet at all. Certainly, the law does undoubtedly apply to the internet.

There have already been cases which have decided that unauthorised use of material from the internet can amount to breach of copyright (see, for example, *Shetland Times Ltd v Wills and Another* [1997] FSR 604, discussed at **A2.6.2**). There is also the opposite situation where copyright material is used on the internet without permission. For example, in January 1999, a considerable number of musicians and pop singers took out advertisements in newspapers to protest against the unauthorised internet use of their material, and to demand tighter legal controls. You may be familiar with the litigation in the USA on the 'Napster' site which various record companies sued for breach of copyright in their recordings. Napster was supposed to be coming back as a licensed site, where you have to pay money to download the recordings. However, other sites have sprung up, such as Gnutella, Blubster, Newtella, MusicCity and KaZaA. These do not use a centralised server so are harder to take action against. They use P2P software which enables one computer to communicate with another computer without going through a centralised server (P2P stand for 'peer to peer').

See the case of *Sony Music Entertainment (UK) Ltd and Others v Easyinternetcafé Ltd* at **13.4.2** for an instance of copyright infringement on the Internet. In the *Daily Telegraph*, 24 April 2003, it was reported that EMI is making 140,000 of its tracks available to customers via the internet. It will charge customers, but less than they would have to pay to buy a CD version.

More recently, the Recording Industry Association of America (RIAA) has instituted proceedings against 261 people in the United States for allegedly using P2P copying.

13.7 PUBLIC PERFORMANCES – THE COLLECTING SOCIETIES

It would be very difficult for the creators of music and songs, in particular, to enforce their rights acting individually, not least as their copyright could be infringed by a public performance anywhere in the country. To overcome this problem, the collecting societies have existed for many years. They operate either as licensees of the relevant copyrights or as agents acting on behalf of the copyright holders. They employ staff to travel round the country to find places where public performances are taking place without a licence from one of the collecting societies. The typical problem locations are pubs and restaurants.

The Performing Rights Society (PRS) and the Mechanical Copyright Protection Society (MCPS) act for writers of music and lyrics and their publishers. The MCPS acts on behalf of its composer and publisher members. It negotiates agreements with those who wish to record the music of its members. It collects and distributes the 'mechanical' royalties which are generated from recording of the music on to many different formats. The PRS collects licence fees on behalf of composers, lyricists and music publishers for public performance or broadcast of their works. They co-operate closely under the name 'The Music Alliance'. Phonographic Performance Limited (PPL) acts for over 3,000 record companies both large and small and deals primarily with the copyright in sound recordings. Video Performance Limited (VPL) is responsible for music videos.

As well as their policing role, the collecting societies license performance of their works, including to broadcasters such as the BBC, ITV and Sky. All the societies co-operate closely to ensure that the copyright holders in each aspect of a work receive their fair share of a licence fee from a user.

In the publishing world, the Copyright Licensing Agency Ltd ('CLA') seeks to enforce its members' copyright in their works. It licenses businesses to copy protected works. The CLA is owned by the Authors Licensing and Collecting Society ('ALCS') and the Publishers Licensing Society ('PLS'). The Newspaper Licensing Agency Ltd ('NLA') was set up in 1996 to enforce newspaper proprietors' rights in their copyright. It licenses businesses to copy newspapers, and was involved in a high-profile case with Marks & Spencer (see **13.4.5**).

13.8 DEVELOPMENTS IN THE LAW OF COPYRIGHT

Directive 2001/29/EC on Copyright and Related Rights in the Information Society ('Copyright Directive') deals with harmonisation of copyright through the EU. In particular, it addresses the issue of copyright protection on the internet and satellite and cable broadcasts. It provides for an exemption from liability for an intermediary which carries out transient or incidental copying as part of a technological process. Articles 6 and 7 of the directive are intended to outlaw the making and selling of devices which circumvent anti-copying technology. Its implementation has been delayed at the time of writing (August 2003).

Directive 2001/84/EC on the Resale Right for the Benefit of the Author of an Original Work of Art is to be implemented in Member States by 1 January 2006.

Chapter 14

THE DATABASE RIGHT

14.1 BACKGROUND

There has been a difference of approach between English law and the Continental civil law systems on the protection of utilitarian information such as lists of customers' names and addresses, or entries in a phone directory. The English approach has been to grant copyright protection, but the Continental view was that such functional documents were not literary works and therefore could not be protected by copyright. This difference of approach was resolved by Directive 96/9/EC on the Legal Protection of Databases ('the Database Directive'). This was implemented by the Copyright and Rights in Databases Regulations 1997, SI 1997/3032. These amended the CDPA 1988.

• What is protected?	• collections of information
• What benefit is there?	• protects against unauthorised copying
• How is it obtained?	• arises automatically (no registration)
• How long does it last?	• 15 years from creation of the database

14.2 DEFINITION OF A DATABASE

A database is defined in CDPA 1988, s 3A as follows:

'3A **Databases**

(1) In this Part "database" means a collection of independent works, data or other materials which—

(a) are arranged in a systematic or methodical way, and

(b) are individually accessible by electronic or other means.

(2) For the purposes of this Part a literary work consisting of a database is original if, and only if, by reason of the selection or arrangement of the contents of the database the database constitutes the author's own intellectual creation.'

The definition of a 'database' covers information held in electronic form and also that held only as paper documents.

In practice, a database could, for example, be information on the daily price of stocks and shares, a telephone directory, Lexis or the CD-ROM law reports. Copyright protection may also be afforded to a database specifically as a literary work, although the standard is not only that of originality, but also that it is the 'author's intellectual creation'. This seems to be a higher standard than for copyright in literary works in general and so a database is unlikely to have copyright protection.

Whether or not it is protected by copyright, a database attracts the database right, which arises automatically. The database right runs for 15 years from the end of the year of completion. It prevents unauthorised use of the database or a substantial part of it.

Under reg 13 of the Copyright and Rights in Databases Regulations 1997, the database right exists where there is:

> 'substantial investment in obtaining, verifying or presenting the contents of the database.'

Thus, data arrangements have the protection of the database right if there is a substantial investment (including any investment, whether of financial, human or technical resources):

- in quality or quantity; or
- in obtaining, verifying or presenting the data.

Further points to consider in relation to database right are as follows.

14.3 QUALIFICATIONS FOR THE DATABASE RIGHT

There are copyright-style qualification requirements (Copyright and Rights in Databases Regulations 1997, reg 18) based on nationality, or corporate seat.

14.4 OWNERSHIP OF THE DATABASE RIGHT

The maker of a database protected by the database right is the person who takes the initiative in obtaining, verifying or presenting the contents of the database and who assumes the risk of investing in that obtaining (see Copyright and Rights in Databases Regulations 1997, reg 14).

The maker is the first owner of the database right (reg 15).

14.5 DURATION OF DATABASE PROTECTION

The database right lasts for the longer of 15 years from the end of the calendar year:

- of completion of the database; or
- during which the database was first made available to the public (reg 17).

A 'substantial new investment', under s 17(3) will 'top up' the right so the period starts again. So, a telephone directory would in effect have a rolling 15-year protection, as a new edition is produced every year.

14.6 INFRINGEMENT OF THE DATABASE RIGHT

Infringement is the extraction or re-utilisation of all or a substantial part of the contents of a database without the consent of the owner (reg 16).

'Extraction' means the permanent or temporary transfer of the contents of a database to another medium by any means or in any form.

'Re-utilisation' means making those contents available to the public by any means.

'Substantial' is in terms of quality or quantity or both.

'Substantial part' can include repeated extraction and/or re-utilisation of insubstantial parts (reg 16(2)).

14.7 EXCEPTIONS FROM THE DATABASE RIGHT

Database rights are not infringed (regs 19 and 20):

- by fair dealing with a substantial part of a database made available to the public if:
  - such dealing is for illustration in teaching or research; and
  - sufficient acknowledgement is given; or
- generally, by copying or use with the authority of the keeper of a database available for public inspection as a statutory record.

The database right can be licensed or assigned (as can the copyright in the database).

14.8 APPLICATION OF THE DATABASE RIGHT

The database right was introduced to give the database owner an action against people who extract information from the database without their permission whether or not this would constitute copyright infringement. See the case below of *British Horseracing Board v William Hill Organisation Ltd* [2001] 2 CMLR 12 on the use of information on the runners and riders. The database right would also have applied to the facts such as those in *Faccenda Chicken Ltd v Fowler* [1986] 1 All ER 617, where the unauthorised use was of a database which was a list of customers' names and addresses.

In *British Horseracing Board v William Hill*, the British Horseracing Board operated a computerised database containing the details of horse owners, trainers and jockeys, racing colours, horses and other information relating to races to be run in Great Britain. Information on the database was updated after each race. William Hill, a bookmaker with 1,500 licensed betting shops in the UK, legitimately used information from the British Horseracing Board service. In 2000, William Hill started an internet betting service which used information from the British Horseracing Board service. This was outside the terms of William Hill's licence agreement. The British Horseracing Board therefore sued for breach of the database right.

It was held at first instance to be a breach and an injunction was granted. The Court of Appeal indicated that it was minded to uphold the judgment at first instance but also referred some matters of interpretation of the underlying directive to the ECJ. The defendants have taken out a conditional licence and the injunction has been discharged for the time being.

Chapter 15

DESIGN RIGHTS

15.1 WHAT IS DESIGN RIGHT?

Registered designs have existed in England since at least the 1830s. They were bolstered at that time to protect the designs of fabrics from being copied by cheap imports. The Registered Design Right was strengthened in the CDPA 1988, with the aim of promoting its use for commercial items. At the same time, copyright was pushed in the direction of artistic output not least to resist the trend that had developed of trying to use copyright for industrial items. Directive 98/71/EC on the Legal Protection of Design (the Design Directive) made further amendments to the legislation governing registered designs, the RDA 1949. (At the time of writing, August 2003, there are believed to be some Member States which have not yet implemented the directive.)

Unregistered design right was created by the CDPA 1988. It has been little used and there are few recorded cases where it has been an important factor. It protects three-dimensional shapes, both pretty ones and those that are merely functional. Usually, people seek to rely on it in the case of the functional items. EC Regulation 6/2002 has introduced an EU unregistered design right.

15.1.1 Overview of registered design right

The CDPA 1988 amended the Registered Designs Act 1949 to strengthen the protection of registered designs. Directive 98/71/EC was implemented by amending again the 1949 Act, in December 2001. Most existing textbooks will therefore be out of date. The cases on registered designs will also be obsolete as the criteria for registerability have changed.

In essence, registered design right protects the appearance of consumer items. The types of articles for which designs have been registered in the past include:

- foodstuffs;
- jewellery;
- clothing;
- travel goods;
- textile goods;
- furniture;
- clocks and watches;
- musical instruments; and
- sales and advertising signs.

• What is protected?	• new designs for consumer items
• What benefit is there?	• monopoly right
• How is it obtained?	• registration
• How long does it last?	• 25 years from registration

15.1.2 Overview of unregistered design right

Unregistered designs were created by the CDPA 1988. They are primarily intended to protect functional objects. Copyright protection for such objects, where it existed, was cut back by the CDPA 1988. Unregistered design right can only be used to protect three-dimensional shapes from copying. It has been used for functional items, where indeed it has been used at all. It is the weakest of the mainstream IP rights.

•	What is protected?	•	3-dimensional shapes
•	What benefit is there?	•	prevents copying
•	How is it obtained?	•	arises automatically (no registration)
•	How long does it last?	•	10 years in most cases

Instances where unregistered design right has been used in disputes are:

- pig 'fenders', for keeping mummy pigs away from the piglets' food;
- a slurry separator, a machine for separating solid and liquid components of slurry resulting from the mixture of animal excreta and washing water; and
- electrical transformers (see **15.3.1**).

Unregistered design right can apply to parts of a machine which are never in public view, as well as to a machine, or any parts of it, that are in the public view. This is in contrast to registered design right where only those aspects on view are capable of being registered.

Let us look at registered and unregistered designs in a bit more detail.

15.2 REGISTERED DESIGN RIGHT

15.2.1 Definitions – 'new' and 'individual character'

Registered design is defined in RDA 1949, s 1(2) as:

> '... the appearance of the whole or part of a product resulting from the features of, in particular, the lines, contours, shape, texture and/or materials of the product itself and/or its ornamentation.'

Product is defined in s 1(3) as:

> 'any industrial or handicraft item other than a computer program; and in particular, includes packaging, get-up, graphic symbols, typographic type-faces and parts intended to be assembled into a complex product.'

This definition now includes things that were not covered before, perhaps most notably the packaging and get-up (presentation) of goods. Thus, it would now be possible to register the appearance of packaging as a registered design. This would give such items the increased protection of a registered right.

A design must be 'new' and have 'individual character', which are defined as follows:

> **'1B Requirement of novelty and individual character**
>
> (1) A design shall be protected by a right in a registered design to the extent that the design is new and has individual character.

(2) For the purposes of subsection (1) above, a design is new if no identical design or no design whose features differ only in immaterial details has been made available to the public before the relevant date.

(3) For the purposes of subsection (1) above, a design has individual character if the overall impression it produces on the informed user differs from the overall impression produced on such a user by any design which has been made available to the public before the relevant date.'

It seems doubtful that 'individual character' adds much to the basic requirement that the design be new.

15.2.2 Wider scope of the prior art

The design must be new at the date of application. Previously, only prior art (existing designs) in the UK was relevant. It is now prior art anywhere in the world, if it could reasonably have been known about in the relevant trade sector in the European Economic Area (EEA). The Patent Office is continuing its policy of not examining applications for registered design against the prior art. It is relying on third parties to object when the application is published.

15.2.3 'Grace period' of 12 months

The amended RDA 1949 now provides a grace period of 12 months during which a designer may disclose the design. This will not affect the design's novelty or the assessment of its individual character in an application for registration by the end of the 12-month period (s 1B(5), (6)). There is no right to claim for infringement before the design has been granted registration (s 7A(6)).

It would still be important to keep evidence of the date of creation of the design (eg by storing original drawings which should be dated and signed). Thus, if someone else claims during the 12-month grace period that they had created the design in question, there would be evidence available to refute that claim. Once the design has been registered, any such disputes would be resolved by the registration, if it is valid.

15.2.4 Designs that cannot be protected

(a) Technical function

There is an exclusion from registerability for features dictated 'solely by the products technical function' but the feeling is that this will be construed less restrictively than was the case under the old law (which simply referred to 'function').

Section 1C(1) states:

'A right in a registered design shall not subsist in features of appearance of a product which are only dictated by the product's technical function.'

(b) Interfaces

This is also an exception for the interface between product and another object. However, it only excludes mechanical fittings. There is a carve-out from this exception in that it does not extend to new modular products (eg a design for stackable chairs).

In effect, it seems that *Amp Inc v Utilux Pty Ltd* [1971] RPC 397 has been overruled. This case held that it was not possible to have a registered design in a functional object.

15.2.5 Designs that can now be protected

Under the old law, it was not possible to have a design registration for a part (see *R v Registered Designs Appeal Tribunal ex parte Ford Motor Co* [1995] 1 WLR 18). However, it is now possible to have such a registration, provided the part is visible during the normal use of the whole product. For example, a new design of radio aerial for a car would be registerable as it would be visible but a new design for an oil filter for a car would not, as it would be hidden during normal use. Thus, s 1B(8), (9) provides:

> '(8) For the purposes of this section, a design applied to or incorporated in a product which constitutes a component part of a complex product shall only be considered to be new and to have individual character—
>
> (a)   if the component part, once it has been incorporated into the complex product, remains visible during normal use of the complex product; and
> (b)   to the extent that those visible features of the component part are in themselves new and have individual character.
>
> (9) In subsection (8) above "normal use" means use by the end user; but does not include any maintenance, servicing or repair work in relation to the product.'

'Normal use' means that a wing mirror, in the *Ford* case, could now be registered as it is visible in the ordinary use of a car.

A design registration cannot be used against someone supplying a spare part for the repair of a complex product (eg the car radio aerial mentioned above (s 7A(5)). So, the registration can be used to stop another manufacturer from using that design for a car radio aerial on their make of car. It cannot be used to stop someone supplying spare aerials.

15.2.6 The scope of the right

The proprietor has the exclusive right to use the design and 'any design which does not produce on the informed user a different overall impression' (s 7(1)). This in effect includes use of the design on any product.

Unlike the situation under the old law, designs no longer have to be registered in regard to certain types of product. So, use of a design intended for crockery on, say, tee shirts would be infringement of the design registration.

15.2.7 Duration of protection

The duration of protection is a maximum of 25 years (s 8).

15.2.8 Scope of protection

The scope of protection includes any design that does not produce on the informed user a different overall impression (s 7(1)).

15.2.9 Ownership of registered designs

If the design is created in the course of someone's employment, the ownership of the design belongs to the employer. This in effect is the same as copyright.

If the design is created as a result of a commission, then the ownership belongs to the commissioner, not to the designer. This is in contrast to the situation with copyright.

15.2.10 Exhaustion of rights

Registered design right cannot be used to hinder parallel importing (s 7A(4)).

15.2.11 Infringement of registered designs

The registration of a design gives the registered proprietor the exclusive right to use the design and 'any design which does not produce on the informed user a different overall impression' (s 7(1)).

'Using' the design is defined in s 7(2) including a reference to:

> '... the making, offering, putting on the market, importing, exporting or using of a product to which the design is incorporated or to which it is applied.'

Infringement is defined in s 7A as doing anything that is the exclusive right of the proprietor without their consent. Exceptions in s 7A(2) include:

> '(a) an act which is done privately and for purposes which are not commercial
> (b) an act which is done for experimental purposes
> (c) an act of reproduction for teaching purposes ...
> (d) ...
> (e) [these concern foreign ships and aircraft]
> (f) ...'

There are qualifications to the exceptions, in subs (3):

> '(a) the act of reproduction is compatible with fair trade practice and does not unduly prejudice the normal exploitation of the design, and
> (b) mention is made of the source'

Damages may not be awarded against an innocent infringer (s 9). It is not enough to mark a design with the word 'registered' to overcome this but rather the registration number of the design must also be marked on the product in question.

Remedies can include:

- an injunction;
- damages;
- an account of profits; and
- an order for delivery up or destruction of the offending items.

RDA 1949, s 26 provides for a remedy for groundless threats of infringement proceedings. These are a declaration, damages and an injunction. The reason for these types of provisions in the legislation governing IP rights is that the threat of an infringement action is a severe threat to a business.

15.2.12 EU-registered design right

Regulation 6/2002 has set up an EU-registered design system. The new system is run by the EU Trade Marks Office (OHIM) in Alicante. For the purposes of this edition we are not dealing with this development, but it will affect you when you are in the office, sooner or later.

15.3 UNREGISTERED DESIGN RIGHT

This is referred to in the CDPA 1988 as 'design right'. 'Design' is defined in s 213(2) as:

> 'any aspect of the shape or configuration (whether internal or external) of the whole or part of an article.'

No right subsists unless the design is recorded in a document or an article has been made to the design (s 213(6)).

15.3.1 Originality

The requirement of originality for unregistered design right (UDR) is twofold:

- that it should be original, in the copyright sense of not itself being a copy; and
- that it should not be 'commonplace in the design field in question' (s 213(4)).

There have been some cases which have considered what it means to be commonplace. The idea is that UDR protects a design against copying. For that concept to work, the design in question has to be distinguishable from all the other goods of that type in the marketplace. For example, see the following cases.

In *Farmers Build Ltd v Carrier Bulk Materials Handling Ltd* [1999] RPC 461 concerning a slurry separator, putting a number of different commonplace features together in a new way can result in a design that is not commonplace.

In *Jo-Y-Jo Ltd v Matalan Retail Ltd* [1999] EIPR 627, it was held that flowers embroidered on vests were commonplace.

In *Ocular Sciences Ltd and Another v Aspect Vision Care Ltd and Others; Galley v Ocular Sciences Ltd (No 2)* [1997] RPC 289, a design for contact lenses was held to be commonplace if trite, common-or-garden, or hackneyed. In that case, many features of the contact lenses were held to be commonplace, or subject to the 'must fit' exclusion (ie must fit the eye – see **15.3.2**).

In *Baby Dan v Brevi* [1999] FSR 377, the existence of UDR in a child safety barrier was upheld. It was also held that the right had been infringed.

In *Lambretta Clothing Company Ltd v Teddy Smith (UK) Ltd & Next Retail plc* [2003] EWHC (Ch), (2003) unreported, 23 May, the subject matter was a 'retro-vintage' track top. On the existence of UDR, it was held that:

- the outline shape of the track top was not original as it had itself been copied from another garment;
- the Lambretta logos were surface decoration and therefore excluded from unregistered design right (see **15.3.2(d)**);

- mere juxtaposition of patches of colour on the garment did not fall within the meaning of 'configuration' in s 213(2), so did not attract UDR; and

- two-dimensional colour applied to the garment did not generate an original three-dimensional design.

Overall, there was no UDR existing in the garment.

In *A Fulton Co Ltd v Grant Barnett & Co Ltd* [2001] RPC 16, there was held to be unregistered design right in the handle of an umbrella, which had been designed by a director of the claimant company. The designs were held to be original and not to be commonplace. They were also held to have been infringed by the defendant.

In *Guild v Eskandar Ltd* [2001] FSR 38, UDR was held to exist in garments based on Iranian ethnic clothing, that is there was sufficient originality in the designs in question (see **13.2.2**).

15.3.2 Exclusions

CDPA 1988, s 213(3) gives the exclusions.

(a) Methods or principles of construction (s 213(3)(a))

These are excluded on the basis that methods of construction are the subject of patent law rather than design law. (Method of construction has been defined as a process or operation by which a shape is produced, as opposed to the shape itself (*Kestos Ltd v Kempat Ltd* [1936] RPC 139)).

In *Christopher Tasker's Design Right References; Re Patent Office* [2001] RPC 3, various aspects of sliding doors for wardrobes were held to be subject to UDR, and therefore to come within s 213(2). However, the hiding from view of aluminium runners by the use of wooden mouldings was a method of construction, and excluded from UDR by s 213(3).

(b) Must fit (s 213(3)(b)(i))

This applies to both types of design right. Functional designs are not excluded from UDR. One of main purposes of this right is to protect functional designs. There is, however, an exclusion for those aspects of the design which 'must fit' with other articles in order that either article may perform its function. It is only the 'interface' that is, excluded from protection, that is the bits that have to fit into the other object.

This exclusion would also apply to human spare parts (prostheses) or contact lenses (*Ocular Sciences Ltd and Another v Aspect Vision Care Ltd and Others; Galley v Ocular Sciences Ltd (No 2)* [1997] RPC 289). Another instance concerned a holder for a mobile phone, many features of which did not get UDR as its shape was dictated by the phone (*Parker v Tidball* [1997] FSR 680).

(c) Must match (s 213(3)(b)(ii))

UDR can not apply if the appearance of the article is dependent on that of a larger article of which it is intended to form an integral part. There could, for example, be no UDR in spare parts (for cars or prostheses for people, eg artificial limbs).

(d) Surface decoration (s 213(3)(c))

Surface decoration is excluded from UDR. This is really part of the definition, as UDR only protects the shape of a product (see the *Lambretta* case at **15.3.1**).

15.3.3 Ownership of unregistered designs

If the design is created in the course of someone's employment, the ownership of the design belongs to the employer (s 215). This in effect is the same as copyright.

In *Ultraframe (UK) Ltd v Clayton and Others; Ultraframe (UK) Ltd v Fielding and Others* [2002] EWHC 1964 (Ch), [2002] All ER (D) 167 (Dec), the claimant company was held to be the owner of unregistered designs created by the person who had been managing director and major shareholder. In *A Fulton Co Ltd v Grant Barnett & Co Ltd* [2001] RPC 16, the claimant company was also held to own an unregistered design created by a director.

If the design is created as a result of a commission, then the ownership belongs to the commissioner, not to the designer. This is in contrast to the situation with copyright.

Ownership is the same for both registered and unregistered designs. Why the difference from copyright? Primarily because design rights are thought of as commercial rights, so it makes sense that 'he who pays the piper calls the tune'. With copyright the position is more subtle. Although it covers other things as well, copyright is often considered to be the realm of the creative artist so here the starting point is that the author should own his own creation.

15.3.4 Duration of protection

UDR lasts for 15 years from the end of the calendar year in which the design was first created, or 10 years from being made available for sale or hire (s 216).

15.3.5 Infringement of unregistered designs

UDR follows copyright in that there is primary and secondary infringement. Secondary infringement requires knowledge.

Primary infringement is, for commercial purposes, making articles to the design or making a design document for the purpose of enabling such articles to be made (s 226(1)).

Secondary infringement includes importation, possessing for commercial purposes, selling and hiring, but is only relevant if the person had knowledge or reason to believe that they were infringing items (s 227).

Remedies are damages, injunctions, accounts of profits (s 229(1)), order for delivery up of infringing articles (s 230), and an order for disposal of infringing articles (s 231). Damages are not available against an innocent primary infringer (s 233).

There is a provision providing a remedy against groundless threats of infringement proceedings (s 253). The remedies are a declaration, injunction and damages.

15.3.6 Overlap with copyright

If copyright subsists in a work which also has UDR, the UDR is suppressed. Only the infringement of the copyright is considered (s 236).

15.3.7 Licences of right

In the last 5 years of the term of an unregistered design, anyone can apply for a licence to use the unregistered design (s 237). If terms cannot be agreed between the parties, then the terms are settled by the Designs Registry, which is part of the Patent Office.

15.3.8 EU-unregistered design right

EU Regulation 6/2002 has introduced an EU-unregistered design right. This right lasts for 3 years. However, it seems that the EU right is merely intended to protect registerable designs in the period before registration is applied for.

15.4 REGISTERED AND UNREGISTERED DESIGNS

	RDR	UDR
Statute	Registered Designs Act 1949 as amended by Registered Designs Regulations 2001	CDPA 1988
Definition	Appearance of whole or part of a product resulting from features of, in particular: • lines • contours • colours • shape • texture or materials • ornamentation 'Product' includes packaging, get up, graphic symbols, typographic type-faces and visible parts	Any aspect of: • shape, or • configuration of the whole or part of an article NB no right subsists unless the design is recorded in a document or an article has been made to the design
Originality	**New**: no identical design/design differing in only immaterial details has previously been made available to public, *and* **Individual character**: overall impression to informed user differs from that of any other design that has been made available to public, and **The design has not been made available to public**: ie not published, exhibited or used in the trade NB 12 months grace period	Must be **original**, ie must be: • **the result of independent effort** ie not copied, and • **not commonplace** in design field in question
Exclusions	• features solely dictated by technical function • interface (mechanical fittings only) (but modular designs are registerable)	• methods of construction • must fit • must match • surface decoration
Ownership	Commissioner; the employer; the designer, in that order	Commissioner; the employer; the designer, in that order

Duration	25 years in total	The shorter of: • 15 years from the end of the year of creation/recording; or • 10 years from the end of the year of first sale/hire
Infringement	Making, offering, putting on market, importing or exporting any product incorporating the design or any design which does not produce a different overall impression. No need to prove copying NB private non-commercial acts are excluded	Primary: making articles to the design/making document for purposes of making articles. Need to prove copying: substantial similarity is enough. Secondary: import, sell, hire, offer, possess with knowledge/reason to believe is an infringing article.

Chapter 16

PATENTS

16.1 INTRODUCTION

Patents are monopoly rights granted by the government to protect inventions under, today, the Patents Act 1977 (PA 1977). If a patent is granted, the inventor gets a monopoly over use of his invention for (generally) 20 years (ie he can stop anybody else using it for this time). The quid pro quo of getting a patent so far as the inventor is concerned is that before the patent is granted, details of the invention go on a public register at the Patent Office so it is available for everyone to study. So, a patented invention cannot be kept secret. The idea is that others should be able to learn from the patent. It contributes to the general body of technological understanding. After the 20 years is up, the invention is available for anyone to use.

The main justification for patents is that if there were no patents, then commercial organisations would not invest in the research needed to produce new inventions. They need to have a chance to recoup their expenditure on the invention that is a success as well as the time spent on abortive projects. The estimated cost of putting a new pharmaceutical on the market is £200 million, and it takes about 12 years. A business will need to recover this cost from its product, hence patent protection is very important in the business world.

There has been an unusual development in recent times. There is a website on which commercial organisations can post details of technology which they wish to put in to the public arena so that someone else cannot patent it. If it is on the website, there can be no arguments that the information is public (and therefore unpatentable).

• What is protected?	•	new invention
• What benefit is there?	•	monopoly right
• How is it obtained?	•	registration
• How long does it last?	•	20 years from application

16.2 OBTAINING A PATENT

The patent system is a 'first to file', not a 'first to invent'. In other words, the crucial step is the bureaucratic step of filing the application at the Patent Office. You may recall the tale of Elisha Gray who filed his application for the telephone 4 hours later than Alexander Graham Bell. Bell therefore was awarded the patent by the US Supreme Court and became famous. Gray has been largely forgotten by history (but he, in fact, patented a telegraph system and founded the Western Electric Company, so do not feel too sorry for him).

A patent for the UK can be obtained:

• by applying to the UK Patent Office;

- by applying to the European Patent Office under the European Patent Convention ('EPC'); or
- via an international application under the Patent Co-operation Treaty ('PCT').

The PCT would be used, for example, if the proprietor of a US or Japanese patent was also seeking to apply for a patent in the UK. They would then be assigned the priority date of the non-UK patent (see **16.4.1**), which is one big advantage of an application through either the PCT or EPC. There are more than 100 countries which are members of the PCT.

The EPC is not a true European Patent (but see below for developments on this aspect). It awards a bundle of national patents for countries which are parties to the EPC. Not all EPC patent applications will specify all the countries of the EPC. It is a European system, not an EU one, and encompasses countries that are not EU Member States (eg Switzerland), though all the EU Member States are individual members of the EPC.

The cost of a European patent (EPC) is high, being about £31,000 as opposed to perhaps £2,000 plus VAT for drafting and filing a UK patent. The headquarters of the European Patent Office are in Munich and its search branch is in The Hague.

The PCT 1970 is administered by the WIPO in Geneva. It provides for a single application and preliminary search. It then sends the application on to national offices for them to decide whether to award a patent for their territory.

There have been discussions at EU level for several years aimed at setting up a Community patent system. The discussions have been dogged by disputes over which languages can be used, and the role of the national patent offices. On 3 March 2003, the Member States finally agreed on the approach to be taken. The key areas are:

- the existing framework of the EPC should be utilised;
- the European Patent Office would run the Community patent system;
- it would grant a patent 'for the territory of the Community';
- the EU as such will need to ratify the EPC, though all current members of the EU are individual members of the EPC;
- the full patent specification could be filed in any one of English, French or German at the European Patent Office with the claims, only, translated into the other two languages; and
- a court to be called 'the Community Intellectual Property Court' will be established by Council Regulation to come into being by 2010 at the latest, though there are hopes it could exist by 2005, but this seems somewhat optimistic.

Patents can be categorised as 'product' patents which claim the end product of a manufacturing process (eg a new drug, or a better vacuum cleaner), or as 'process' patents which claim the manufacturing process itself (eg the method for making 'Goretex' waterproofing for outdoor clothing). It would of course be sensible to try to patent both the product and the method of making it. This would have to be done in separate patents.

16.3 PATENTABILITY

An invention will be patentable if it satisfies four conditions, in that it must:

- be new;
- constitute an inventive step;
- be capable of industrial application; and
- not be within any of the exclusions in PA 1977, s 1(2).

We will take each of these in turn.

16.3.1 New

Novelty is judged by reference to the 'state of the art' at the priority date. Under Article 54(2) of the EPC:

> 'The state of the art shall be held to compromise everything made available to the public by means of a written or oral description, by use, or in any way, before the date of filing of the European patent application.'

The information sources utilised would be:

- other granted patents or published applications, both UK and relevant foreign jurisdictions;
- published descriptions of relevant technology, eg in scientific journals or PhD theses; and
- existing products or processes that are in the public domain.

As a matter of practicality, these are matters known about within, or are accessible from, the jurisdiction. Third parties can bring material to the attention of the Patent Office when the application is published, see below.

So this involves a factual investigation (ie has the invention been thought of before and been made public?). The investigation will be carried out by the Patent Office in its initial examination of the patent application. Third parties can also object after publication of the application by the Patent Office. The whole topic of novelty is also highly relevant in patent infringement actions when the usual defence of the alleged infringer is to challenge the validity of the patent.

This means that the topic of the prior art is examined again, but this time in retrospect, perhaps 20 years or more after the original patent application (see **16.8**).

An invention will not be regarded as forming part of the state of the art unless there has been an 'enabling disclosure'. As the name suggests, an enabling disclosure means a disclosure that would enable somebody to make the product or work the process, as the case may be. The question the Patent Office asks is whether, at the priority date, a skilled worker could by observation or analysis reproduce the applicant's invention from the disclosure in question. So, if a newspaper reports that Professor X has created a new process for cloning sheep, this would not be an enabling disclosure. For it to be an enabling disclosure the report would have to describe the process in a way that would allow others to reproduce the invention. (A detailed scientific paper would undoubtedly give such information.)

In *Vericore Ltd v Vetrepharm Ltd and Another* [2003] EWHC 111 (Ch), (2003) unreported, 6 February, a patent for a pesticide to attack sea lice infestation in farmed salmon was held to be invalid on the grounds of anticipation and obviousness. In other words, it was not 'new' and there was no 'inventive step' (see **16.3.2**). In particular, the patentee had failed to restrict his claims to synthetic pyrethroids and had impliedly claimed natural pyrethroids as well. The prior art already disclosed the use of natural pyrethroids for treatment of fish, so the patent claims were not 'new' as at the priority date of the patent (see **16.4.1**).

In what circumstances might an enabling disclosure arise? In the case of product patents, disclosure of the product will usually be an enabling disclosure, especially where the invention is a mechanical device. An obvious example is where there is already a product on the market which discloses the invention. For example, if the patent application is for a bagless vacuum cleaner and there is already a bagless vacuum cleaner on the market. This is clearly an enabling disclosure because anyone taking the vacuum cleaner apart can see how the invention works. Similarly if a vacuum cleaner embodying the invention had been exhibited at a trade fair, then this would be an enabling disclosure (but some trade fairs are specifically excluded under PA 1977). The enabling disclosure could arise from a third-party product where the third party had thought of the idea first (eg *Windsurfing International Inc v Tabur Marine* [1985] RPC 59). Alternatively, it could be the applicant for the patent marketing/exhibiting his invention before the filing date. This is called 'self-publication'.

In one case, the invention was a hay-raking machine in which the rake wheels were turned by contact with the ground rather than by an engine (*C Van der Lely NV v Bamfords Ltd* [1963] RPC 61). A photograph of the machine was printed in a newspaper. The question was whether the photograph was clear enough to show how the invention worked. If so, it was an enabling disclosure, and in this case it was held to be so.

In some cases the product may not disclose the invention. This would often be the case in relation to process patents. The end product of the patented process will not necessarily reveal the process itself. A consequence is that it may be possible to disclose the existence of a new product without showing how the process works. An example is *Quantel Ltd v Spaceward Microsystems Ltd* [1990] RPC 83, where the demonstration at an exhibition of a complex computer for creating visual effects on television would not have enabled someone to work out how it operated. Falconer J said in relation to this aspect:

> 'Demonstration of a prototype of the claimed invention at an exhibition where no-one was allowed near the actual machine and no engineering description was given, although individuals were allowed to use the stylus to draw a picture, could not possibly have been an enabling disclosure so as to anticipate any claim.'

16.3.2 Inventive step

An invention might be new but it also needs to be a quantum leap over the existing technology. This second criterion for patentability is that the invention should involve an 'inventive step' (ie be clever enough). The question asked here is whether the invention would be obvious to a person skilled in the art, taking into account the state of the art at the priority date (see the *Vericore* case at **16.3.1**). The person skilled in the art refers to the 'uninventive technician'. This is someone who is knowledgeable, but lacking that inventive spark.

In using the 'uninventive technician', the following limitation was referred to by Aldous LJ in *Amersham Pharmacia Biotech AB v Amicon Ltd and Others* [2001] EWCA Civ 1042, (2003) unreported, 5 July:

> 'A fiction in patent law is that the notional uninventive skilled man in the art is deemed to have read and assimilated any piece of prior art pleaded by the party attacking the patent claim …
>
> The more distant a prior art document is from the field of technology covered by the patent, the greater the chance that an intelligent but uninventive person skilled in the art will fail to make the jump to the solution found by the patentee.'

In other words, the prior art being used in an attempt to strike out a patent has to be highly relevant to the patent in question.

The test is in *Windsurfing International Inc v Tabur Marine* [1985] RPC 59. Here, Oliver LJ described the test as having four stages:

(1) the court must identify the inventive concept embodied in the patent;
(2) it must assume the mantle of the normally skilled but unimaginative addressee in the art at the priority date and impute to him what was, at that date, common general knowledge in the art in question;
(3) it must identify what, if any, differences exist between the matters cited as being 'known or used' and the alleged invention; and
(4) it must ask itself whether, viewed without any knowledge of the alleged invention, those differences constituted steps which would have been obvious to the skilled man or whether they required any degree of invention.

Put simply what you have to do is first, identify what the invention adds to the state of the art. If this new bit is not obvious to the uninventive technician then you have inventive step.

The classic case was the 'sausage machine case'. A patent was struck out for lack of inventive step because it was simply the combination of two known machines, a mincing machine and a sausage-filling machine. There were also arguments along these lines in the case of *Hickman v Andrews and Others* [1983] RPC 174 concerning infringement of the patent for the Black and Decker 'Workmate', invented by Ron Hickman. Clamping arrangements of this type were known before Ron Hickman invented the Workmate. However, the Court of Appeal upheld the patent.

Commercial success of the product is taken as being a good indicator of the patent having an inventive step. So is fulfilling a 'long felt want', that is plugging a gap in the market. In other words, if it was an obvious step from the existing technology why had no one done it before the patentee had come up with his invention?

In *Biogen v Medeva* [1997] RPC 1, the House of Lords held:

> 'Anything inventive done for the first time was the result of adding a new idea to the existing stock of knowledge. If it was the idea of using established techniques to do something which no one had previously thought of doing, the inventive idea would be doing the new thing.'

In other words, the inventive step could be a very small one and yet create a valid patent. For the record, the case concerned genetic engineering, and the patent was found to be invalid. The *Biogen* case concerned a novel method of producing a vaccine for viral hepatitis B. Genetic engineering and computer programs are the big areas in patent practice at the moment (notwithstanding that computer programs are not patentable, strictly speaking). The first patent case since *Biogen* to reach the House of Lords is also on genetic engineering (*Kirin-Amgen Inc v Hoechst Marion Roussel Ltd*, unreported).

The question of inventive step is, of course, a question of fact in each case.

16.3.3 Industrial application

It must be possible to make the product/carry out the process. Patents are not about abstract ideas. The invention must be able to be put into practice. In effect, this requirement is taken care of by the exclusions in PA 1977, s 1(2) and (3).

16.3.4 Exclusions

These are listed in s 1(2) and (3):

'(2) It is hereby declared that the following (among other things) are not inventions for the purposes of this Act, that is to say, anything which consists of—

(a)   a discovery, scientific theory or mathematical method;
(b)   a literary, dramatic, musical or artistic work or any other aesthetic creation whatsoever;
(c)   a scheme, rule or method for performing a mental act, playing a game or doing business, or a program for a computer;
(d)   the presentation of information;

but the foregoing provision shall prevent anything from being treated as an invention for the purposes of this Act only to the extent that a patent or application for a patent relates to that thing as such.

(3) A patent shall not be granted—

(a)   for an invention the publication or exploitation of which would be generally expected to encourage offensive, immoral or anti-social behaviour;
(b)   for any variety of animal or plant or any essentially biological process for the production of animals or plants, not being a micro-biological process or the product of such a process.'

Paragraph (2)(a) deals with discoveries of natural phenomena. These have not been invented by any human, so are not patentable.

Paragraph (2)(b) deals with aesthetic creations which are protected by another IP right, that is copyright.

Paragraph (2)(c) deals with mental acts. How would you know if someone else was performing the mental act in question? Obviously, you could not, so making such matters patentable would be impractical.

Computer programs are also in theory excluded. However, this does not actually mean that computer programs can never be patented. The tendency in recent years has been to grant patents to more and more computer programs. Very broadly, the test is whether the program has a 'technical effect', that is – has it a practical application? One example is *Vicom's Application* [1987] OJ EPO 14 where a program for doing computer-aided design (CAD) of engineering products was held to be patentable.

The approach of the European Patent Office ('EPO') has been more inclined toward granting computer patents since its decisions in two cases – T 935/97 *IBM/Computer Programs* [1999] EPOR 301 and T 1173/97 *IBM/Computer programs* [1999] EPOR

219. The EPO technical board of appeal held that the 'technical effect' requirement simply meant that to be patentable, the application had to go beyond the mere routine operation of a computer. The UK Patent Office has issued a notice on its practice following these EPO decisions, which in effect states that it will follow the EPO's new approach ([1999] RPC 563). Even before then, in *Merrill Lynch's Application* [1989] RPC 561, the applicant did eventually succeed in amending their patent application and being granted a patent for a computer system for executing transactions of Stock Exchange securities (GB 2 180 380B). Overall, therefore, many types of computer programs are in fact patentable.

Paragraph (2)(d) deals with presentation of information. This could not constitute an 'invention'.

Paragraph (3)(b) excludes some biological processes. However, genetic engineering inventions are patentable and indeed are a major area of activity for patent agents and lawyers (see **16.3.2**). Also, producing new varieties of plants is protectable under the Plant Varieties and Seeds Act 1964, which is outside the scope of this book. In the US case on gene engineering (*Diamond v Chakrabarty* 65 Law Ed (2d) 144 (1980)), the Supreme Court held that 'anything under the sun', apart from a human being, should be regarded as patentable.

16.4 THE PATENT SPECIFICATION

The documents required for filing an application are a request for grant and the patent specification. A request for grant is what it says it is. The specification contains an abstract, the description and the claims. The abstract is a summary which is used for reference purposes. The description must disclose the invention sufficiently for it to be performed by a skilled person. The description and the claims must be a consistent match for each other. A case needs to be shown for the grant of a patent, in particular that there has been an inventive step above and beyond the existing technology. The description also needs to provide support for the claims, especially the broadest ones. (Strictly speaking, the 'specification' is the term used for the descriptive part of the application or granted patent, but in common parlance amongst IP lawyers the term 'patent specification' is used to describe the whole document.)

A patent specification is a complex technical and legal document. A patent agent normally drafts it. This is someone with a scientific or engineering qualification, depending on the particular field they are working in. The costs of drafting a specification and dealing with the initial filing of the application are about £2,000 plus VAT. If there are queries from the patent examiner in the Patent Office then this will increase that cost.

If the patent is granted then it is the claims that define the scope of the monopoly granted to the inventor. The analogy of a fence is sometimes used. The idea is that the claims form a fence that surrounds the area which the inventor claims as his own. For someone to be liable for patent infringement, it is enough to infringe one claim in the patent specification (ie to have crossed the fence in only one place).

In drafting the claims, the aim is to include all possible alternatives whilst excluding those that already exist or are obvious. If an alternative is omitted, a competitor could claim that to be their own invention or could use the gap to exploit the technology themselves. On the other hand, if too much is said in the claims, one danger is that improvements in the technology may not be patentable when they arise in the future. The reason is that a patent specification itself becomes part of the state of the art once it is published, so a new application would have to show that it has achieved an inventive step over the previous patent.

The first claim will be the widest. It will state the invention claimed in fairly general terms. Subsequent claims refine the first claim. Each claim usually narrows the invention down a bit. The final claims usually describe the commercial product that is going to be on the market.

The idea is that the wider the area of technology which is claimed, the further away the patent owner can keep rival inventors. In patent litigation, an inevitable area of dispute is that some of the patent claims are too wide and need to be narrowed, or struck out, as being unjustifiable.

The invention must be described in enough detail to allow a person with the requisite skills to carry out the invention. So, if the patent is for interleaving chocolate and ice-cream, the specification must describe the process in sufficient detail to allow a skilled ice cream maker to set up the process.

You should be aware of the difference between this and manufacturing 'know-how'. Manufacturing know-how is the extra tricks of the trade that help you make the process run with greatest efficiency. For example, it might be the speed of the production line to get the most cost effective results, how much air to blow into the ice-cream, or the temperature the room should be at. So, even though the patent specification describes the basic invention, the know-how is often also needed for a licensee because it makes it economically feasible to set up and run the process.

16.4.1 The priority date

The 'first to file' basis of the patent system increases the pressure to be the first person to reach the Patent Office with an application.

Normally, the application or 'filing' date is the patent's priority date. The priority date is the date on which we judge whether the invention is new. The usual reason for the priority date being earlier than the date the papers were filed is that the proprietor is claiming priority from an earlier overseas patent under one of the international conventions (see **16.2**). (An alternative reason which is much less common is that PA 1977, s 15 allows the inventor to file an 'outline application' at an early stage in order to secure an early priority date. The outline application will be less detailed than a full application. A full application must be filed within 12 months.)

16.4.2 Timescale

The Patent Office takes about 18 months to do the initial examination. It is then published as an application and is on the public register (ie the invention can no longer be kept secret). Third parties then have the opportunity to object to the grant of the patent. If there are no major problems then the patent will be granted 6 months or so after publication, that is 2 years after filing the papers. This period counts as part of the 20-year period for the life of the patent. If there is a major problem that delays grant of the patent, then the useful life of the patent once granted could be severely reduced. However, the maximum period between publication and grant of the patent is now 36 months. In addition, there can be other regulatory problems which reduce the useful life of the patent such as obtaining permission to market a new pharmaceutical, or plant protection product. There are EU provisions which allow for an extension of up to 5 years to the life of a pharmaceutical patent (Regulation 1768/92), or to the life of a patent for a plant protection product (Regulation 1610/96). These are intended to compensate for the regulatory delays.

16.5 WHO IS ENTITLED TO GRANT OF A PATENT?

The general rule is that the inventor is the first person entitled. The inventor is the person who devised the invention. This can be more complicated than it seems, for example if there are multiple parties involved (eg *Henry Bros (Magherafelt) Ltd v Ministry of Defence* [1999] RPC 442, where the Court of Appeal held that the test was to determine who had contributed to the main concept of the invention).

16.5.1 Employees

Under PA 1977, s 39, if the inventor is an employee, the patent will belong to the employer if the invention is made in the course of the employee's normal duties, provided an invention might reasonably be expected to result from his duties. This is also the outcome if he owes the employer a special duty (eg a director's duty to his company). In *Greater Glasgow Health Board's Application* [1996] RPC 207, it was held that a hospital doctor who had invented a new device for examining eyes owned the invention himself. He was employed to treat patients, not employed to invent, so the invention did not belong to his employer.

The rule is slightly different from the rule for ownership of copyright but the result is similar. Copyright also does not have any equivalent of the provision relating to employees with a special duty (PA 1977, s 39(1)(b)).

Another important difference is that PA 1977, s 42 does not allow contracting out of these provisions. With copyright there is nothing to stop the employer from putting a provision in the contract of employment that all copyright relevant to the employer's business will belong to the employer. With patents any such provision would be void. However, there is nothing to stop the employer drafting the job description to emphasise that the employee is employed to make inventions.

16.5.2 Compensation for employee inventors

Under PA 1977, s 40, an employee who invents something may be entitled to compensation where the patent belongs to the employer. This is the case if:

- the patent is of outstanding benefit to the employer; and
- it is just that compensation is awarded.

The statutory test is awkward to apply in practice because the criterion is the benefit of the patent, not the benefit the product which was sold on the marketplace. In the case of *Garrison's Patent* [1997] CIPA 297, an invention which provided 2%–3% of the turnover of a small company was held not to be of outstanding benefit, and therefore no compensation was awarded.

In determining the amount of compensation, s 41 gives guidance including factors listed in s 41(3) (eg the nature of the employee's duties and the amount of his remuneration).

Disputes of this type are often settled, and recorded cases are rare (but see **16.10**).

16.6 INFRINGEMENT

16.6.1 Definition of infringment

Infringement arises where a third party engages in the acts prohibited under PA 1977, s 60. As patents are national rights, to infringe a UK patent, the prohibited acts have to occur within the UK:

> **'60 Meaning of infringement**
>
> (1) Subject to the provisions of this section, a person infringes a patent for an invention if, but only if, while the patent is in force, he does any of the following things in the United Kingdom in relation to the invention without the consent of the proprietor of the patent, that is to say—
>
> (a) where the invention is a product, he makes, disposes of, offers to dispose of, uses or imports the product or keeps it whether for disposal or otherwise;
> (b) where the invention is a process, he uses the process or he offers it for use in the United Kingdom when he knows, or it is obvious to a reasonable person in the circumstances, that its use there without the consent of the proprietor would be an infringement of the patent;
> (c) where the invention is a process, he disposes of, offers to dispose of, uses or imports any product obtained directly by means of that process or keeps any such product whether for disposal or otherwise.'

You should note the distinction between infringing acts for a product patent and for a process patent. However, even with a process patent, dealing with the products of that process will be infringement even though the products themselves are not patented.

Section 60(2) makes it an offence to supply or offer to supply 'any means ... for putting the invention into effect'. So, in *Lacroix Duarib SA v Kwikform (UK) Ltd* [1998] FSR 493, the supply of a kit of parts would have infringed the claims in a patent for the completed article.

16.6.2 How do you judge if infringement has occurred?

The first thing to establish is whether the allegedly infringing product or process comes within one of the claims in the patent specification. That is, has the third party crossed the 'fence line' which is constituted by the claims and stepped on to the patentee's monopoly? It is enough for patent infringement if one of the patent claims is infringed.

Patent specifications are drafted with conflicts in mind. Even in the context of patent licensing, the specification only really becomes relevant when the collaboration starts to fall apart.

The first claim is often the most important as it will be the broadest. So why bother then with the other claims that narrow this down? The reason is that when you sue somebody for patent infringement they will invariably counterclaim by saying that the patent is invalid. The patentee then has to defend his claims, particularly in relation to novelty and inventive step. (The 'infringer' will go digging round in the prior art to try to find reasons why the patent should never have been granted in the first place.) The broader the claim the more difficult it is to defend. So, that is why you have the narrower claims too. If claim 1 falls by the wayside, then you may still be able to defend one of the later claims.

16.6.3 Interpreting the claims in the patent specification

How does the court approach the interpretation of the claims? The court takes a 'middle road' between interpreting the claims strictly literally and taking into account what the patentee must have intended. Although the courts are said to be taking the 'purposive' approach from *Catnic Components Ltd and Another v Hill & Smith Ltd* [1982] RPC 183 they tend to be a lot less generous to patentees than this might appear. In effect, the courts tend to hold the view that if the patentee meant to cover a particular variation then they should have claimed it expressly. (It should be remembered that *Catnic* was decided under PA 1949. It concerned a patent for steel lintels for use above doors and windows. The patent claimed a right angle in the cross-sectional shape of the lintel. The defendants lintel was 4–5 degrees away from a right angle but was still held to infringe.)

Improver Corporation and Others v Remington Consumer Products Ltd and Others [1990] FSR 181 was a case which reformulated the test. This was the case about the 'Epilady' device for removing hair. Here, the patented device featured a rotating spring mechanism. The defendant's device performed the same task but a rubber tube mechanism with slits removed the hairs.

Hoffman J restated the issues as two of fact and one of construction:

(i)   does the variant have a material effect upon the way the invention works? If yes, the variant is outside the claim; if no

(ii) would this (ie that the variant had no material effect) have been obvious at the date of publication of the patent to a reader skilled in the art? If no, the variant is outside the claim; if yes

(iii) would the reader skilled in the art nevertheless have understood from the language of the claim that the patentee intended that strict compliance with the primary meaning was an essential requirement of the invention? If yes, the variant is outside the claim.

There was held to be no infringement. It is regarded as an example of poor drafting by the patent agent who apparently did not draft the first claim widely enough to catch the rubber tube variation but restricted it to a helical spring. This is a good illustration of how patent infringement litigation hinges on the precise wording of the claims in the patent specification (see also *Vericore* at **16.3.1**).

It is in the extension of the *Improver* questions away from the area of mechanical devices to chemical compounds that greatest difficulties have arisen (eg *Pharmacia Corporation and Others v Merck & Co Inc and Another* [2001] EWCA Civ 1610, [2001] All ER (D) 227 (Dec)). The Court of Appeal has re-affirmed the *Improver* approach in *Wheatley v Drillsafe Ltd* [2001] RPC 133, though the tests are now referred to as the 'Protocol questions', after the protocol on the interpretation of Article 69 of the European Patent Convention (see **16.2**). This corresponds to PA 1977, s 125(1) on how to interpret the word 'invention'.

On the construction of the claims generally, in *Dyson Appliances Ltd v Hoover* [2001] EWCA Civ 1440, (2001) unreported, 4 October, the Court of Appeal said that construction of the claims was a matter for the judge. Evidence as to the factual situation was helpful, especially to explain the technology, but it was not acceptable to have expert witnesses who gave their own interpretation of the meaning of the claims.

It is also worth noting the words of the Court of Appeal in *Scanvaegt International AS v Pelcombe Ltd* [1998] FSR 786:

> 'lack of clarity ... can result in the patentee being unable to establish infringement. If you cannot define the invention claimed, you cannot conclude that it is being used.'

16.7 INFRINGERS

The acts listed in s 60 would cover those making a product, using a process or disposing of the product of a process. Section 60 covers disposing and keeping, so would cover all the parties in a supply chain, even including the ultimate customer. Do not forget that the acts have to take place in the UK for there to be infringement of a UK patent. In the case of *Stena Rederi Aktiebolag and Another v Irish Ferries Ltd* [2002] EWHC 737 (Ch), [2002] RPC 990; [2003] EWCA Civ 66, (2003) unreported, 6 February, the infringing article, a high-speed passenger ship, only came into UK waters for periods of three hours at a time. The defendants were able to use the provisions in PA 1977, s 60(5)(d) which give exemptions for temporary entry into the UK of ships and aircraft.

16.8 DEFENCES

The first possible defence is that the patentee has consented to the use by granting a licence.

The chief line of defence is an attack on the validity of the patent, in part or in total. If the patent can be proved to be invalid, or at least some claims can be struck out, then the defendant could not be liable for having infringed an invalid claim.

A major use for trainees in an IP department is to have them spend weeks in the bowels of the libraries looking for documents on the topic in question which have been date stamped with a date earlier than the priority date. The patentee is fixed with such knowledge in any language provided the document is within the jurisdiction. The documents may help to strike out some or all of the claims of the patent.

Another defence is that the alleged infringer is in fact a co-owner of the patent, and therefore is entitled to work the patent themselves (PA 1977, s 36).

The use in question could be the subject of an implied licence under the patent (eg *Betts v Wilmott* [1871] 6 Ch App 239). Likewise, repair of a patented product is not infringement of the patent. However, reconditioning the patented article may be regarded as going too far and be an infringing act (*Sirdar Rubber v Wallington, Weston & Co* [1907] 24 RPC 539).

Goods sold on other markets by the patentee or its licensees may be parallel imported into the UK from other EU Member States, under Articles 28 and 30 of the Treaty of Amsterdam. The cases that arise usually concern pharmaceuticals which are high value items and often have their price regulated by national governments (eg *Centrafarm BV and Adrian de Peijper v Sterling Drug Inc* (Case 15/74) [1974] ECR 1147). The exercise of patent rights was held to be incompatible with the free movement of goods in that case. (Centrafarm bought a Sterling product in the UK and re-sold it in the Netherlands for twice the UK price.)

The PA 1977 provides for two general defences in s 60(5):

> 'An act which, apart from this subsection, would constitute an infringement of a patent for an invention shall not do so if—
>
> (a)   it is done privately and for purposes which are not commercial;
> (b)   it is done for experimental purposes relating to the subject matter of the invention.'

The activities in subs (5) are regarded as being for the public good, and therefore the patent system should not be a restraint. The type of activities covered include research by scientists in universities and research institutes.

Section 64 allows a defence of prior use where the defendant was using the relevant technology before the priority date. In practice, this is a very limited defence, as you cannot expand your use, only go on using the process or product exactly as you did before the priority date.

16.9 REMEDIES

Under s 61, the claimant may seek:

- an injunction restraining the defendant;
- an order for delivery up or destruction of the offending goods;
- damages;
- an account of profits (but not as well as damages); or
- a declaration that the patent is valid and has been infringed by the defendant.

Section 62 states that damages may not be awarded against an innocent infringer.

Section 72 allows the court or the Patent Office to revoke a patent on the grounds of failing to meet the criteria for patentability in s 1(1). Section 75 allows for the amendment of patents under the control of the court or the Patent Office.

You need to beware of a threats action under PA 1977, s 70. This is where the patentee can be held liable for a threat to sue someone for patent infringement if the threat turns out to be unjustified. The person threatened can sue for a declaration (that the threats are not justifiable), injunction and damages. Consequently, initial letters in patent disputes are very restrained! There is also a similar provision in relation to various IP rights (see **11.13**, **15.2.11** and **15.3.5**).

16.10 PROPOSED PATENTS ACT (AMENDMENT) BILL

Various revisions to the PA 1977 are being considered.

Changes to ss 39-42 would make it easier for an employee inventor to claim compensation.

The scope of a 'threats' action under s 70 will be reduced, so that a manufacturer or importer cannot use it in regard to possible infringement proceedings against them. The aim is to promote settlement of actions in line with the spirit of the Civil Procedure Rules 1998.

The concept of co-ownership of a patent will be clarified following the criticism of the current law by the Court of Appeal in the *Henry Brothers* case (see **16.5**).

The revisions to the European Patent Convention, which were agreed between the parties in 2000, need to be brought into the PA 1977.

Also, references in the PA 1977 to the Community Patent Convention of 1975 are being removed. The Convention has never been ratified, so the relevant sections have never been brought into force. It looks as if the Community Patent which has now been tentatively agreed (see **16.2**), will come into effect by Council Regulation which will, of course, have direct effect.

Chapter 17

BASICS OF THE LAW OF CONFIDENTIAL INFORMATION

17.1 THE LAW OF CONFIDENTIAL INFORMATION

Basically, the law will uphold a person's obligation to keep a secret, in certain circumstances. The law of confidence is not an IP right in a pure sense but is often classified with some of the mainstream rights. For example, maintaining confidentiality before submitting a patent application is vital to avoid destruction of the invention's novelty.

On the other hand, the law here can give protection in its own right. For example, the owner of confidential information relating to a product or process may decide to keep this 'know-how' secret, rather than formalise matters by seeking formal patent protection. The benefit of this is that a well-guarded secret may be protected indefinitely, rather than simply for the limited period afforded to IP rights (eg 20 years for patents).

Case-law rather than statute govern the law of confidence and, as you would expect, the vast majority of cases relate to circumstances where express obligations of confidence are lacking and implied duties of confidentiality have to be considered. It is, however, important to remember that express obligations can (and often should) be imposed on (eg key employees or independent contractors). See for example *Attorney-General v Observer Ltd and Others; Attorney-General v Times Newspapers Ltd and Another* [1990] AC 109, which concerned the book *Spycatcher* written by Peter Wright, an ex-employee of the security services.

• What is protected?	• secret information
• What benefit is there?	• protects against unauthorised disclosure
• How is it obtained?	• arises automatically (no registration)
• How long does it last?	• indefinitely

17.2 THE ELEMENTS OF CONFIDENTIALITY

The case of *De Maudsley v Palumbo and Others* [1996] FSR 447 demonstrates the difficulties faced by a claimant where no express obligation of confidentiality has been imposed. The facts related to the Ministry of Sound, the celebrated nightclub in Southeast London. The case report states:

'At a supper party held on November 1, 1989 between the plaintiff, the first defendant and the latter's girlfriend, the plaintiff communicated to the first defendant his idea for a night club which he claimed had five novel features:

(1)   it would be legally open all night long;
(2)   of large size with decor of a "high tech industrial" warehouse style;

(3) it would have separate areas for dancing, resting and socialising, and a VIP lounge;

(4) an enclosed dance area of acoustic design ensuring excellent sound quality, light and atmosphere, with no leakage of those elements beyond its environment; and

(5) it would employ top disc jockeys from the United Kingdom and around the world.'

In the autumn of 1991 the defendants opened a nightclub called the Ministry of Sound, featuring some but not all of the claimant's ideas. The claimant was excluded from the project and subsequently sued for (inter alia) breach of confidence.

The judge (Knox J) relied on the three-point test from *Coco v AN Clark (Engineers) Ltd* [1969] RPC 41. This is as follows.

17.2.1 First element: Did the information have the necessary quality of confidence about it?

Knox J stated:

> 'Before the status of confidential information can be achieved by a concept or an idea, it is necessary to have gone far beyond identifying a desirable goal. A considerable degree of preliminary development of a definite product needs to be shown.'

He found that the claimant's ideas were too vague to constitute confidential information.

He also found that, in order to merit protection, the idea must contain some element of originality. He took each element of the claimant's proposal and criticised them for lack of novelty and/or vagueness.

He accepted Hirst J's analysis in *Fraser and Others v Thames Television Ltd and Others* [1984] 1 QB 44 of the requirements for a literary, creative or entertainment idea to be protected as confidential information. This case concerned use of the law of confidential information to protect an idea for a television series about a female pop group. (Copyright will not protect a mere idea in these circumstances, see *Green v Broadcasting Corporation of New Zealand* [1989] 2 All ER 1086, which concerned the format for a game show.)

Hirst J said that the idea must:

(a) contain some element of originality;

(b) be clearly identifiable (as an idea of the confider);

(c) be of potential commercial attractiveness; and

(d) be sufficiently well developed to be capable of actual realisation.

17.2.2 Second element: Was the information imparted in circumstances importing an obligation of confidence?

The problem here for the claimant was that the relevant occasion on which he had imparted the information was a social one, not a business context. The claimant acknowledged in his evidence that he had deliberately refrained from explaining that the information was confidential 'because [he] did not want to blow the deal there and then'. Finally, there was no accepted trade practice in this area to substantiate the claimant's claim.

17.2.3 Third element: Was there any unauthorised use of the information?

Here, the judge held that the claimant's ideas and the defendant's club did not overlap to a sufficient degree to constitute unauthorised use.

The claimant's action therefore failed on all three counts. However, the judge summarised the situation as follows:

> 'Mr de Maudsley was in my view rather shabbily treated in that he was encouraged to think that he would be part of the enterprise but was only told that this would not be so, long after Mr Palumbo and Mr Waterhouse had decided, almost certainly justifiably because of Mr de Maudsley's rather difficult character and limited abilities, that he would not be included in their project.'

The moral of the story is not to rely upon an implied duty of confidence. It is far better to inject certainty into the situation with the use of a written confidentiality agreement.

In *Cray Valley Ltd v Deltech Europe Ltd and Others* [2003] EWHC 728 (Ch), (2003) unreported, 16 April, an action for breach of confidence in relation to the manufacture of industrial resins failed. There were no express undertakings of confidence by the former employees in question. It was held that the information did not have the necessary quality of confidence, not least as much of it had been published already and was easy to reverse engineer. It was not imparted in circumstances importing an obligation of confidence, but merely in the normal running of a factory without any express instructions to employees to treat it as confidential. A claim for breach of copyright did succeed.

17.3 REMEDIES

The most important measure will often be an injunction to prevent disclosure of the information, that is a restraining order in advance. Once the information has been released it is usually too late to seek an injunction. However, an injunction may be granted in regard to confidential information that is of commercial value where:

(a) there are two rival businesses and not to grant an injunction would give the wrong-doer an advantage (eg *Speed Seal Products Ltd v Paddington and Another* [1986] 1 All ER 91); or

(b) use of the 'springboard' doctrine where one business would gain an unfair advantage over its rivals because of unauthorised disclosure to it of commercial information (eg *Roger Bullivant v Ellis* [1987] FSR 172).

Compensatory damages are available for breach of confidence (see *Seager v Copydex Ltd* [1967] 2 All ER 415).

An account of the defendant's profits is also possible (see *Peter Pan Manufacturing Corporation v Corsets Silhouette Ltd* [1964] 1 WLR 96).

An order for delivery up, or destruction under oath, of the offending document or articles made by use of the information is also possible (see *Industrial Furnaces Ltd v Reaves and Another* [1970] RPC 605).

17.4 A RIGHT OF PRIVACY AND THE HUMAN RIGHTS ACT 1998?

In the somewhat unusual case of *Douglas and Others v Hello! Ltd and Others* [2003] EWHC 786 (Ch), [2003] All ER (D) 209 (Apr), breach of confidence was used to prevent publication by a rival magazine of wedding coverage granted by two film stars to a magazine. It was held that the photographs of the event had the necessary quality of confidence about them, and deserved protection as a trade secret. The illicit photographer from the rival magazine (the defendant) had been under a duty of confidentiality when attending the wedding. The defendant knew of the arrangement between the couple and the other magazine, but had deliberately ignored how the photographs were taken. The law of confidence was held to have protected the claimants' privacy rights under Human Rights Act 1998, Sch 1, Part 1, art 8. It was therefore held that it was unnecessary to consider whether the Act had created a new right of privacy.

In *A v B (A Company) and Another* [2002] EWCA Civ 337, [2002] 2 All ER 545, the Court of Appeal refused to uphold an injunction under the privacy provisions of the Act restraining two newspapers from publishing details of the extra-marital affairs of the claimant, a professional footballer.

In *Campbell v MGN Ltd* [2002] ECWA Civ 1373, [2003] QB 633, the Court of Appeal again refused to uphold an injunction against a newspaper restraining publication of sensitive information about a well-known media personality. She had been having treatment for drug addiction having previously denied drug abuse. The court held that the public interest in publishing the story overrode her privacy rights under the Human Rights Act 1998.

PART IV

COMPETITION LAW

Chapter 18

COMPETITION LAW AND COMMERCIAL AGREEMENTS

18.1 INTRODUCTION

The topic of EC competition introduced in the LPC Resource Books *Pervasive and Core Topics* and *Business Law and Practice* (Jordans).

This chapter aims to place it into context by considering the ways in which it may affect the drafting and operation of commercial agreements. In addition, the chapter also briefly considers the current state of English competition law and its impact on commercial agreements. Before looking at these two areas of competition law, however, it may be useful to consider some of the general points which arise when advising on competition law in the context of commercial agreements.

18.1.1 Advice to clients

It is important for the solicitor to appreciate the different ways in which competition law may be relevant to a client's business, and to be able to advise accordingly. For example, a client who is expanding his business into continental Europe may realise that there could be competition law difficulties and seek advice specifically on this point, but what about the client who is simply expanding within the UK? What if a client intends to make a deal with another company in the UK which will effectively keep competitors based in other EU Member States out of the UK market in a particular product?

It is also important for the solicitor to keep the client's documentation under review. For example, it may be necessary to advise a client that a particular commercial agreement can be used for deals which have no connection at all with the EU, but must not be used for deals which may affect trade and competition within the EU, or even for deals outside the EU which could have some impact within the EU. The solicitor may wish to 'audit' the client's documentation from time to time, checking that each document is still suitable for the client's purposes, is being used by the client in the correct way (and, of course, that it still complies with EC law).

18.1.2 Which law applies?

A commercial agreement between two parties based in the UK might, of course, be affected by English competition law (see **18.2**). However, because the relevant Articles of the European Community Treaty (often still referred to as the 'Treaty of Rome') have direct effect in each Member State, these may apply to the agreement as well. It is important to remember that an agreement does not have to be between businesses based in different Member States for EC competition law to apply; broadly speaking, as long as the agreement may affect the natural flow of trade between Member States, EC competition law is potentially relevant. Thus, even where both parties are based in the same Member State, the solicitor must be aware of its possible impact. EC competition law could also apply to an agreement made between a business based within the EU and one based outside if there is a strong trading interaction between the markets involved. Although the Commission would normally have practical problems in enforcing EC competition law in these circumstances, this will not stop it becoming involved. In addition, it should be noted that parts of the EC Treaty, including its competition law rules, (in effect) formally apply to certain non-EU countries following the creation of the European Economic Area (see **18.1.3**).

Now that the Competition Act 1998 (CA 1998) (see **18.2**) has been in force for some time, the English and EC competition authorities are working out how to draw the dividing line between the ambit of EC competition law and English competition law. It is, however, still likely to take some time for this to become really clear.

18.1.3 The European Economic Area

The impact of EC competition law widened when the EEA, came into existence on 1 January 1994. The Member States of the EEA are the Member States of the European Union (which are (at the time of writing), in alphabetical order, Austria, Belgium, Denmark, Finland, France, Germany, Greece, the Republic of Ireland, Italy, Luxembourg, The Netherlands, Portugal, Spain, Sweden and the UK) and Iceland, Liechtenstein and Norway. Broadly speaking, the EEA Agreement extends many of the basic legal rules of the EC to all nations within the EEA, including the principles of free movement of goods, persons, services and capital, and competition law. As far as competition law is concerned, Articles 53 and 54 of the EEA Agreement are similar to Articles 81 EC and 82 EC (Articles 85 and 86, prior to the coming into force of the Treaty of Amsterdam in May 1999), except that they apply where an agreement may affect trade between the countries of the EEA.

Note that, as from 1 May 2004, the European Union will expand by 10 new Member States: Cyprus, the Czech Republic, Estonia, Hungary, Latvia, Lithuania, Malta, Poland, Slovakia and Slovenia.

18.1.4 Drafting and competition law

The solicitor should always consider how competition law problems can be minimised by appropriate drafting. If an agreement is likely to be affected by EC competition law, the solicitor should at least be able to avoid obvious drafting pitfalls (such as drafting export bans and price-fixing clauses) and should also consider taking advantage of any relevant block exemption (see **18.3.6**). However, both solicitor and client must appreciate that with many agreements, it is difficult to be certain that problems with EC competition law will not arise. This is also true of the system of English competition law introduced by the CA 1998: see **18.2.1**.

18.1.5 Types of agreement

This chapter is concerned exclusively with individual vertical commercial agreements (those between parties at different levels of supply, such as manufacturer and wholesaler, supplier and distributor, principal and agent). It does not consider horizontal agreements (those between parties at the same level of supply, such as manufacturers). It also concentrates on the distribution agreement (in particular, the exclusive distribution agreement, where the supplier agrees that the distributor will be the only authorised reseller of the supplier's goods within a defined territory).

18.1.6 The relevant competition law

English law

This chapter is concerned entirely with the (still relatively new) system of competition law introduced by the CA 1998 (see further **18.2**).

EC law

In relation to EC law, this chapter is primarily concerned with Article 81 EC. It is the Article most likely to apply to individual commercial agreements, as it applies to agreements and other arrangements which may affect trade between Member States and which have as their object or effect the prevention, restriction or distortion of competition within the common market (see further **18.3**).

18.2 ENGLISH COMPETITION LAW

18.2.1 The Competition Act 1998

A complete reform of English competition law relating to individual commercial agreements was officially proposed as long ago as 1989. Numerous criticisms had been levelled against the system of competition law embodied in (primarily) the Restrictive Trade Practices Act 1976 (RTPA 1976): in particular, that it was too complex, involved a bureaucratic registration system, lacked effective enforcement provisions and, because of its concentration on the formal provisions of an agreement, was capable of catching harmless agreements and letting through anti-competitive ones. It was not until the autumn of 1997, however, that a Competition Bill was finally presented; it received Royal Assent as the CA 1998 on 9 November 1998.

The CA 1998 (subject to transitional provisions) repealed the Restrictive Trade Practices Acts 1976 and 1977, the Resale Prices Act 1976 (RPA 1976) and most of the Competition Act 1980. Its main provisions are modelled very closely on EC competition law in the form of Articles 81 EC and 82 EC. These provisions are known in practice as the Chapter I and Chapter II Prohibitions. The Chapter I Prohibition (contained in s 2) is the equivalent of Article 81 EC, and the Chapter II Prohibition (contained in s 18) is the equivalent of Article 82 EC.

The CA 1998 came into force on 1 March 2000.

The UK authorities must deal with cases under the Act in a way that ensures consistency with EC competition law (CA 1998, s 60, the 'governing principles' section), both in interpreting and applying the Act.

The Office of Fair Trading (OFT) is responsible for administering the CA 1998; there is a Competition Commission to hear appeals from its decisions.

18.2.2 The Chapter I prohibition

The Chapter I prohibition, contained in s 2 of CA 1998, is almost identical in its wording to Article 81 EC; the main difference is that the Act refers to 'the UK', where Article 81 EC refers to 'the common market' or 'Member States'. Like Article 81 EC, the prohibition applies to both informal and formal arrangements, whether or not they are in writing. Also, like Article 81(1) EC, CA 1998 lists specific types of arrangement which are caught by the prohibition (eg agreeing to fix purchase or selling prices or other trading conditions).

However, as with Article 81 EC, the list merely provides guidance; the important thing is whether the arrangement between the parties falls within the prohibition.

An agreement, decision or concerted practice prohibited by s 2(1) is void (s 2(4)).

18.2.3 The Chapter II prohibition

This prohibition, contained in s 18 of CA 1998, is almost identical in its wording to Article 82 EC. It covers the abuse by one or more undertakings of a dominant position within the UK in the relevant market (in Article 82 EC, 'market' covers both the relevant product market and relevant geographical market: the position will be the same under the Chapter II prohibition) if it may affect trade within the UK.

Dominance will be assessed in the same way as it is under Article 82 EC, and market share will often be the most significant factor. Generally, an undertaking is unlikely to be considered dominant if it has a market share of less than 40%. However, as in EC law, other factors will also be relevant when assessing dominance. For example, an undertaking with a lower market share may be considered dominant if it structures the market in such a way to enable it to act independently of its competitors. Like Article 82 EC, CA 1998 gives specific examples of types of conduct that are likely to be considered an abuse (eg imposing unfair purchase or selling prices).

However, as with the Chapter I prohibition, this only provides guidance; it is whether or not the prohibition itself actually applies which is important.

18.2.4 Investigative powers

The OFT has wide-ranging investigative powers under the CA 1998 (ss 25–31 of Chapter III cover these powers). These include the power to enter premises and to require the production of documents that he considers relevant to the investigation (cf the Commission's powers of investigation under Articles 81 EC and 82 EC).

18.2.5 Consequences of infringement

Enforcement

The rules on enforcement are in ss 32–41 of Chapter III of CA 1998, and give the OFT substantial powers. For example, an offending agreement may be terminated or amended by order of the OFT. Any offending conduct may also be ordered to cease.

The OFT has the power to order interim measures which require an undertaking to refrain from engaging in suspected illegal activity while he investigates the matter. This power will only be exercised when he considers it necessary to take urgent action to protect third parties from suffering serious irreparable damage, or to protect the wider public interest.

Financial penalties

Under s 56 of CA 1998, infringing undertakings may be fined up to 10% of their UK turnover for infringement of either Chapter I or Chapter II prohibitions.

18.2.6 Methods of avoiding infringement

There are various ways in which an agreement may avoid infringement (primarily infringement of the Chapter I prohibition, but in one case, the Chapter II prohibition).

Limited immunity

Section 39 of CA 1998 provides a 'limited immunity' from the Chapter I prohibition for what it refers to as 'small agreements'. This means that the agreement is immune from penalties (ie fines) under s 36. A 'small agreement' is one where the parties' joint turnover does not exceed £20 million (s 39(1)(a) and the Competition Act (Small Agreements and Conduct of Minor Significance) Regulations 2000, SI 2000/262). It is very important to note, however, that a 'price-fixing agreement' cannot be a small agreement (s 39(1)(b)). A 'price-fixing agreement' is defined by s 39(9) as:

> 'an agreement which has as its object or effect, or one of its objects or effects, restricting the freedom of a party to the agreement to determine the price to be charged (otherwise than as between that party and another party to the agreement) for the product, service or other matter to which the agreement relates.'

Even where the agreement qualifies as a small agreement, the OFT has power to withdraw the immunity if as a result of an investigation, it considers that the agreement is likely to infringe the Chapter I prohibition (s 39(3), (4)).

Section 40 provides a limited immunity from the Chapter II prohibition where there is 'conduct of minor significance'; this applies where an undertaking's turnover is less than £50 million (s 40(2) and Competition Act 1998 (Small Agreements and Conduct of Minor Significance) Regulations 2000, SI 2000/262: see above). As with s 39, the immunity given is immunity from fines, and can be withdrawn if, following an investigation, the OFT considers that conduct of minor significance is nevertheless likely to infringe the Chapter II prohibition (s 40(3) and (4)).

Appreciability

In administering CA 1998, the OFT and the courts will also respect an 'appreciable effect' test, the principle of which is imported from EC law (it is not specifically provided for in the Act). This means that an agreement will not infringe the Chapter I prohibition where the parties' joint market share does not exceed 25% (cf the EC threshold under the Notice on Agreements of Minor Importance – see **18.3.5**).

It appears that if the parties' joint turnover does not exceed £20 million, and there is no price-fixing, the agreement will be immune from fines under s 39 unless limited immunity is withdrawn (it is possible that the 25% 'appreciability' threshold will then be relevant): in any other case, the 'appreciability' test above will apply.

Vertical agreements

Vertical agreements (eg distribution agreements) are excluded altogether from the Chapter I prohibition as a result of the Competition Act (Land and Vertical

Agreements) Order 2000, SI 2000/310. It is important, however, to note that this exclusion does not apply where the agreement fixes prices.

Individual exemption

Individual exemption is available from the OFT under CA 1998, s 4 on broadly the same terms as it is under Article 81 EC (see s 9). It must be applied for (s 4(1)), and can be cancelled (s 5) if, for example, circumstances change.

Block exemption

Exemption for particular categories of agreement can be given by the Secretary of State for Trade and Industry on the recommendation of the OFT (s 6(1), (2)). An agreement which falls within a category specified in a block exemption order is exempt from the Chapter I prohibition (s 6(3)). Criteria for making a block exemption order are the same as those for granting individual exemption (s 9). In practice, it is likely that parallel exemption (see below) will be more significant than block exemption. An example of block exemption made under the CA 1998 is that granted for public transport ticketing schemes, which came into force on 1 March 2001.

Parallel exemption

Under s 10 of CA 1998, an agreement, decision or practice is exempt from the Chapter I prohibition if it is exempt from 'the Community prohibition' (ie Article 81 EC) for one of the following reasons.

(a)   It falls within an EC block exemption (eg Regulation 2790/99: see **18.3.9**).
(b)   It has been given individual exemption by the Commission.
(c)   It has been exempted by virtue of an opposition procedure (see **19.4**).

Section 10(2) further provides that an agreement is exempt from the Chapter I prohibition if it does not affect trade between Member States, but otherwise falls within a category of agreement which is exempt from Article 81 EC by virtue of a Regulation.

It is not necessary to apply for a parallel exemption.

Guidance

Sections 13 and 15 of CA 1998 cover the ability of the OFT to give 'guidance' about an agreement. A party to an agreement who thinks that the agreement may infringe the Chapter I prohibition may notify the agreement to the OFT and ask for guidance as to whether there is an infringement. If the OFT gives guidance that the agreement is unlikely to infringe, or is likely to be exempt, then by s 15(2), it 'is to take no further action' in relation to the agreement unless, for example, circumstances change, or it has reasonable suspicion that the information on which it based its guidance is false, misleading or incomplete.

18.2.7 Procedures

Undertakings do not generally have to notify the OFT of any agreements or conduct (although there are exceptions to this; for example, individual exemption can only be granted following notification). As noted above, they may, for example, seek guidance as to whether a particular agreement infringes the Chapter I prohibition or may benefit from an exemption.

18.2.8 Transitional provisions

For a year after the coming into force of the CA 1998, transitional provisions applied to 'old' agreements (very broadly, agreements which were already in existence before the Act). Although problems relating to these provisions may still be relevant in practice for some time after their expiry, consideration of these provisions is outside the scope of this book.

18.2.9 The Enterprise Act 2002

This Act contains significant competition law provisions which came into force in June 2003. Much of the Act is concerned with instituting a new merger control regime within the UK, and is therefore outside the scope of this course. However, it is important to note that Part 6 of the Act creates (for the first time) a criminal offence in relation to certain types of anti-competitive arrangement.

By s 188, it is a criminal offence (the 'cartel offence') for an individual dishonestly to agree with one or more other persons to make or implement certain types of cartel arrangements. These include agreements which directly or indirectly fix prices for the supply of goods or services in the UK, and agreements to share markets or customers in certain circumstances.

The offence can only be committed where those participating in the arrangements are at the same level of the supply chain (ie it only applies to horizontal agreements).

By s 190(4), the Office of Fair Trading can issue a notice to prevent proceedings (known as a 'no action letter') against a person who would otherwise be liable to prosecution for the offence; the idea is to encourage 'whistleblowers' who have been participating in a cartel to come forward and give details about the cartel to the OFT. The OFT is given extensive powers to investigate persons suspected of committing the offence.

18.3 EC COMPETITION LAW

18.3.1 The relevant competition law

This chapter concentrates on Article 81 EC; as indicated previously, it is the Article which is most likely to be relevant when drafting a commercial agreement. However, when considering the general impact of EC competition law, the solicitor should also be aware of the following Articles.

(1) Article 3(1)(g) EC, which provides that the activities of the EC shall include a system ensuring that competition in the internal market is not distorted.
(2) Articles 28–30 EC (formerly Articles 30–36 of the EC Treaty), which prohibit restrictions imposed by import and export controls (and measures having equivalent effect) on the free movement of goods around the common market. These Articles will be only indirectly relevant to most individual commercial agreements, but can be significant where the licensing of intellectual property rights is concerned. This topic is considered further in Chapter 19.

(3) Article 82 EC, which prohibits the abuse by one or more undertakings of a dominant position within the common market or a substantial part of it insofar as it may affect trade between Member States. This Article, which is covered more fully in the two Resource Books mentioned at **18.3.2**, is not considered further in this chapter, because it will usually apply to the activities of one undertaking rather than to an agreement between undertakings. The solicitor should always be aware, however, that even the most careful drafting of an agreement cannot prevent Article 82 EC from applying if one of the parties is dominant within a particular product and geographical market, and the Commission finds that there is abuse of that dominant position.

18.3.2 Article 81 EC – a brief reminder

The basic principles of EC competition law are considered in the LPC Resource Books *Pervasive and Core Topics* and *Business Law and Practice* (Jordans). However, a brief reminder of Article 81 EC may be useful. It is important to note that the Treaty of Amsterdam simply re-numbered this Article; it did not make any changes to the substance of it.

Article 81(1) EC prohibits as incompatible with the common market any agreements, decisions by associations of undertakings and concerted practices which may affect trade between Member States and which have as their object or effect the prevention, restriction or distortion of competition within the common market. The Article contains a non-exhaustive list of the types of business practice which are likely to infringe this prohibition. Agreements need not be formal or legally binding for Article 81 EC to apply, and both actual and potential effects on trade can be considered. It is also important to remember that the Article can apply to agreements confined to one Member State (or where one or more parties are based outside the EU altogether), and that it is not necessary for the parties to intend to restrict competition. It is not always easy to predict when Article 81 EC will apply to vertical agreements, but distribution agreements which contain territorial restrictions are especially at risk. For example, a distribution agreement between an English supplier and a French distributor, which gives the distributor 'exclusive territory' (ie the distributor is the only authorised seller of the supplier's goods in France) is potentially likely to infringe Article 81(1) EC. The agreement may affect trade and competition within the common market if, for example, it makes it more difficult for other businesses to break into the French market for the product in question or it cuts down on the sources of supply for French customers. (However, note that this potential infringement of Article 81 EC may in fact be sanctioned by block exemption: see **18.3.9**.)

18.3.3 Effect of infringing Article 81 EC – a brief reminder

It may be possible to sever terms which infringe Article 81 EC from an agreement without invalidating the rest of the agreement. Whether this can be done is a matter of national law, not EC law: it will therefore depend on what the governing law of the agreement provides about severance. If the offending terms cannot be severed, however, the whole agreement will be void: Article 81(2) EC. Note that it may be impossible to sever offending provisions from a distribution agreement if they are 'exclusive territory' provisions as described above, because they will normally be part of the consideration for the agreement. There may also be other consequences of infringement. For example, the Commission can impose fines on the parties for infringement of Article 81 EC, and undertakings which have been affected by an infringement may be able to take proceedings in their national courts to obtain damages and/or an injunction.

18.3.4 The Commission's powers

The Commission (strictly speaking, the Competition Directorate-General, formerly known as DG IV) has wide powers to enforce EC competition law, including the power to obtain information about undertakings and their agreements and business practices. Until recently, these powers were contained in Regulation 17/62; however, from 1 May 2004, they are to be found in Regulation 1/2003.

Under the old enforcement regime, the Commission (and only the Commission) had power to grant individual exemption under Article 81(3) EC to an agreement which infringed Article 81(1) EC. To gain this individual exemption, an agreement had to satisfy the conditions laid down in Article 81(3) EC; broadly speaking, this meant the parties notifying the agreement to the Commission, and the Commission being satisfied that the operation of the agreement benefited consumers without unduly restricting competition.

In practice, the old enforcement regime was unsatisfactory in a number of respects, in particular, those relating to individual exemption and the notification system. The Commission could not cope with all the requests for individual exemption, very few were actually granted, and the Commission usually responded to requests with a comfort letter (a non-binding but persuasive statement of the Commission's opinion about the status of an agreement in relation to Article 81 EC).

Under the new regime, notification to the Commission and grant of individual exemption by the Commission cease to exist. Instead, the Regulation introduces a process of what is in effect self-assessment by the parties to an agreement to gain exemption from the provisions of Article 81(1) EC. Undertakings will have to assess for themselves whether their agreement satisfies the conditions set out in Article 81(3) EC (note that these conditions are not in any way altered by the new Regulation). If disputes arise as to whether an agreement fulfils the Article 81(3) EC conditions, these will be settled by national competition authorities (in the United Kingdom, this is the Office of Fair Trading), and, ultimately by the national courts. The Commission retains a residual power to declare that Article 81 EC is inapplicable in cases where the Community public interest requires it, but it is expected that this power will be used only rarely.

At the time of writing (September 2003) the Commission is beginning to issue further guidance on a number of important aspects of the Regulation's operation, including the precise role of national competition authorities and courts, and how enforcement policy will be co-ordinated between Member States. It is also likely that with the greater emphasis on the role of national authorities and courts in enforcing EC law, that some overlaps will arise between EC and national competition law which will need to be resolved. In the UK, for example, the OFT is proposing to abolish the individual exemption and notification procedure under the Competition Act 1998.

18.3.5 Avoiding the impact of Article 81 EC

Because the operation of Article 81 EC is effects-based rather than form-based, it is difficult to be sure of avoiding infringement simply by drafting an agreement in a particular way. However, depending on the circumstances and the type of agreement, there are various ways in which the solicitor can minimise the risks of infringement. This section considers the most important ways in the context of the Wood Magic example from Chapter 5.

Example

Assume that before seeking advice on their proposed distribution agreement, Wood Magic and Bois Massif had in principle agreed the following terms:

(1) Wood Magic agreed that Bois Massif would get France as its exclusive territory.
(2) In return, Bois Massif agreed that:
  – it would not export the goods from France;
  – it would not solicit orders from outside France;
  – it would not meet unsolicited orders from outside France;
  – it would not sell below the prices set by Wood Magic.

Would an agreement on these terms run into difficulties with Article 81(1) EC, and, if so, would it be possible to avoid this happening?

Article 81(1) EC problems

Although it may seem obvious to say so, the solicitor first needs to assess whether Article 81(1) EC would apply to the proposed agreement before looking for ways round it. In particular, it is important to remember that Article 81(1) EC will not apply to a distribution agreement simply because it *is* a distribution agreement. The question is whether the agreement and its terms may affect trade and competition within the common market. The proposed agreement here certainly has the capacity to do so, because its terms amount to territorial restrictions, export bans (direct and indirect) customer restrictions and price-fixing. How (if at all) could Wood Magic and Bois Massif contract on those terms without infringing Article 81(1) EC? This requires consideration of the various ways of avoiding the impact of Article 81 EC.

Parent and subsidiary companies

An agency or distribution agreement made between a parent and a subsidiary company will fall outside Article 81 EC. The companies will be taken to be one undertaking, and so the Article cannot apply; there is no 'agreement between undertakings'. This is a potentially useful way of avoiding the impact of Article 81 EC, but is clearly irrelevant to Wood Magic and Bois Massif.

Agency agreements

As already noted in Chapter 5, many agency agreements will fall outside Article 81 EC because they are covered by paras 12–20 of the Commission's Notice of May 2000 which provides guidelines on vertical restraints. It may be possible, therefore, to avoid problems by drafting the agreement to be a 'genuine' agency agreement if this is commercially appropriate. Again, however, this will not be of use to Wood Magic and Bois Massif, who have chosen to enter into a distribution agreement.

The 'de minimis' provision

The agreement may be covered by the Notice on Agreements of Minor Importance. The Commission adopted its most recent version of this Notice (OJ 2001/C 368/07) in December 2001. As a basic proposition, if the Notice applies to an agreement the Commission will not take proceedings against the parties for infringement of Article 81 EC.

Under Point 7 of the Notice, the Commission accepts that, in certain circumstances, agreements between undertakings which affect trade between Member States nevertheless do not appreciably restrict competition within the meaning of Article 81(1) EC. These circumstances are:

(1) where the agreement is made between undertakings which are actual or potential competitors (known as 'agreements between competitors') the agreement does not appreciably restrict competition if the aggregate market share of the parties does not exceed 10% on any of the relevant markets affected by the agreement;

(2) where the agreement is made between undertakings which are not actual or potential competitors (known as 'agreements between non-competitors'), the agreement does not appreciably restrict competition if the market share held by each of the parties to the agreement does not exceed 15% on any of the relevant markets affected by the agreement.

A footnote to Point 7 of the Notice indicates that guidance on whether businesses are actual or potential competitors can be found in a set of Commission guidelines on the applicability of Article 81 EC to horizontal co-operation agreements (OJ C3 6.1.2001). However, broadly speaking, horizontal agreements are likely to be 'agreements between competitors', and vertical agreements are likely to be 'agreements between non-competitors'.

If an agreement is difficult to classify, the 10% threshold is applicable.

Point 4 of the Notice clearly states that in cases covered by the Notice, 'the Commission will not institute proceedings' (ie for infringement of Article 81 EC). Although strictly speaking, the Notice does not bind the Commission, Point 4 is so clearly expressed that it is likely to be difficult in practice for the Commission to go back on it. The Notice will not, however, automatically bind national courts, nor will it prevent third parties from making a claim based on infringement of Article 81.

To benefit from the Notice, the agreement must not contain any hardcore restrictions: Point 11(2) of the Notice makes it clear that for agreements between non-competitors, these hardcore restrictions are the same as those in Article 4 of the vertical agreements block exemption (see **18.3.7**) which include price fixing and certain customer/territorial restrictions. In addition, Point 8 of the Notice seems to reserve a certain amount of discretion to the Commission where certain market conditions ('cumulative foreclosure effect') apply.

Could Wood Magic and Bois Massif benefit from the Notice? It seems likely that this is an agreement between non-competitors; however, we do not currently know the market share which each of them enjoys in the relevant market (Point 10 of the Notice gives some guidance on the calculation of market share: in particular, the Commission's Notice on market definition (OJ C372 9.12.1997, p 5) is relevant). However, even if the shares are within the 15% threshold, there is a problem as the proposed agreement contains hardcore terms (eg fixed minimum prices, export ban). As long as the hardcore terms remain in the agreement, the Notice will not apply.

18.3.6 Block exemption

The general principle behind block exemption is to ensure that the Commission does not have to investigate agreements which may at first sight appear to infringe Article 81(1) EC, but do not in practice impose serious restrictions on competition (and which may in fact stimulate trade and benefit consumers), thereby satisfying the conditions under Article 81(3) EC. Block exemption is given in the form of Commission Regulations, most of which essentially provide guidance on which terms are acceptable (and which are unacceptable) in particular agreements (a rather different approach is taken by the relatively new block exemption given by Regulation 2790/99; see **18.3.7**).

Block exemption should be unaffected by the new enforcement regime introduced by Regulation 1/2003. It will remain the case that if an agreement falls squarely within the terms of a block exemption, it will fall outside Article 81(1) EC, and the Commission will take no interest in it (unless circumstances change). It is therefore advantageous for the parties to draft an agreement to fall within any relevant block exemption; the existing block exemption Regulations all give relatively clear guidance (albeit in a variety of ways) as to when they will (and will not) apply, and, at least while the operation of the new regime is worked out in practice, this is likely to be easier and safer than relying on the new 'self-assessment' regime introduced by Regulation 1/2003.

18.3.7 Block exemption and vertical agreements

The position in relation to vertical agreements changed substantially in 2000 with the introduction of a new style of block exemption.

This block exemption, contained in Regulation 2790/99, was adopted on 22 December 1999.

Strictly speaking, the block exemption came into force on 1 January 2000. However, it did not begin to apply to agreements until 1 June 2000 (see note on Article 13 below).

As previously noted in relation to agency agreements, the Commission has produced a Notice giving guidelines on vertical restraints generally; the bulk of these guidelines relate to this block exemption and its application. These guidelines are likely to be helpful in practice as an indication of the Commission's thinking, but cannot be a substitute for study and application of the text of the Regulation itself.

Two features of Regulation 2790/99 are particularly significant.

(a) By Article 3, the block exemption does not apply where the market share of the relevant party (usually the seller: see the discussion of Article 3 below) exceeds 30%.

(b) Unlike its predecessors (and most other existing block exemptions), this block exemption has no list of permissible terms (a so-called 'white list'). Instead, it proceeds on the basis that a term is acceptable unless specifically forbidden (see the discussion of Articles 4 and 5 below). This is confirmed by para 21 of the guidelines, which actually state that the Regulation 'creates a presumption of legality for vertical agreements, depending on the market share of the supplier or buyer' (referred to as the 'safe harbour' created by the Regulation).

The block exemption in outline

PREAMBLE

As is customary with block exemptions, the initial recitals explain the Commission's reasons for granting block exemption in the way in which this Regulation has done (eg Recitals 8 and 9 explain the policy behind the market share threshold in Article 3). It is therefore helpful to study the preamble carefully before going on to the Articles themselves.

Broadly speaking, the block exemption applies to vertical agreements for the sale of goods/supply of services where the relevant party has a market share of no more than 30%.

ARTICLE 1

This is the block exemption's 'definitions section'. Note, in particular, the definitions of 'non-compete obligation' (see the note on Article 5 below), 'exclusive supply obligation' (important for the application of Article 3: see below) and 'selective distribution system' (important for the application of Article 4: see below).

Note also that the vital definition of 'vertical agreement' does not appear here; it is found in the next Article.

ARTICLE 2

This Article states the scope of the exemption provided by the block exemption. Article 2(1) in effect provides that Article 81(1) EC will not apply to:

- agreements or concerted practices,
- entered into between two or more undertakings,
- where the undertakings operate in such a way that the agreement or practice satisfies the definition of a 'vertical agreement'.

For an agreement to be a vertical agreement within the meaning of Article 2(1), the parties must operate at a different level of the production or distribution chain, and the agreement or practice must relate to the conditions under which the parties may 'purchase, sell or resell certain goods or services'. This will cover, for example, all types of distribution agreements, franchising agreements and agency agreements.

Note that Regulation 2790/99 is capable of applying to a situation where more than two undertakings are involved, and that it extends to the provision of services.

Article 2(2) allows the block exemption to apply (subject to certain conditions) to vertical agreements between, for example, a trade association and its members or suppliers.

Article 2(3) allows the block exemption to cover vertical agreements under which IP rights are licensed or assigned, as long as the IP provisions of the agreement do not constitute the 'primary object' of the agreement.

Article 2(4) provides specific rules for vertical agreements between competing undertakings. Article 2(5) means that this block exemption cannot apply where the subject-matter of the agreement is dealt with under another block exemption (eg technology transfer under Regulation 240/96; see **19.4**).

ARTICLE 3

This is a crucial element of the block exemption; using market share to determine its applicability.

In most cases, the block exemption applies only if the *supplier's* share of the relevant market does not exceed 30% (Article 3(1)). However, where the agreement contains 'exclusive supply obligations' (see definition in Article 1; broadly, a situation where the seller is selling to one buyer only), it is the market share of the *buyer* which must not exceed 30% for the block exemption to apply.

Note that Article 9 sets out how to calculate market share: see the note on this Article below.

ARTICLE 4

This is the list of forbidden restrictions (referred to in the guidelines, although not in the regulation itself, as 'hardcore restrictions'); if the vertical agreement has as its object any of the matters listed here, the block exemption will not apply to the agreement as a whole.

4(a) outlaws price-fixing (although note that the possibility of imposing a maximum sale price, or recommending a sale price still remains).

4(b) outlaws restrictions on the buyer in relation to the territory into which the buyer can sell, or the customers to which the buyer can sell (so, eg, straightforward export bans are outlawed). However, note that there are some exceptions (ie certain restrictions can legitimately be imposed on the buyer, notably the restriction of certain types of active sale).

4(c) and (d) relate only to selective distribution systems (see definition in Article 1); restrictions on active and passive sales to end users, and cross-supplies between members of the system. Selective distribution is discussed in more detail at **18.4**.

4(e) also relates to a specific situation: a restriction agreed between a supplier and buyer of components limiting the supplier's freedom in relation to sales of spare parts to repairers or service providers.

ARTICLE 5

Note the wording of the first two lines of Article 5: if any of the three obligations listed in Article 5 is included in the agreement, then *that obligation* will not have the benefit of the block exemption; the rest of the agreement can still benefit (as long as there are no hardcore restrictions, of course).

Article 5 is generally concerned with restrictions of competition. Note that under Article 5(a), a non-compete obligation (see definition in Article 1: it need not be total) therefore loses the benefit of the block exemption if it is for an indefinite period, or a period exceeding 5 years (subject to an exception where the supplier provides the buyer with premises – eg a 'tied' pub).

ARTICLE 6

All block exemptions have the equivalent of this provision, giving the Commission power to withdraw the exemption from a particular agreement if necessary. The power is, however, rarely used.

ARTICLE 7

This provision, however, is novel; granting power to Member States to withdraw the block exemption from a particular agreement if necessary. It is expected that the power will be used sparingly.

ARTICLE 8

This gives the Commission the power to withdraw the block exemption from a particular sector of business. Again, it is expected that the power will be used sparingly.

ARTICLE 9

As noted above, this indicates how to calculate market share for the purposes of Article 3. Note that the test in Article 9(1) is based on substitutability (ie the test used for defining markets under Article 82 EC). Rules for the actual calculation of the figure are in Article 9(2).

ARTICLE 10

This indicates how to calculate 'total annual turnover' for the purposes of Article 2(2) and (4).

ARTICLE 11

This indicates that when the Regulation uses the terms 'undertaking', 'supplier' and 'buyer', connected undertakings (as defined in Article 11) are included.

ARTICLES 12 AND 13

These articles provide for the commencement of the Regulation and set out transitional provisions relating to the block exemptions which this Regulation replaced.

A block exemption checklist

The following checklist may be useful in applying the block exemption (it is still vital, however, to apply Article 81 EC first to determine whether there is a problem with EC competition law; there may also be other relevant ways of avoiding infringement of Article 81 EC which should be investigated on any given set of facts).

(1) Are you dealing with a 'vertical agreement' as defined in Article 2(1) of the block exemption (eg a distribution agreement (sole or exclusive), an exclusive purchasing agreement, a franchising agreement)?

(2) If so, check the market share threshold in Article 3 (usually the supplier's share of the relevant market, but if the agreement is an exclusive supply agreement, it will be the buyer's market share).

(3) If the relevant market share does not exceed 30%, the block exemption is potentially applicable.

(4) Does the agreement have as its object any of the restrictions listed in Article 4 (eg price-fixing, export ban)?

(5) If so, the block exemption does not apply.

(6) If not, the agreement benefits from the block exemption. (NB be careful of Article 5: the obligations in that Article are not themselves exempted, although

their inclusion does not stop the block exemption applying to the agreement as a whole.)

18.4 SELECTIVE DISTRIBUTION

18.4.1 What is a selective distribution agreement?

This name is given to the type of distribution agreement in which the supplier specifies the persons to whom the distributor can supply the goods. This type of distribution agreement is often considered to be essential by manufacturers of specialist and luxury goods (eg cameras, perfume) in order to maintain the brand image and reputation of the goods, ensuring that the goods are only sold through outlets which the manufacturer deems suitable. A classic selective distribution arrangement would operate as follows. A manufacturer enters into distribution agreements with a number of different wholesalers (in other words, there is usually a 'network' of agreements), appointing them as distributors for its products. In each agreement, the manufacturer specifies the retail outlets which the wholesalers can supply; this is usually done by the manufacturer laying down conditions which the retail outlets must satisfy before the wholesaler is permitted to sell to them. Depending on how these conditions are expressed (see **18.4.2**), competition law problems may result, especially if the manufacturer is using the agreement simply to stop certain outlets selling its products. An extensive network of similar distribution agreements can effectively close off a particular market to potential resellers.

18.4.2 The attitude of the Commission and the courts

The Commission has not been particularly consistent in its attitude towards selective distribution agreements. It has, for example, sometimes been prepared to agree that Article 81 EC does not apply at all to a particular selective distribution agreement (or network). However, this will only be the case if the supplier's criteria for selecting the person to which the distributor can sell are purely qualitative (ie based on those persons' suitability to sell the product, taking into account such matters as the standard of their premises, their qualifications and the expertise and training of their staff) rather than quantitative (ie simply based on restricting the number of outlets for the supplier's product in a particular area). In addition, the selection criteria must be applied without discriminating against particular outlets. In other cases, the Commission has concluded that Article 81(1) EC does apply and that it has been infringed.

It is interesting to note that both the Court of First Instance and European Court of Justice appear, in certain circumstances, to accept the principle that selective distribution arrangements are not only acceptable but necessary in respect of certain types of goods. For example, this was borne out in the *Galec* case (*Groupement d'Achat Edouard Leclerc (Galec) v Commission of the European Communities* (Case T-19/92) [1996] ECR II–1851. The case was, in fact, about the grant of individual exemption (under the system which was then in force) to a selective distribution system for Yves Saint Laurent perfumes. However, it is interesting to note that, as part of its ruling, the court accepted that most of YSL's selection criteria for outlets were necessary and in the interests of the consumer; the court commented that these were products in respect of which maintaining 'an aura of luxury and exclusivity' was vitally important.

As noted above, Regulation 2790/99 is capable of applying to selective distribution as long as the agreement satisfies the relevant conditions.

Chapter 19

EC LAW AND INTELLECTUAL PROPERTY RIGHTS

19.1 INTRODUCTION

This chapter looks at the relationship between EC law and intellectual property rights. It concentrates on the competition law problems which may arise in relation to the exploitation of intellectual property rights (with particular reference to the licensing of patents), but also briefly considers the ways in which intellectual property rights may come into conflict with the provisions of the European Community Treaty relating to the free movement of goods (Articles 28 EC–30 EC).

19.1.1 Exploiting intellectual property rights

Assume that Frodsby Engineering Ltd, a small company, has developed a revolutionary new machine, in respect of which it has obtained patents in the UK and other Member States, including France. Frodsby's directors are now looking for ways to make money out of the 20-year monopoly right which English law has conferred on the company (not least to get a return on the time and money spent on developing the machine; the directors see this as a just reward for the company's creativity and effort).

Their two main options are:

(1) make money by Frodsby manufacturing and selling the machine itself;
(2) make money by licensing the right to other businesses to manufacture and sell the machine (ie allowing other businesses to make use of the patent).

The advantages of licensing are covered in Chapter 35 of the LPC Resource Book *Business Law and Practice* (Jordans). Briefly, it is possible here that Frodsby may choose to license the patent because it is not geared up to manufacture the machine in sufficient quantities, or in other ways lacks the resources to exploit the patent fully, or because it finds a licensee with a better knowledge of the machine's target market.

19.1.2 How might Frodsby's actions cause competition law problems?

English law gives Frodsby as patent holder a right which arguably in itself could restrict trade and competition. Frodsby can rely on the patent to stop anyone else making or selling the machine, or even developing a similar machine which comes too close to the patent. Even if Frodsby allows other businesses to use the patent (by licensing it out), it could directly or indirectly restrict trade and competition by the terms which it includes in the licence; for example, it could grant a licensee exclusive territory, or stop a licensee exporting the machine from that territory.

19.1.3 The response of EC law

EC law has a balancing act to perform in this situation. It must try to deal fairly with two potentially conflicting situations; on the one hand, the desire of the patent holder to be rewarded for its creativity (failure to permit this could stifle innovation and the development of new markets) and on the other, the need to stop intellectual property rights granted under national law interfering with trade and competition within the common market.

The EC Treaty does not try to stop Member States passing laws which grant intellectual property rights (although, increasingly, attempts are being made to harmonise national systems). Article 295 EC (formerly Article 222 of the EC Treaty) provides that the Treaty 'shall in no way prejudice the rules in Member States governing the system of property ownership', which has led the EC competition authorities to take the view that it is not the mere existence of intellectual property rights which EC law should seek to control. What the law does seek to control is the exploitation (or as it is more commonly expressed, the 'exercise') of rights (see further **19.2**).

19.1.4 Which rights may cause problems?

Many of the points covered by this chapter are relevant to all types of intellectual property right. However, problems arise most often in relation to three of the rights because of their particular characteristics. Patents (on which the chapter concentrates) are particularly likely to pose problems because of their monopoly aspect. Trade marks can, if regularly re-registered, last for an indefinite period of time. Copyright cannot last indefinitely, but at 70 years in most cases, has the longest period of guaranteed validity of any intellectual property right.

19.2 ATTEMPTING TO RESOLVE THE CONFLICT

The distinction mentioned in **19.1.3** between the existence of an intellectual property right and its exercise was developed by the European Court of Justice as an attempt to reconcile Article 295 EC with other, possibly conflicting, Treaty provisions. Briefly, the ECJ's interpretation is that Article 295 EC is concerned with safeguarding the existence of national intellectual property rights; other Articles (such as Articles 28 EC–30 EC and 81–82 EC) with controlling their exercise. As a basic rule, if the exercise of an intellectual property right interferes with a Treaty provision (other than Article 295 EC), that right will be compromised; its exercise will be forbidden or restricted.

19.3 ARTICLE 81 EC AND THE EXPLOITATION OF INTELLECTUAL PROPERTY RIGHTS

If the holder of an intellectual property right licenses it out, as Frodsby is contemplating doing in the example above, this will involve an agreement between the holder and the licensee (a patent licensing agreement, sometimes simply called a 'patent licence'). Because there is an agreement, Article 81 EC may apply (depending, of course, on the terms of the agreement). The existence of the intellectual property rights which are being licensed will not, as such, infringe Article 81(1) EC. However, the licence agreement itself might, if it may affect trade and competition within the common market. In addition, the bringing of an action to stop infringement of an intellectual property right may infringe Article 81(1) EC if the action itself may affect trade within the common market, and is brought as a result of an agreement. In other words, exercise of the right may be restricted if there is evidence that the exercise infringes Article 81(1) EC. (Note that if Article 81 EC applies to an agreement and the Commission suspects a breach, the Commission can take action because of its duty to enforce Article 81 EC. The Commission has no similar power to intervene where Articles 28–30 EC are at issue; see **19.6**.)

Assume that Frodsby is contemplating licensing the patent for the machine to Megaco, a French company. The parties have agreed the following licence terms in principle.

(1) Frodsby has agreed that it will not appoint any licensees in France other than Megaco.
(2) Megaco has agreed that it will pay royalties on the use of the patent of a minimum of £10,000 per month.
(3) Megaco will not seek to challenge the validity of the patent in any way.
(4) Megaco will sell the machines at a price which Frodsby will determine.

Would an agreement on these terms run into difficulties with Article 81(1) EC, and if so, would it be possible to avoid this happening?

19.4 PATENT LICENSING AGREEMENTS AND COMPETITION LAW

19.4.1 Likely competition law problems

As explained in **19.3**, if a proposed patent licensing agreement may affect trade within the common market, it may infringe Article 81(1) EC. If so, (assuming that the agreement does not fall within the Notice on Agreements of Minor Importance), the parties will normally have two main ways of trying to resolve this problem. Either they can assess their agreement to see if it is likely to get the benefit of Article 81(3) EC, or they can try to redraft the agreement in order to get the benefit of the relevant block exemption (see **19.4.2**). As indicated at **18.3.6**, the latter is likely to be preferable, if at all possible.

Patent licensing agreements give rise to many of the competition law problems associated with distribution agreements; in particular, the grant of territorial protection to the licensee. This could therefore be a problem for Frodsby and Megaco. However, the parties often regard having some sort of territorial protection as an essential term of the agreement; the licensee in particular may not be prepared to get involved on any other basis because of the financial risks of exploiting the licence. It is also important to realise that, in some circumstances, the grant of protection may actually stimulate trade and competition despite its restrictive appearance; it may lead to more efficient exploitation of the patent and better marketing of the patented item, with benefits for consumers (who might not get the item at all if the protection were not permitted).

Generally, in deciding whether or not an agreement (or any given term such as exclusive territory) does infringe Article 81(1) EC, the Commission recognises the distinction drawn by the European Court of Justice between the existence and the exercise of rights. There are cases (eg *Nungesser (LC) AG and Kurt Eisle v Commission for the European Communities* (Case 258/78) [1982] ECR 2015) where the Court appears to have decided that the terms of a licence agreement did not infringe Article 81(1) EC at all. However, the case-law can be difficult to interpret, and it can be difficult to decide which terms in an agreement relate to the existence of the right and which to its exercise. Broadly, the former are terms which are necessary for protecting the very essence, or 'specific subject-matter' (see **19.7.3** for further discussion of this concept) of the rights, and will not infringe Article 81(1) EC. The latter are terms relating to exploitation of the right rather than the right itself, and are capable of infringing Article 81(1) EC. In practice, most terms in a patent licensing agreement are likely to fall into the second category, which means that it is very important to consider ways of avoiding infringement of Article 81 EC.

Frodsby and Megaco are proposing to enter an agreement containing terms which will restrict each party's commercial freedom, and which could cause competition law problems (territorial restrictions, fixed minimum payment by one party to the other, a 'no-challenge' clause and price-fixing). The solicitor must therefore now consider ways of avoiding infringement of Article 81(1) EC. It will be worth checking whether the parties satisfy the conditions for the Notice on Agreements of Minor Importance to apply; the other line worth proceeding with is drafting the agreement to fall within the relevant block exemption.

19.4.2 Block exemption

The current block exemption relating to intellectual property licensing came into force in 1996. This is Regulation 240/96, usually referred to as the 'Technology Transfer Regulation'. It covers three types of agreement: patent licensing agreements; know-how licensing agreements (in this context, broadly speaking, 'know-how' is important and secret information relating to how to manufacture an item or carry out a process; it can be licensed out by its owner in much the same way as a patent); and 'mixed' agreements (where a patent and related know-how are licensed out together). Article 10 of the Regulation gives a list of relevant definitions, including 'know-how'.

After a preamble explaining the purpose of the block exemption, Article 1 of Regulation 240/96 sets out the types of agreement to which the block exemption applies ('pure' patent or know-how licensing agreements and mixed agreements) and the main conditions which need to be satisfied before the block exemption will apply. Article 2 sets out a list of permitted terms (described as 'generally not restrictive of competition'), use of which will not stop the block exemption applying. This list is often referred to as the 'white list'. Article 3 contains a list of prohibited clauses (or situations) which will stop the block exemption applying (commonly known as the 'black list').

Article 4 of the block exemption contains what is known as an 'opposition procedure'. This applies to clauses in the agreement which are potentially restrictive of competition, but which are neither specifically permitted nor specifically forbidden by the block exemption. The parties may notify such clauses to the Commission; if within 4 months of notification the Commission does not oppose exemption, the clauses will have the benefit of the block exemption. Regulation 240/96 contains some guidance as to when the Commission may oppose exemption or withdraw the benefit of the block exemption; note Article 7(1), which deals with situations where the goods are not being exposed to sufficient competition, and which indicates that this may happen particularly where the licensee's market share exceeds 40%.

Applying the block exemption

To apply the block exemption correctly, it is important to follow Article 1 particularly carefully; note that the conditions which need to be satisfied to make this block exemption apply are considerably more complicated than, for example, those relating to the vertical agreements block exemption (contained in Regulation 2790/99, and discussed at **18.3.7**), and are applied in a very different way.

A checklist may assist in working through Article 1:

(1) What type of agreement is being considered?

Like all block exemptions, Regulation 240/96 provides that Article 81(1) EC (Article 85(1) of the EC Treaty when the block exemption was adopted) shall not apply to certain categories of agreement, namely:

- pure patent licensing agreements;
- pure know-how licensing agreements;
- mixed patent and know-how licensing agreements (ie agreements under which a patent and relevant know-how are licensed together).

As previously noted, 'know-how' is defined in Article 10; Article 1 also provides that the block exemption will also apply to 'agreements containing ancillary provisions relating to intellectual property rights other than patents' (eg an agreement under which the licensor licenses its trade mark as well as a patent and/or know-how).

(2) How many parties are there?

The block exemption will apply only to an agreement to which two undertakings are party.

(3) Does the agreement contain one or more of the obligations listed in Article 1(1)?

Article 1(1) contains a list of eight obligations, including sole and exclusive territory obligations (Article 1(1)(1) and (2)) and obligations in relation to active and passive sales (Article 1(1)(5) and (6)). For the block exemption to apply, the agreement must include one or more of these eight obligations.

(4) Are the parties entitled to have exemption for the obligations in Article 1(1)?

It is vitally important to be aware at this point that it is not enough for the parties to show that they have accepted one or more of the obligations listed in Article 1(1); they can have exemption for those obligations only if they comply with the rules laid down in Article 1(2) (for pure licensing agreements), 1(3) (for pure know-how licensing agreements) or 1(4) (for mixed agreements).

For example, Article 1(2) states that, in a pure patent licensing agreement, exemption for sole or exclusive territory obligations:

> 'is granted only to the extent that and for so long as the licensed product is protected by parallel patents in the territories ... of the licensee.'

It is also important to note that 'parallel patents' is defined in Article 10; they are patents which protect the same invention in different Member States. Thus, a licensing agreement for an English company to license its patent to a French company can have exemption for its terms (for example, for a term giving the French company exclusive territory) *only* if the invention is protected by a French patent (a 'parallel patent' in the territory of the licensee).

There are no short cuts here; the only way to be certain that the block exemption actually grants exemption in the circumstances to the Article 1 terms is to study Articles 1(2), 1(3) or 1(4) (as appropriate) very carefully, and to consult the definitions in Article 10.

(5) After applying Article 1 as above, consult Articles 2, 3 and 4

This should be a more straightforward exercise. As noted above, Article 2 is the 'white list' setting out permitted terms, and Article 3 the 'black list' setting out terms and situations which will stop the block exemption applying. Article 4 contains the opposition procedure, relating to what are sometimes called 'grey clauses'.

Does the Frodsby–Megaco agreement fall within the block exemption?

Frodsby appears only to be licensing the patent (and not any know-how or related intellectual property rights) to Megaco. This makes it a 'pure patent licence' to which only two undertakings are party (Article 1(1)). As previously explained, for the block exemption to apply, the agreement must contain one or more of the eight 'obligations' listed in Article 1(1). This agreement contains the obligation in Article 1(1)(1); 'an obligation on the licensor not to license other undertakings to exploit the licensed technology in the licensed territory' (ie what is usually referred to as the grant of sole territory); Frodsby has agreed that it will not appoint any licensees in France other than Megaco. However, before concluding that the block exemption does grant exemption for this term, it is vital to check Article 1(2); this stipulates that the obligation in Article 1(1)(1) is only exempted insofar as the licensed product is protected by 'parallel patents' (ie patents which protect the same invention in various Member States in the territory of the licensee). Frodsby's machine is protected by a patent in France, the licensee's territory, so the proposed term does satisfy Article 1(2).

The obligation on Megaco to pay a minimum royalty per month is permissible under Article 2(1)(9). However, the remaining two terms are not permitted by Articles 1 and 2. The price-fixing term is in fact outlawed by Article 3.1, and the parties must not include this if the block exemption is to apply.

The term which forbids Megaco from challenging the validity of the patent falls within Article 4(2)(b). The parties could therefore make use of the opposition procedure in Article 4: if they notify the agreement to the Commission, which does not oppose exemption within a period of 4 months, the term will be exempted.

(As noted above, that terms which fall within the ambit of the opposition procedure are sometimes described as 'grey clauses' or 'grey-listed'. Confusingly, however, the expression 'grey clause' or 'grey list' is also sometimes used to describe the terms which fall within Article 2 of this block exemption.)

19.4.3 Drafting a patent licensing agreement

Both *Practical Commercial Precedents* (Section G), and the *Encyclopaedia of Forms and Precedents* (Volume 21 on Intellectual Property, updated by Service Volume B) provide complete precedents for patent licensing agreements, and indicate how an agreement can be tailored to gain the benefit of the existing block exemption.

19.5 ARTICLE 82 EC AND INTELLECTUAL PROPERTY RIGHTS

The ownership of intellectual property rights may confer a dominant position on an undertaking within a particular geographic or product market. For example, a business may become dominant in a relevant product market by acquiring a patent; the patented item may form a market by itself if its novelty and inventiveness mean that consumers do not regard any other product as a substitute for it. However, this of itself (ie the existence of the intellectual property right) will not infringe Article 82 EC. Infringement requires abuse of a dominant position, which would mean improper exercise of the right in question. Not all exercises will be improper and, therefore, 'abusive'; it will depend on the circumstances, and in particular the effect on competition in the markets concerned. These general principles were confirmed by the ECJ in *Radio Telefis Eireann and Another v Commissioner of the European Communities and Another* (Cases C-241/91P and C-242/91P) [1995] ECR 1-801 (the 'Magill' case). However, this case still leaves some uncertainty about the relationship between Article 82 EC and the exercise of intellectual property rights; notably how far a right-holder's refusal to license its right to others amounts to abusive behaviour.

19.6 ARTICLES 28 EC–30 EC AND INTELLECTUAL PROPERTY RIGHTS

19.6.1 Introduction

The competition authorities of the EC cannot resolve all the problems which arise from the existence and exercise of intellectual property rights by using the specific competition law Articles of the European Community Treaty (Articles 81 EC and 82 EC). For example, in many cases, Article 81 does not apply because the situation does not involve a business arrangement of the type to which Article 81 EC can apply. It will then be necessary for the authorities to control the exercise of intellectual property rights by relying on the principles of free movement of goods (Articles 28 EC–30 EC).

19.6.2 How Articles 28 EC–30 EC may be relevant

Assume that Frodsby Engineering Ltd puts its patented machine on the market in Germany as well as in the UK. Market conditions in Germany mean that Frodsby can afford to sell the machine more cheaply there than it can in the UK. Fred, a businessman, realises that he can make money by (lawfully) buying the machine in Germany and reselling it in the UK at a price which still undercuts Frodsby's UK price. What if Frodsby were to try to rely on its patent rights under English law to prevent Fred from importing the machines into the UK, claiming that those rights give it absolute control over what happens to the machines at all times?

Fred may try to argue that English patent law is a 'measure having equivalent effect' to a quantitative restriction on imports under Article 28 EC, as the patent holder is attempting to use the law to stop imports of patented goods into the UK. Article 28 EC prohibits such measures, so use of the UK patent rights to stop the imports may not be justified, being incompatible with the free movement of goods around the common market.

However, Article 28 EC must be read subject to Article 30 EC. This permits derogations from Article 28 EC in certain circumstances, such as where the measure is necessary for 'the protection of industrial or commercial property rights', an expression which will cover intellectual property rights such as patents. Thus, under Article 30 EC, the national measure (ie the law on patents) may be justified if it protects something about the patent which needs protection.

There are, in turn, however, limits on the use of Article 30 EC. The Article itself provides that it cannot be invoked to justify a measure which amounts to 'arbitrary discrimination' or 'a disguised restriction on trade', and the European Court of Justice has used this to ensure that any derogations from Article 28 EC do not go too far. In particular, the Court has developed the doctrine that Article 30 EC can only be invoked by the holder of an intellectual property right if the infringement action is necessary to protect the 'specific subject-matter' of the right. In other words, although EC law recognises that national intellectual property rights need protection in certain circumstances, it also attempts to ensure that they do not interfere too much with trade within the common market.

19.6.3 Specific subject-matter

What constitutes the specific subject-matter of an intellectual property right will vary according to the right concerned. The European Court of Justice has held that the specific subject-matter of a patent is 'the guarantee that the patentee, to reward the creative effort of the inventor, has the exclusive right to use an invention with a view to manufacturing industrial products and putting them into circulation for the first time, either directly or by the grant of licences to third parties, as well as the right to oppose infringement' (*Centrafarm BV and Adrian de Peijper v Sterling Drug Inc* (Case 15/74) [1974] ECR 1147). For a trade mark, however, the specific subject-matter is 'the guarantee that the owner of the trade mark has the exclusive right to use that trade mark, for the purpose of putting products protected by the mark into circulation for the first time, and is, therefore, intended to protect him against competitors wishing to take advantage of the status and reputation of the trade mark by selling products illegally bearing that trade mark' *(Centrafarm BV and Adrian de Peijper v Winthrop BV* (Case 16/74) [1974] ECR 1183). The position in relation to copyright is less clear; this is at least partly because national systems of copyright law within the EU still vary quite considerably. The specific subject-matter of an intellectual property right may, therefore, be seen as a limit on the use of the principles relating to free movement of goods. The Court recognises that there is something central to each intellectual property right which needs protection, but is reluctant to allow the right to be exercised in an uncontrolled manner; the Court will always be prepared to stop the use of intellectual property rights if they are being used to restrict trade and competition within the common market.

19.6.4 Exhaustion of rights

This is further illustrated by the concept of 'exhaustion of rights', which the European Court of Justice has applied to most intellectual property rights, including patents, copyright and trade marks. Its effect is that when goods which are subject to an intellectual property right are lawfully put on the market for the first time in the EEA (either by the right holder or with its consent), this 'exhausts' the right holder's opportunities to control what subsequently happens to the goods. In particular, the right holder cannot use the right to prevent the goods being imported into another Member State. However, note that this only applies to attempts by the right holder to control the movement of the goods around the EEA; it does not take away the holder's right to take action if the right has actually been infringed. The case of *Silhouette International Schmied GmbH and Co KG v Hartlauer Handelsgesellschaft mbH* (Case C-355/96) [2000] All ER (EC) 769 showed the doctrine at work in relation to trade marks. The European Court of Justice interpreted Article 7 of the Trade Marks Directive (89/140/EEC) to mean that exhaustion only occurred in the circumstances described above (lawful marketing in the EEA by the owner or with the owner's consent). Thus, the owner of a trade mark would be entitled to stop products bearing the mark being imported into the EEA from outside that area (in this case, spectacle frames bearing Silhouette's mark being imported from Bulgaria into Austria). However, even after the *Silhouette* case, this area continued to prove problematic, particularly on the issue of the trade mark owner's consent. For example, how far could the owner's consent to imports of its goods into the EEA be implied when the owner had put its goods on the market outside the EEA without express restrictions as to where they could be re-sold?

The questions relating to consent now appear to have been answered by the ECJ's ruling in the joined cases of *Zino Davidoff SA v A & G Imports Ltd; Levi Strauss & Co and Another v Tesco Stores Ltd and Another; Levi Strauss & Co and Another v Costco Wholesale UK* (Joined Cases C-414/99, C-415/99 and C-416/99) [2002] All ER (EC) 55.

The Court in effect ruled that there had to be some positive expression of consent by the trade mark owner to its goods being imported into the EEA from outside. Consent cannot be implied from silence; there would have to be some unequivocal demonstration from the circumstances that the trade mark owner had given up its right to control the import into and marketing of the goods within the EEA. This ruling appears greatly to have strengthened the hand of trade mark owners: for example, it appears that there is now no need to state expressly in an agreement for goods which are to be sold outside the EEA that they must not be imported into and sold in the EEA.

19.7 ARTICLE 28 EC AND ARTICLES 81 EC–82 EC: RELATIONSHIP

It seems clear that any attempt to use intellectual property rights to prevent the import of goods from one Member State into another is at least capable of infringing both Article 28 EC and Article 81 EC (or Article 82 EC) *(Nungesser (LC) and Kurt Eisle v Commission for the European Communities* (Case 258/78) [1982] ECR 2015: the 'Maize Seeds' case). Application of the rules on free movement of goods to a case does not preclude the application of the competition rules, although in practice it is comparatively rare for both to be argued actively in the same case.

19.8 EC COMPETITION LAW AND FRANCHISING AGREEMENTS

Like the other types of agreement considered in Chapters 18 and 19, franchising agreements have the potential to infringe Article 81(1) EC. They will frequently contain terms restricting the parties' commercial freedom (eg territorial restrictions, restrictions on the use that can be made of the intellectual property rights which are part of the franchise package). If the agreement is capable of affecting trade and competition within the common market, then the parties will need to consider how to avoid infringing Article 81(1) EC.

All the normal methods of avoidance are available, including block exemption. Prior to 1 June 2000, franchising agreements were covered by a specific block exemption, granted by Regulation 4087/88. This has, however, now been replaced by the vertical agreements block exemption, Regulation 2790/99, so franchising agreements can enjoy block exemption on the terms of that Regulation (see **18.9**).

APPENDICES

INTRODUCTION TO APPENDICES

The two Appendices which follow (on the Consumer Credit Act 1974 and on information technology) are designed to supplement and act as background to certain areas of the main part of the course. The material which they contain is not examinable in the College of Law's Commercial Law elective. It is primarily designed to raise awareness of points which are likely to be of importance to the commercial solicitor in practice, but which it is not possible to cover in detail within the constraints of the Commercial Law course.

Consumer Credit

This topic provides important background information in relation to financing commercial agreements (see Chapter 9): as explained in **A1.1.1**, issues raised by the Consumer Credit Act 1974 are likely to be of importance to commercial solicitors.

Information Technology

This Appendix is designed to provide background to a number of the issues involved in the Intellectual Property chapters, as well as to consider how issues involved in general commercial contracts (eg for the sale of goods) apply to software and hardware contracts. It now includes e-commerce.

Appendix 1

CONSUMER CREDIT ACT 1974

This Appendix aims to provide a brief guide to the Consumer Credit Act 1974 (the Act) by summarising the main provisions of the Act, and indicating how it may be relevant to commercial practice. The points which it makes should be considered when studying the sections of the main book which touch on the financing of commercial agreements (eg in Chapter 9). Note that, at the time of writing, there are proposals for changes to the EC Consumer Credit Directive, and a number of ongoing DTI consultations about consumer credit law, which may lead to changes in the Act (see, eg, **A1.3.1(5)**). However, it is not clear when these changes might take effect.

A1.1 THE CONSUMER CREDIT ACT AND COMMERCIAL WORK

Despite the reference to 'Consumer' in its title, the Act is frequently relevant to commercial practice, and it is important for the commercial solicitor to have at least an outline knowledge of its provisions. The main points to be aware of are as follows.

A1.1.1 The Act may be relevant when advising commercial clients who are finance providers ('creditors')

This point makes it very important for the commercial solicitor to be aware of the scope and effect of the Act. As explained in more detail below, the Act (and secondary legislation made under it) lays down many rules which creditors must observe in relation to credit agreements, and the consequences of infringement of these rules can be severe (eg inability to enforce any agreement against the debtor, which in practice may make it impossible for a creditor to recover money lent under the agreement or enforce the payment of interest). It is therefore vital for the solicitor to know when the Act will apply: all sorts of finance-providing clients, such as banks, finance houses and credit card companies are potentially within its scope.

A1.1.2 The Act may be relevant when advising certain commercial clients who wish to obtain finance for their business activities

As explained in more detail below, the Act applies to credit transactions between a business ('the creditor') and an individual ('the debtor') where the creditor provides credit not exceeding £25,000 to the debtor. Thus, some commercial clients (eg sole traders) can benefit from the Act's protection when entering into credit agreements (eg bank loans) because they will qualify as debtors under the Act.

A1.2 AN OUTLINE GUIDE TO THE ACT

It is very important to remember that the main objective of the Act is the protection of the debtor. It seeks to achieve this objective in two ways:

- the regulation of the consumer credit 'industry' (this is done by way of a licensing system and the provision of detailed rules covering how creditors can advertise and seek business generally); and
- the control of individual agreements.

A1.2.1 Regulation

(1) Licensing (CCA 1974, ss 21–42)

A creditor who wishes to carry on a consumer credit or consumer hire business (see below), must obtain a licence from the Office of Fair Trading (OFT) (s 21(1)). Licences last for 5 years, and can be revoked or varied if, for example, the OFT believes that the licence-holder is acting improperly. Any agreement made by an unlicensed trader is unenforceable without a validating order from the OFT (s 40). In practice, this means that the creditor will, for example, be unable to demand payments of interest or repayment of the credit without the OFT's sanction. Schedule 1 to the Act also makes unlicensed trading a criminal offence.

(2) Restrictions on advertising and seeking business

The Act itself contains a general prohibition on false or misleading advertising. However, the detailed rules on this point can be found in the Consumer Credit (Advertisement) Regulations 1989, SI 1989/1125.

A1.2.2 Control of individual agreements

The Act covers:

- consumer credit agreements (s 8);
- consumer hire agreements (s 15);
- certain 'linked transactions' (s 19).

In practice, the Act is capable of covering virtually all forms of consumer credit, including hire purchase, conditional sale and credit sale agreements, loans and most credit cards. Certain mortgages are also covered. There is a summary at the end of this Appendix of how the main forms of credit work.

The following summary concentrates on the consumer credit agreement. Note, however, that by s 15, the Act will apply when an individual or partnership enters into certain agreements to hire goods; this could cover commercial clients who hire business equipment.

A1.3 CONSUMER CREDIT AGREEMENTS

Section 8 defines a consumer credit agreement as a personal credit agreement (ie an agreement under which the person receiving credit is an individual) whereby a person (the creditor) provides credit not exceeding £25,000 to a debtor.

By s 9, 'credit' includes a cash loan or any other form of financial accommodation; this is wide enough to cover any circumstances in which a customer is allowed time to pay.

Such an agreement is 'regulated' by the Act unless it is exempt. Exempt agreements are defined by s 16 of the Act and the Consumer Credit (Exempt Agreements) Order 1989, SI 1989/869, as amended. They include, for example, agreements for normal trade credit, and credit card agreements such as American Express, where all the debtor's indebtedness must be discharged by a single payment.

A1.3.1 The Act's protection for individual agreements

The Act aims to provide protection for the debtor at every stage of an agreement's 'lifetime'.

(1) Prior to making the agreement

Both parties need to be aware that the potential debtor has certain important rights even before the agreement has been concluded:

- the right to withdraw (s 57): this allows the debtor to withdraw from a transaction before it has become binding, and makes communication of withdrawal easier;
- a special right, in land mortgage cases, for the potential debtor to reflect on the wisdom of entering into the transaction before becoming bound by it (s 58) (NB in practice, the Act applies to comparatively few land mortgages: many are exempt, and obviously any agreement where the credit exceeds £25,000 is outside the scope of the Act);
- by s 56, antecedent (ie pre-contract) negotiations conducted by a supplier or credit-broker (a credit-broker is someone who puts potential debtors in touch with sources of credit) are deemed to be conducted by that person as agent for the creditor as well as in the supplier or broker's own capacity.

An example of this last point may assist:

Assume that a sole trader wishes to buy a van on hire-purchase. This sort of agreement works in such a way that, although there will be a contract (the hire-purchase agreement) between the sole trader and the finance company and also between the garage and the finance company (in HP, the credit-broker literally sells the HP goods to the creditor, who is the person who actually supplies them to the debtor), there is no direct contract between the sole trader and the garage. This could cause a problem for the sole trader if the garage makes false or misleading statements about the van during pre-contract negotiations. Section 56 improves the debtor's position by deeming that such negotiations are conducted by the credit-broker as agent for the creditor, thus giving the debtor a right of action against the creditor in relation to the garage's false or misleading statements.

(2) On making the agreement

Sections 60–64 of the Act and the Consumer Credit (Agreements) Regulations 1983, SI 1983/1555, as amended, lay down numerous formalities which an agreement must satisfy, relating to, for example:

- the size and legibility of print used;
- the contents of the agreement;
- the prominence of certain information.

It is vital for creditors to comply with these formalities. If they do not, the agreement is 'improperly executed' and unenforceable by the creditor without a court order under s 127. In the case of *Wilson v First County Trust* [2001] All ER (D) 28, the Court of Appeal held that s 127(3) of the CCA 1974 was incompatible with Article 6 of the European Convention for the Protection of Human Rights and Fundamental Freedoms 1950 and Article 1 of the First Protocol to that Convention, on the grounds that the absolute bar on enforceability by the creditor contained in s 127(3) disproportionately infringed the creditor's ECHR rights in relation to the policy aim of the section. The court made a declaration of incompatibility under the Human Rights Act 1998. However, on appeal to the House of Lords (*Wilson v First County Trust Ltd* [2003] UKHL 40, [2003] All ER (D) 187 (Jul)), the House of Lords ruled that the Court of Appeal had been wrong to make the declaration of incompatibility in relation to s 127(3). This was primarily because the cause of action in the case arose before the Human Rights Act came into force. However, the House of Lords was also of the opinion that even if s 127(3) did have the effect of interfering with rights under the Convention, the interference was justified.

There are also detailed rules on how many copies of the agreement the debtor must receive and when they must be provided; the sanction for non-compliance by the creditor is, again, unenforceability without a court order.

Both parties to a regulated agreement must also be aware that, in certain circumstances, the debtor has the right to cancel (without penalty) an agreement which has become binding upon him. The detailed rules on cancellation are outside the scope of this Appendix, but the relevant provisions can be found in ss 67–71.

(3) During the agreement

The debtor has the following rights:

- to receive certain information about the agreement (ss 77–79);
- in certain cases, to take action against the creditor for breach of contract or misrepresentation committed by the supplier (s 75).

An example of s 75 will be useful.

It is very important to be aware that the section only applies to the kind of agreement where the creditor and supplier are different people. In consumer credit jargon, this is the type of agreement is often referred to as a 'three-party debtor-creditor-supplier agreement' or 'three-party DCS' agreement.

This includes most credit cards and certain types of loan agreement, but not hire purchase (which is a 'two-party DCS' agreement) or ordinary bank loans where the debtor is actually given cash or a cheque (this is a 'debtor-creditor' or 'DC' agreement; for a fuller explanation of DC and DCS agreements, see **A1.5.2**).

Assume that a sole trader uses a credit card to buy goods from a retailer which cost £5,000. The goods turn out to be defective.

Obviously, the sole trader has a contract with the retailer, and could sue the retailer in relation to the defective goods in the usual way. However, s 75 provides that the credit card company is jointly and severally liable for breaches of contract committed by the retailer. This means that the sole trader could sue the credit card company in addition to, or even instead of the retailer. This is often particularly useful if the retailer has gone out of business.

Note:
- the same rule applies to misrepresentations made by the retailer;
- the goods bought must have a cash price of more than £100 but less than £30,000.

(4) Ending the agreement

The Act also gives protection to a debtor on the ending of the agreement. This is a difficult topic to summarise briefly, because the protection given may vary according to what type of agreement it is, and why it is being brought to an end. A solicitor advising either of the parties must always check these two points very carefully. In particular, a debtor under a DC agreement (eg an ordinary bank loan) receives less protection than a debtor under a DCS agreement. The following main points are, however, worth noting:

- in many cases, the debtor is entitled to a warning in the form of a 'default notice' from the creditor (s 87) if the creditor wishes to do more than simply sue for arrears under the agreement (eg terminate the agreement or repossess goods);
- debtors who are in possession of goods which they do not own (under HP or conditional sale agreements) have special protection against repossession under ss 90 and 92;
- the debtor may be able to cancel the agreement under ss 67–71 without penalty (see above);
- the Act provides that, in many situations associated with the ending of agreements (eg service of a default notice, creditor attempting to repossess goods), the debtor will have the right to apply to the county court, which has wide powers to look at the situation and make orders to sort it out (eg a 'time order', which allows the debtor extra time to pay what he owes).

(5) Extortionate credit bargains

One potentially important power of the court to assist debtors who have made bad credit bargains is to find that there is an 'extortionate credit bargain' under ss 137–140. An extortionate credit bargain (ECB) is one which either requires grossly exorbitant payments or otherwise grossly contravenes the ordinary principles of fair dealing. A major factor in this (although not the only one) will be whether the agreement charges a very high rate of interest. If the court finds an ECB, it can reopen the agreement so as to 'do justice between the parties'.

Debtors and creditors should always be aware of these provisions. Creditors should note in particular that they apply in two situations where the Act normally would not apply:
- where the credit exceeds £25,000;
- where the agreement is exempt.

However, the little case-law that exists indicates that the court will, in practice, be very reluctant to find that an agreement is an ECB. Note that this is one of the areas in relation to which the DTI is consulting interested parties: the DTI's view is that the present law relating to ECBs is ineffective in protecting debtors.

A1.4 COMMON FORMS OF CONSUMER CREDIT AGREEMENTS

A1.4.1 Hire-purchase

A hire-purchase agreement is a contract for the bailment of goods (ie the debtor gets possession, but not ownership of the goods) in return for periodical payments by the debtor (the hire-purchase instalment payments). Ownership of the goods does not pass to the debtor unless and until the contract terms are fulfilled, and one or more of the following occurs:

(1) the exercise of an option to purchase by the debtor;
(2) the doing of any other specified act;
(3) the happening of any other specified event.

The most common of these in practice is probably (1): in effect, the debtor notifies the creditor on payment of the last instalment that he now wishes to 'buy' the goods from the creditor and become their owner.

> *Example*
> Billy, a sole trader, wants to buy a van on hire-purchase for making deliveries. He selects the van from stock at Ace Motors, which puts him in touch with Mammoth Credit, a finance house. Mammoth Credit is prepared to give Billy credit by entering into an HP agreement with him. The arrangement which now results is often called the 'HP triangle'. In Consumer Credit Act terms, Billy is the debtor, Mammoth Credit the creditor, and Ace Motors the credit broker. Note that Mammoth is legally also the supplier of the goods under the agreement. Ace Motors will actually sell the van to them, and Mammoth will then bail the van to Billy, who makes instalment ('periodical') payments to them. Mammoth remains the owner of the van until one of the events noted above takes place.

A1.4.2 Conditional sale

A conditional sale is an agreement for the sale of goods (or land) with the price payable by instalments, and under which ownership does not pass to the buyer until certain conditions are satisfied (eg payment of the last instalment). Consequently, conditional sales are similar to hire-purchase agreements, and because ownership of the goods is retained by the creditor, extra protection for debtors under these agreements is incorporated into the CCA 1974.

A1.4.3 Credit sale

A credit sale is similar to a conditional sale, except that ownership of the goods passes immediately to the buyer at the time of the contract, without any preconditions. The creditor allows credit to the buyer, who is allowed to pay the price by instalments.

A1.4.4 Loan

The term 'loan' is generally used to denote a fixed-term loan by a bank or finance company, repayable by instalments. Loans may be secured or unsecured. They are often secured so that if the borrower defaults with payment, the lender can realise the security to recoup the money lent. A loan is often given to finance a particular transaction, for example, the purchase of a car, as an alternative to buying the car under a hire-purchase or credit sale agreement. In a business context, however, the debtor may simply be obtaining the money for general business purposes (eg a sole trader or partnership may borrow money from a bank to improve the business's general cash flow).

Example

Alma, a sole trader, arranges a loan of £10,000 from Midwest Bank to help improve her cash flow position. Midwest opens a loan account for her and puts the £10,000 into it. In Consumer Credit Act terms, Midwest Bank is the creditor and Alma the debtor, and the agreement is a DC agreement. Note that there is a variation on this situation called the 'connected loan', where the creditor does not provide the credit directly to the debtor, but instead provides it to a supplier of goods or services to assist the debtor with the purchase of those goods or services. For example, Ethel wants to buy a carpet from Floorworld; she arranges a loan from Tonto Credit, which pays the loan money directly to Floorworld. Ethel can now get her carpet (Floorworld has been paid), and she will make repayments of the loan to Tonto Credit. A connected loan is a DCS rather than DC agreement (see **A1.5.2**).

A1.4.5 Credit card

A credit card can be used to obtain cash, goods or services up to a stipulated credit limit. The supplier is subsequently paid by the credit card company (eg Barclaycard), which, in due course, is reimbursed by the credit card holder, who will be charged interest at the end of the credit period if any money is still owing. Some card agreements demand payment in full at the end of a specified period (eg Diner's Club and American Express). These are commonly known as charge card agreements, and are exempt under CCA 1974, s 16.

Care must be taken to distinguish between a genuine credit card (eg Barclaycard) and a card which does not, on closer investigation, involve the provision of credit. Examples of the latter include:

(1) a cash card used to obtain cash from an automated teller machine (ATM) or cash machine;

(2) a debit card used in conjunction with a current account. These cards dispense with the need for cheques. The card-holder's bank account is debited when the card is presented to pay for a transaction and there is no pre-set transaction limit. The only limit on the card's use is the amount of funds available to the card-holder under his current account. The most common examples of debit cards are Switch and Delta cards;

(3) a cheque guarantee card issued by a bank or building society for use in connection with a cheque. The bank or building society guarantees payment of individual cheques in the amount shown on the card (usually £50, but sometimes up to £200);

(4) a pre-payment card issued in respect of a certain sum against the pre-payment of that sum. Examples include phone cards for use in connection with pay phones and cards to pay for photocopying.

The CCA 1974 will not apply to any of these types of card, as there is no 'credit' involved.

A1.4.6 Bank overdraft

A bank overdraft occurs when a bank allows a customer to overdraw against his current account. The customer is regarded as owing money on the account, and this may be seen as the equivalent of a bank loan (the finance is simply being provided in a slightly different way).

A1.5 TERMS AND EXAMPLES

Consumer credit is a topic with its own particular jargon. This paragraph aims to define and explain some of the terms which you are most likely to come across, either in the Act or in relation to consumer credit generally.

A1.5.1 Types of credit

(1) Fixed-sum and running-account credit

FIXED-SUM CREDIT

As its name suggests, this is where the credit which the creditor provides to the debtor is a fixed sum (eg loans, hire-purchase, conditional and credit sales).

RUNNING-ACCOUNT CREDIT

In this sort of agreement, the amount of credit advanced will fluctuate from time to time, the amount available depending upon what transactions and what repayments have been made. Credit card and overdraft agreements fall into this category: both are, of course, normally subject to 'credit limits'.

(2) Restricted and unrestricted use credit

The Act defines unrestricted-use credit (UUC); everything else is restricted-use credit (RUC).

UNRESTRICTED-USE CREDIT

In this case, the credit is provided in such a way that the debtor is free to use it as he sees fit (ie he gets his hands on money or the equivalent of money, as with a bank loan provided in the form of a cheque payable to the debtor, or money paid into an account in the debtor's name; overdrafts also fall into this category).

RESTRICTED-USE CREDIT

In this case, the credit is provided in such a way that the debtor is not free to use it as he sees fit, chiefly because he does not get his hands on money or the equivalent of money. Examples include HP, conditional sale and credit cards being used to buy goods. In this last case, the credit is restricted in the sense that the card can only be used at outlets which accept that card.

NB It is irrelevant for the purpose of deciding if credit is RUC or UUC whether the agreement stipulates how the credit is to be used (eg a bank loan advanced on condition that the debtor buys a car). If the debtor puts the credit to a different use, this will be breach of contract, but it does not stop the credit being RUC.

A1.5.2 Classification of agreements

The Act makes a number of important distinctions between DC and DCS agreements. For example, it is crucial to know whether an agreement is DC or DCS when considering whether it is regulated or exempt. In addition, many important provisions of the Act (notably ss 56 and 75) only apply to DCS agreements.

The key factor is the relationship between the supplier of the credit and the supplier of the goods, land or services.

(1) Where they are the same person

In this case, the agreement is a DCS agreement (commonly known as a 'two-party DCS' agreement, although the Act does not in fact use this term). Examples include credit sale agreements (eg where a shop sells goods and allows the buyer to pay for them in instalments) and HP agreements (where the finance company provides credit and supplies the goods to the debtor, having previously bought them from the retailer).

(2) Where they are not the same person, but have business arrangements between themselves

This type of agreement is commonly known as a 'three-party' DCS agreement. Most credit card agreements work in this way: the credit card company has contractual arrangements with a wide variety of outlets (shops, garages, theatres, etc) under which the outlet is authorised to accept the card. (Note that a three-party DCS situation contains two other contracts: the credit card agreement between the card company and the debtor and the contract between the debtor and the supplier, known as a 'linked transaction' in Consumer Credit Act terms. Both of these contracts will normally be regulated by the Act.)

(3) Where they are not the same person, and have no business arrangements

This is a DC agreement. Many loan agreements work in this way; eg a sole trader gets a bank loan and then uses the money to buy a car from a garage. There will be no 'business arrangements' between the bank (creditor) and the garage (supplier). Although the matter is not entirely free from doubt, it is normally assumed that when a credit card is used to obtain cash, this is a DC agreement.

(4) Types of credit activity

The Act applies to all types of credit transactions and also to certain 'ancillary credit businesses'. By s 145, this is defined as any business which comprises or relates to:

- debt-adjusting (renegotiation of debts on debtors' behalf);
- debt-counselling (advising debtors on the payment of debts);
- debt-collecting;
- the operation of a credit reference agency (ie the kind of business which collects financial information on debts for the purpose of providing it to others, eg potential creditors).

(5) Working out what 'credit' is

As the amount of credit is one of the factors which determines whether or not an agreement is regulated, it is important to be able to identify the various sums which are likely to be involved in a credit transaction, and to appreciate which of these sums constitute the 'credit'. This is best done by way of example:

Tom wishes to buy a new car with a cash price of £15,000, but cannot afford to pay for it all out of his own resources. The garage therefore arranges for him to enter a hire-purchase agreement with a finance company on the following terms:

(a) he will pay a cash deposit of £2,000;
(b) he will receive a part-exchange allowance of £7,000 for his existing car;
(c) he will pay 40 monthly instalments of £200 each; and
(d) he will pay an administration fee of £50.

The total payable is £17,050 (ie the aggregate of everything he has to pay to the finance house). This figure is also known as the total price.

The total charge for credit is £2,050 (ie the total price less the cash price of the car (£17,050 – £15,000).

The credit advanced under the agreement is £6,000 (ie the total price, less the total charge for credit and less any sums which Tom himself is providing (ie £17,050 – (£2,050 + £2,000 + £7,000)).

A1.6 FURTHER READING

Goode *Consumer Credit Law and Practice* (Butterworths, 2000)

Appendix 2

A GUIDE TO THE LAW OF INFORMATION TECHNOLOGY

A2.1 INTRODUCTION

The computer is a universal presence in offices, homes and schools throughout the developed world. The increase in computer use in the last 20 years or so has come about through the amazing reduction in the price of computing power. For comparison, if a new Jaguar car had decreased in price to the same degree that computers have over the 20-year period, the car would now cost about £20, rather than £35,000.

However, it should not be forgotten that a computer is basically a stupid adding machine with a very large memory. It needs to be told what to do. Appendix 2 addresses some of the main legal and related issues which this raises:

- IP issues;
- semiconductor chip protection;
- hardware contracts;
- software contracts;
- the Internet;
- computer crime;
- data protection; and
- rights in databases.

Many of these issues are relevant to areas of law already covered in the body of the Resource Book, so where appropriate, the Appendix is cross-referenced to that material.

A2.2 IT AND INTELLECTUAL PROPERTY RIGHTS

All the major forms of legal protection of intellectual property rights predate the electronic computer by a century or more. As they were not developed with the computer in mind, there have therefore been many problems in deciding whether a particular activity comes within the remit of the existing intellectual property law. Indeed, there has been a considerable need to produce new forms of legal protection to deal with problems that have emerged. The following paragraphs summarise the way in which the various IP rights may be relevant to computer software and hardware.

A2.2.1 Copyright

For the main points on the law of copyright itself, see Chapter 13. The relevance of copyright to computers is as protection for the software; in other words, the instructions required to enable the computer to perform the desired task. In order to be protected, the software would have to have been 'written down' on paper at some stage of its existence, although of course, when bought by the customer, the software will usually be on floppy disks or a CD. (For the avoidance of doubt, note that 'software' = 'computer programs'.)

A computer program is a series of written instructions telling a computer what to do. It will contain thousands of lines of instructions, each one of which relates to a simple step, but put together as a program, it enables the computer to be used, for example, for word processing. As already noted in Chapter 13, copyright exists in software as a literary work (CDPA 1988, s 3(1)); see further **A2.5.3**.

Unauthorised use of a computer program is therefore breach of copyright. The commercial arrangement for use of software is usually a licence; that is, a copyright licence.

(For the law on copyright in databases, and the relatively new 'database right', see Chapter 14 and **A2.9**.)

A2.2.2 Patents

As noted in Chapter 16, PA 1977 s 1(2) excludes 'computer programs' from the remit of the patent system (although, as indicated in **16.3.4**, this does not necessarily mean that a program can never be patented).

However, patents for computer programs are being granted in increasing numbers. The attitude of the UK Patent Office and the European Patent Office has become more relaxed over recent years, though not to the extent of the 'open doors' policy of the US Patent Office.

Patents do, of course, have relevance to protection of inventions in relation to computer hardware (ie the electronics) if the necessary conditions for patentability are satisfied.

A2.2.3 Trade marks

Trade marks are covered in Chapter 11. This becomes particularly relevant in the context of Internet 'domain' names where trade mark infringement and passing off are the relevant causes of action (see further, **A2.6**).

(Trade marks are, of course, also relevant in the usual context of being used in relation to goods and services, for example Microsoft, Dell, Compaq and so on will have various registered and unregistered marks which they use in connection with their businesses.)

A2.2.4 Design rights

Registered and unregistered design rights (see Chapter 15) are intended to protect the outward appearance of items. The design rights are not often directly relevant to IT (although they may be used to protect the outward appearance of a piece of hardware). However, note that the right which protects semiconductor chips is akin to a design right (see next paragraph).

A2.3 SEMICONDUCTOR CHIP PROTECTION

The chip is the brain of the computer. It is made up of millions of transistors and other electronic components, yet is only 2cm by 2cm or so in size. The 'Pentium' chip, made by Intel is the commonest chip in desktop computers.

Obviously, such a marvel of miniaturisation could not be made by sitting at a work bench and soldering all the bits together. Rather, chips are made by a special type of photographic process whereby the design of the circuit is etched on to the blank chip. As it is made by such a process, it can be copied in a similar manner.

The design of chips is protected in the EU by Directive 87/54/EEC. This has now been implemented in the UK by the Design Right (Semiconductor Topographies) Regulations 1989, SI 1989/1100. Regulation 2(1) defines a semiconductor topography as a design within s 213 of the CDPA 1988 and which relates to a semiconductor product or component thereof. The design has to be recorded in a design document.

Under the 1989 Regulations, there is prohibition of:

- unauthorised copying of a chip; and
- importation into, or sale in, the UK of unauthorised copy chips (but note that exhaustion of rights applies to sales within the EU; see further on this, Chapter 19).

Note that reverse engineering is not prohibited, so it is permissible for a third party to work out from the chip topography how it works, and then to produce a chip that performs the same function.

The right lasts for 15 years from creation of the design or 10 years from first sale of objects made to that design, whichever is the shorter (cf the period for UDR; see further Chapter 15).

A2.4 HARDWARE CONTRACTS

The 'hardware' is the computer equipment. If you buy a computer, you are simply buying electrical equipment; therefore the contract for the purchase of computer hardware is a contract for sale of goods, and is in principle the same as, for example buying a fridge from Comet. However, there is one important practical difference: it is fairly obvious when a fridge is not working properly, but it is more debatable whether or not a particular computer is doing all the things it is supposed to. Part of this problem is that it is the software which tells the hardware what to do (for more detail on software, see **A2.5**).

Consequently, it is suggested that in producing a specification for a new computer system, it is better to specify the software first and then specify that the hardware to be supplied has to be able to run it (ie make the buyer's particular purpose expressly known).

Note that, in practice, it is possible either to buy or to lease hardware. With the decrease in the cost of hardware, buying has become more common in recent years. However, if the system is a major installation, then leasing would still be encountered. In this case, the contract would be of a different type (see **A2.4.2**).

The remainder of this section considers some of the legal issues which may arise in relation to computer hardware.

A2.4.1 Pre-contract issues: negotiation

In *Mackenzie Patten & Co v British Olivetti Ltd* [1984] 1 CL & P 92, a firm of solicitors bought a computer system to run their accounts. The sales representative made various claims for the system. However, there was an exclusion clause in the contract in relation to his statements. The firm signed the contract. The system proved to be slow and hard to use. It was held that Olivetti were bound by the representative's claims, on the basis of a collateral contract.

A2.4.2 Leasing

With a lease of computer hardware, the lessee has the right to use the equipment, but the lessor remains the owner of it. The SGSA 1982 is relevant here (the SGSA 1982 characterises a contract of this type as a contract of hire, but the term 'lease' is more commercially usual in practice).

Most computer leases will be 'finance leases'. This is a commercial term used to distinguish it from an 'operating lease'. With an operating lease, the equipment is hired out to the user (the lessee) for a short period of time, returned to the lessor and then hired out to another user (this is, eg, how a tool-hire shop would normally operate). With a finance lease, the equipment is supplied only to one user, who retains possession of it for substantially the whole of its working life.

A finance lease basically works as follows. The finance company (lessor) acquires the computer hardware by buying it from a supplier.

The finance company pays the supplier for the hardware. It then leases the hardware to the user, and the user pays the finance company a leasing payment, probably monthly. At the end of the lease, the hardware will have little residual value and will be sold off by the lessor. The lessor may credit the user with the sale proceeds (depending on the terms of the lease) but the user must not have the right to acquire title to the hardware, otherwise it will be a hire purchase contract, not a lease.

With a finance lease, note that there is no contractual relationship between the user and the supplier of the hardware. Therefore, it can be difficult for the user to obtain redress against the supplier. This problem can be solved by:

- *assignment of rights* by the finance company to the user, but the user's damages would be limited to those recoverable by the finance company, which could be nothing;
- *partial novation*, where the deal is structured as a sale to the user from the supplier to the user, followed by novation of the financial terms between the finance company and the seller, leaving the seller liable to the user for, for example, the warranties on the system; and
- *a direct collateral contract*, where a collateral contract dealing with, for example the warranties which cover the hardware, is created between the user and the seller.

Note that the lease should provide for the following matters where the user breaches the lease:

- the lessor to have the right to repossess the equipment (so the lease should include a right of entry on to the premises);
- a liquidated damages clause; this is more appropriate than unliquidated damages which would be difficult to calculate, as the lessor has a duty to mitigate; or
- minimum payments, including accelerated payment of all future payments on default.

A2.4.3 Sale

As noted above, a contract for the sale of hardware is in principle the same as for the sale of any other electrical item. However, the following points will require particular care.

(1) Delivery

Depending on the terms of a sale of goods contract, non-delivery or late delivery may entitle the buyer of goods to reject them. Remember, however, that this is only possible if the time for delivery is of the essence (ie a condition of the contract). Problems with hardware contracts can arise if the equipment is being specially produced or modified, or because the supplier is itself waiting for supplies of parts. In such cases, it may not be feasible for the parties to nominate a specific delivery date. It then has to be decided whether the goods have been delivered within a reasonable time. If the delay means that the intended use is no longer practicable, then a reasonable time has elapsed. It is advisable for the buyer to inform the supplier at the outset of the intended uses of the equipment. However, it would be best also for the buyer to specify an end-stop date after which the equipment will not be accepted.

(2) Payment and changes of specification

Terms on price and payment will need careful consideration.

In major hardware contracts, some changes of specification are likely (eg it emerges in discussions between the supplier and the buyer that the buyer's future business plans make it advisable to increase the number of file servers, or specification of the desktop computers). Changes should be categorised as those which are at the buyer's expense and those which are at the seller's expense.

Payment under hardware contracts is commonly made in instalments as the various parts of the system are delivered. The buyer normally retains part of the total price until the complete system has been successfully tested.

Remember that SGA 1979, s 10(1) provides that time is not of the essence in a sale of goods agreement unless otherwise agreed; thus late payment does not entitle the seller to treat the contract as at an end unless the contract provides that the seller has this right.

(3) Passing of risk and property

SGA 1979, s 20(1) provides that risk (of accidental loss or damage to the goods) passes at the same time as property (ie ownership). Sections 16–19 dictate when the property in the goods passes. The issue is important in deciding which party should bear the risk, and therefore the cost of insurance, so remember that ss 16–20 can be ousted by contrary agreement. The parties should consider what is important to them, and provide accordingly.

(4) Retention of title

A properly drafted retention of title clause provides added protection for the seller.

(5) Seller's obligations

Remember that in a sale of goods agreement, various conditions will be implied into the agreement by the SGA 1979:

- s 12 – that the seller will give good title and quiet possession (eg the hardware will be free of third-party IP rights);
- s 13 – sale by description (the Misrepresentation Act 1967 could also be relevant);
- s 14(2) – satisfactory quality (it is, however, normally better to define 'quality' in the contract than to rely on the statutory complied condition); and
- s 14(3) – reasonable fitness for buyer's purpose (remember that the buyer has to make his purpose known to the seller).

Note that because the functioning of hardware is controlled by the software (ie the program), it is often difficult to assess the hardware independently in relation to quality issues.

The implied terms in ss 13 and 14 can be excluded from the contract subject to UCTA 1977. This would often be done in computer supply contracts. In their place, the supplier would offer a warranty that the system complies with the specification agreed with the customer.

(6) Buyer's remedies

Under SGA 1979, s 11(3), the buyer can reject the goods for breach of condition.

Rejection of the goods is the buyer's primary remedy if the seller commits breach of condition. However, this may not be feasible commercially (eg if the hardware is specially adapted or made so that it would be difficult for the buyer to find an alternative supplier at short notice, or possibly at all).

In any event, the right to reject is lost if the goods have been accepted (see SGA 1979, s 35). Acceptance may arise in the following ways:

(i) Hardware contracts will contain acceptance-testing clauses, which would require that the hardware is able to perform certain defined tasks which demonstrate its capabilities. Passing the tests constitutes acceptance. Ordering more hardware from the same seller would normally also constitute acceptance.

(ii) Using the goods beyond mere testing may also constitute acceptance.

(iii) Retaining the goods beyond a reasonable time could also be acceptance. This could happen if the hardware is delivered in instalments.

Note that a buyer can elect not to reject the goods, and can claim damages instead (SGA 1979, s 11(2)). A buyer could waive his right to reject, for example where the hardware is not delivered on time and the buyer presses the seller to make delivery as soon as possible.

(7) Seller's remedies

If the buyer refuses to accept the goods, the seller can sue for the price, but will have to mitigate by trying to re-sell the hardware. The question will then arise: is there a market for this particular hardware, and will the seller be able to get the same price? The seller could be awarded his lost profit under SGA 1979, s 50(2) if he can show that there are few alternative buyers.

(8) Exclusion clauses

In many cases, UCTA 1977 will apply to a hardware contract. The most likely application is in relation to attempted exclusions of SGA 1979, ss 13–14 (ie the implied conditions of description, satisfactory quality and reasonable fitness for purpose). In a commercial sale, the test will be one of 'reasonableness' (UCTA 1977, s 6).

The leading computer case on exclusion clauses is *St Albans City and District Council v ICL* [1996] 4 All ER 481. The loss suffered by St Albans District Council as a result of the computer system supplied by ICL failing to work properly was £1.3m, but the contract contained an exclusion of loss clause for losses over £100,000 (ie compensation for loss caused was limited to this sum). This was held to be unreasonable because:

- ICL had more resources than the council did;
- ICL had product liability insurance of £50m worldwide;
- ICL could not justify the £100,000 limit;
- the contract was signed on superseded standard terms;
- local authorities are limited in what they can insure against;
- St Albans received no inducement to agree; and
- ICL had said that negotiation over terms would delay implementation of the deal.

Since the *St Albans* case was decided, the restrictive interpretation of exclusion clauses was extended in *South West Water Services Ltd v International Computers Ltd* [1999] Build LR 420. The defendant was held to be dealing on standard terms even though the terms had been varied by negotiation. The terms were therefore subject to the reasonableness test under UCTA 1977, s 3(1). (The terms also purported to exclude liability for fraudulent misrepresentation and were held unreasonable under s 3 of the Misrepresentation Act 1967.)

The tide has gone the other way to an extent with the case of *Watford Electronics Ltd v Sanderson CFL Ltd* [2001] 1 All ER (Comm) 696. An interesting point that went against the claimants is that they themselves used a limitation of liability clause in their own terms. They were therefore held to be aware of the commercial considerations and the effect on the price agreed for the job.

A2.4.4 Maintenance agreements

Computer hardware will normally come with a guarantee (usually called a warranty); an express promise from the supplier that it will do or provide certain things if the hardware goes wrong.

After the warranty expires, it makes sense for a buyer to set up a maintenance agreement for commercial hardware.

The key points for the owner of the hardware and the provider of the maintenance to consider when setting up such an agreement are:

- should it provide for repair on site or return to base?
- the desired response time from the provider (the faster it is, the more expensive it is);
- is replacement equipment to be provided in the interim whilst repair is carried out?
- duration of the contract – the older the equipment, the more repairs it will need and the more it will cost to maintain; and
- is transfer of the agreement to a new owner of the hardware permitted, as this will increase the second-hand value of the hardware?

A2.4.5 System supply contracts

A system supply contract is where the buyer receives some or all of the following:

- hardware;
- software;
- cabling, power supply;
- services (eg installation, maintenance, support, systems integration).

Note that in a 'turnkey' contract (where the system is supplied ready to run, usually with all software and peripherals such as printers), the supplier may buy in various aspects of the goods or services, almost certainly including the software. This would be licensed direct to the user, rather than by licence to the supplier and sub-licence from him to the user. It is important that the user evaluates the terms of the licences to see if they are suitable for his purposes.

A2.5 SOFTWARE

'Software' means the computer program(s). It is the instructions which tell the hardware what to do.

Software can be 'off the peg' (ie a standard package) or 'made to order'. Standard package software will be cheaper than made to order, but may not fulfil the user's requirements adequately. A middle way for the buyer of software to choose is to adapt standard software, in effect customising it. The trend is toward increased sales of standard software.

There is also a distinction between system software, which organises the way the hardware operates, and applications software, which performs the function required by the user (eg 'Word' or 'Powerpoint' are applications software). System software is normally supplied by the maker of the hardware (eg the BIOS – the Basic Input/Output System).

A2.5.1 The functional specification

Before selecting (application) software, a user will write down his requirements in a detailed document. This is known as the functional specification, and is central to the tendering process (that is, when the user is seeking quotations for the work) and to the contract for the supply of the software itself.

In *Micron Computer Systems v Wang (UK) Ltd* (1990) unreported, 9 May, the user failed in a claim against a supplier because it had failed to make known its requirement that 'transactional logging' (in effect, a sophisticated backup program) be included in the system.

In *St Albans City and District Council v ICL* (see above), the invitation to tender was incorporated into the contract. The relevant requirements had been included, so the supplier was in breach of the contract.

A2.5.2 What is software?

The problem is whether, legally speaking, software is classified as goods or services, and therefore which implied terms are relevant. This makes it necessary to consider the nature of software.

Software consists of many thousands of lines of written instructions, and is usually sold on floppy disks or CD-ROM disks. The disks themselves are clearly 'goods', but what about the instructions (the program)? In the *St Albans* case, Glidewell LJ said that:

> 'A computer disk is within the definition of goods contained in s 61 of the Sale of Goods Act 1979 and s 18 of the Supply of Goods and Services Act 1982. A computer program, however, is not. Nevertheless, if a disk onto which a program designed and intended to instruct or enable a computer to achieve particular functions has been encoded is sold or hired but the program is defective, so that it will not instruct or enable the computer to achieve the intended purpose, the seller or hirer of the disk will be in breach of the terms as to quality and fitness for purpose implied by s 14 of the 1979 Act and s 9 of the 1982 Act.'

(Remember that both SGA 1979, s 14 and SGSA 1982, s 9 (the '1982 Act' mentioned above) deal with satisfactory quality and reasonable fitness for the buyer's purpose.)

On the other hand, if the software was regarded as services, the standard which the provider of the services would have to reach is that of providing those services with reasonable skill and care under SGSA 1982, s 13.

In practice, the legal status of software remains something of a grey area.

A2.5.3 Software licensing

Software licensing came about with the appearance at the end of the 1960s of writers of software who were independent of the hardware manufacturers. Before then, the hardware manufacturers included the software with their systems. (Remember that, at that time, there were no desktop computers – the 1960s computers filled entire rooms, cost a fortune and did little more than a modern calculator would.)

It was not clear that copyright existed in software at that time, so licensing contracts treated software like confidential information (see Chapter 17) and therefore had restrictions on disclosure and copying. Today's software supply contracts are basically copyright licences (see Chapter 13), but also contain terms dealing with the supply of the physical manifestations of the software (eg sometimes retaining title to the disks, or forbidding the possession of more than one set of back-up disks, or forbidding use other than on specified hardware).

As noted at **A2.2.1**, there is specific legal provision on the IP position for software. Originally, the Copyright (Computer Software) Amendment Act 1985 provided that copyright exists in software as literary works. This was superseded by s 3(1) of the CDPA 1988, but the position remains the same. Under s 17(2) of CDPA 1988, unauthorised storage of a program in a computer is copyright infringement. EC Directive 91/250/EEC specifies further legal protection for software. It is implemented in the UK by the Copyright (Computer Programs) Regulations 1992.

Even where software is sold over the counter, licensing is still relevant. In this case, the software house tries to impose a licence on the user by specifying that opening the cellophane in which the software is wrapped constitutes acceptance of the terms of the standard-form licence visible through the wrapper (this is known as a 'shrink-wrap' licence, and is considered further at **A2.5.6**).

(What will in practice happen in this sort of 'consumer' sale of software and shrink-wrap licence is that the software creator (eg Microsoft) will sell the software to a retailer (eg computer shop). The shop sells the software on to the customer; it is, however, Microsoft which imposes the shrink-wrap licence on the customer.)

A2.5.4 Principal commercial terms in a software contract

(1) Delivery

Software is usually delivered as 'object code'. In this form, it can be read by a computer and put into operation. However, software is actually written in source code (that is, the lines of instructions written by the programmer). In order to correct or update the software, access to the source code is needed. Hence the software supplier will only supply the object code to its customers, specifically so the customer cannot alter the software (the contract usually provides (in effect) that the source code will not be supplied; in fact, what will most commonly happen is that it will provide expressly if the code *is* to be supplied).

(2) Acceptance

The software contract should specify the tests which the software has to pass in order to be accepted by the user. One important matter which will be dependent on acceptance is payment for the software. Acceptance will trigger payment of the whole fee or the final instalment (as the case may be) of a lump sum fee or the start of payments in the case of a periodic fee (see *(3)* below).

After acceptance, the licensee's remedy will be for breach of warranty if problems arise with the software.

(3) Payment

Obviously, under a commercial deal, the licensee will have to pay the licensor for the software. The contract could provide for a lump sum (which may be broken down into instalments) or a periodic fee.

With a lump sum, instalments may be payable on each of the following events: signature of contract, delivery of software, and software acceptance. Problems may arise because the parties' 'ideal' situations on payment are likely to differ considerably. Normally, for example, the licensor will be keen to be paid as soon as possible but the licensee will not pay until it is happy with the software (in practice, what the contract actually provides on payment will depend on bargaining power; in other words, it is like any other commercial agreement).

With the periodic fee, there may be provisions to increase the fee (eg once a year). There is often a provision for interest on overdue payments.

(4) Term and termination

The licence will often be perpetual, subject to termination on reasonable notice.

(5) Warranties

NB Contract terms in this context are often referred to as 'warranties', regardless of their statutory status as conditions.

(A) IMPLIED TERMS

When title to (ie ownership of) the software is transferred, a sale of software is sale of goods under SGA 1979. When title is not transferred, the deal is a hiring under the SGSA 1982. The relevant implied terms therefore apply:

- right to sell or grant possession – SGA 1979, s 12(1) and (2); SGSA 1982, s 7(1) and (2); and
- description, satisfactory quality and reasonable fitness for buyer's purpose – SGA 1979, ss 13(1), 14(2), and 14(3); SGSA 1982, ss 8 and 9.

A problem with software is to what extent 'satisfactory quality' includes the 'bugs' (that is, the faults in the program).

In *Saphena Computing Ltd v Allied Collection Agencies Ltd* [1995] FSR 616, it was held that software should be reasonably fit for any purpose which the user has made known to the supplier.

(B) EXPRESS TERMS

Most software licences will exclude the implied statutory terms (within the limits of UCTA 1977) and will substitute express terms ('warranties').

Express terms fall into two categories:

- that the software will comply with the functional specification or the user manual, or meet specified performance criteria; or
- that defects in the software will be corrected by the supplier.

However, a key problem is deciding what constitutes a defect. Is failure to perform a certain task a 'defect', or is a defect an operation that is outside the capabilities of this software?

(C) LIMITATIONS ON 'WARRANTIES'

Common limitations are:

- any warranty relating to quality will have a duration of 3–12 months. Thereafter, a maintenance contract applies;
- the licensor's only liability is to correct the defect (ie it excludes the licensor's liability for damages); and
- warranties cease to apply if the licensee makes any additions or modifications to the software.

(6) Exclusion of liability

Where a contract term purports to exclude liability in relation to the implied terms of description, satisfactory quality or reasonable fitness for the buyer's purpose, the reasonableness test will apply where the buyer does not deal as consumer (UCTA 1977, s 6 for sale contracts and s 7 for a hiring). Note that the exclusion in Sch 1 to UCTA 1977 (contracts to which UCTA 1977 does not apply) in relation to IP issues does not apply to UCTA 1977, ss 6 and 7.

Remember that the implied terms in relation to title, freedom from charges and encumbrances, and quiet possession cannot be excluded in a sale contract. However, with a hiring, the right to give possession and quiet possession can be excluded if reasonable.

A2.5.5 Source code escrow

If the licensor fails for some reason to provide agreed software maintenance to the licensee (eg because the licensor goes out of business, or simply breaches its contractual duty to provide the maintenance), it would cause serious problems for the licensee, because the licensee will not normally be given the source code (see above).

A common way round the problem is to put the source code into escrow. Under the terms of the escrow agreement, the source code is released by the escrow agent (that is, a third party with whom the program is deposited) to the licensee on the occurrence of a specified event (eg the appointment of a receiver over the assets of the licensor). The National Computing Centre and the Computer Services Association both provide escrow services. The arrangements work successfully.

However, there is the potential for a receiver or liquidator to challenge release under an escrow agreement as a 'preference' under the Insolvency Act 1986, s 239, or disclaim the agreement as an 'unprofitable contract' under s 178 of that Act. It could also be a breach of the *pari passu* principle under s 107 (that is, the principle that the company's assets are distributed equally subject to the claims of the preferential creditors). It is also arguable that release under escrow would require a court order under s 127 of the Insolvency Act 1986.

A2.5.6 Shrink-wrap or click-wrap licensing

Most software today is bought off the shelf; that is, the software is a standard product, such as the 'Word' program used to create this document. As noted at **A2.5.3** above, in order to create a licence between the software creator and the user, the device known as a 'shrink-wrap licence' is used (there would otherwise only be a contractual link between the user and the retailer). This means that terms of use can therefore be imposed by the software creator on the user.

The terms of the licence are set out on the outside of the packaging and are visible through the clear wrapping. The licence purportedly comes into being when the user opens the packaging, supposedly having read the terms and agreed to them (see below for potential problems of enforceability).

A licensing method which has become more common in recent years, both with software downloaded through the internet and being downloaded from a CD-ROM, is that of the 'click-wrap' licence. This is where customers are faced with the text of a licence agreement on screen. The customers have to click on the 'I agree' button before they are allowed access to the software.

(1) Terms

Typical terms in a consumer licence include that:

- the licence is for use on one computer only;
- the software must not be copied (save for one back-up copy);
- the software must not be altered; and
- the licensor will replace defective disks and supply updates.

All other warranties or conditions are excluded (subject, of course, to the impact of UCTA 1977 or other provisions controlling exclusion or restriction of liability). As the licence will be a pure licence of the software creator's intellectual property rights, so the only heads of liability for the software creator are likely to be negligence or product liability. (Remember that exclusion of negligence will be subject to UCTA 1977, s 2; product liability cannot be excluded under s 7 of the Consumer Protection Act 1987.)

If the sale of software is a consumer sale, the Consumer Transactions (Restrictions on Statements) Order 1976 will apply. This requires there to be a statement that any warranty given does not affect the consumer's statutory rights. The Unfair Terms in Consumer Contracts Regulations 1999 may also be relevant in this situation (as noted in Chapter 2, these Regulations can only apply to consumer agreements).

(2) Enforceability

The shrink-wrap or click-wrap licence purports to be a bilateral contract. However, remember that an offeror (in this situation, the licensor) cannot unilaterally decide that silence will constitute acceptance. In the absence of an act by the user (eg signing a user registration card), the enforceability of the licence by the licensor is therefore dubious.

In the Scottish case of *Beta Computers (Europe) Ltd v Adobe Systems (Europe) Ltd* [1996] FSR 367, it was held that if the user had accepted the licence terms by opening the wrapping, then the licensor must be able to rely on the licence as a third party beneficiary under Scottish law.

Under English contract law, the doctrine of privity of contract caused problems in constructing valid contracts between the software creator and the retail customer. However, the Contracts (Rights of Third Parties) Act 1999 has solved many of the problems in this type of situation. Under the Act, the contract can only impose a benefit under the contract, not a burden though there is nothing to stop a third party from voluntarily accepting a burden, for example an obligation to provide 'hotline' support to sort out problems with software on customers' computers. The Act only applies to contracts entered into after 11 May 2000.

A2.5.7 Bespoke software

Bespoke software (ie software 'tailored' to the precise needs of a particular user) is expensive, and will be the subject of a specific contract negotiated between the software house and the user, who in legal terms is the commissioner of the software (this is relevant to the ownership of the IP rights in the software; see below).

In this case, software is written to fulfil the functional specification put forward by the user. The software house will depend on the user supplying information on its business and how it is run in order to create a satisfactory program.

The specification may change during the design of the program, and the costs of such alterations need to be allocated between the parties.

Acceptance tests will need to be devised. The user will not accept the software until these have been passed.

A key problem will be that of ownership of the copyright in the program. As noted in Chapter 13, the copyright will (subject, of course, to any contrary agreement) vest in the creator (ie author) of the work, not the person who commissions it. However, this may not fulfil the desires of the parties to the agreement here; the user might ideally want to have exclusive rights to the program which it paid the creator to devise, even if only to prevent third parties from benefiting from the program. The creator, on the other hand, would want to have the right to use at least some aspects of the program in future programs which they may write, not least because they regard it as part of their evolving expertise. In practice, this is another matter which will be determined by bargaining power; basically, users are unlikely to get exclusivity unless they are prepared to pay a substantial amount for it.

A contract for bespoke software will probably be construed as a contract for the supply of services and some ancillary goods. The SGSA 1982 will imply that the services be provided with reasonable skill and care, and that the materials must be reasonably fit for the user's purpose and of satisfactory quality. Specific warranties will often be included in the contract, for example that the software will meet the functional specification. As far as exclusion of terms is concerned, remember that UCTA 1977, s 2 provides that liability for negligence causing damage other than personal injury or death can only be excluded to the extent it is reasonable.

A2.5.8 Software maintenance

Software maintenance comprises:

* the correction of errors (so-called 'bugs') in the software; and
* providing enhancements and updates.

There will be a free warranty for the first 3–12 months after supply of the software. Thereafter, the user will need to take out a maintenance agreement if it wishes to ensure the continued running of that software.

As noted above, users of software will not normally be able to undertake maintenance themselves, as they will not have been supplied with the 'source code' of the software (ie the form in which the software is written and can be corrected). However, this is not always so. In *Andersen Consulting v CHP Consulting Ltd* (1991) unreported, 26 July, ChD, it was held that as the contract in that case provided for the supply of the source code to the user, there must have been the intent that the user was to be able to do the software maintenance.

Usually, under the contract, the supplier will only be obliged to provide those updates which it is making generally available to its customers. On the other hand, the user will be obliged to utilise all the updates made available to them, so that the supplier's customer base will all be operating with the same versions of the software. This will make life easier for the supplier.

A2.6 THE INTERNET

The internet is a system of linked computers throughout most of the world. It started off in the United States as a means of minimising the effects of a nuclear strike on the command system of the armed services, but has grown vastly since then, and is expected to continue to grow. It can be regarded as a sort of electronic post office and library.

A2.6.1 Using a name

In order to send a message over the internet, it has to have an address to go to. An Internet Protocol address has the form '130.132.59.234'. As the Internet Protocol addresses are essentially forgettable, the Domain Name System (DNS) was devised. 'Domain names' are names rather than numbers, and are translated into Internet Protocol addresses by some of the computers in the internet. An example of a domain name is 'lawcol.co.uk'. So, for example, a message could be sent to Trevor.Adams@lawcol.co.uk.

Domain names have different 'levels'; for example, the top-level domain name in the above example is 'uk'. Obviously, this is the country where the relevant party is located. Other examples of top-level domain names are '.com', '.gov' or '.org'. There is little dispute about these. Rather, the problems which arise in relation to domain names usually concern the second-level names, especially where that name is the trade mark, registered or not, of a commercial product or organisation, (eg 'McDonalds.com'). Clearly, unauthorised use of that domain name would upset a certain chain of burger restaurants.

In the UK, the organisation known as Nominet allocates domain names and does so on the basis of first come, first served. It is located at www.nic.uk.

In the United States, and in effect internationally as well, the body known as the Internet Corporation for Assigned Names and Numbers (ICANN) deals with many domain name issues also and is located at www.icann.org. It has just set up some new top-level domain names at the time of writing, for example '.pro' for lawyers and accountants. WIPO also has an input into domain name issues especially from the trade mark perspective, and runs a dispute resolution procedure.

In England, in the case of *British Telecommunications and Others v One in a Million Ltd; Marks & Spencer plc v One in a Million Ltd; Virgin Enterprises Ltd v One in a Million Ltd; J Sainsbury plc v One in a Million Ltd; Ladbroke Group plc v One in a Million Ltd* [1999] 1 WLR 903, the Court of Appeal held that the use of various business names as domain names without consent was passing off and infringement of the registered trade marks under the Trade Marks Act 1994. The claimants were BT, Sainsbury's, Virgin, Ladbrokes and Marks and Spencer. Following this case, it seems clear that unauthorised use of a business name as a domain name will be taken by the English courts as being passing off and trade mark infringement (assuming that there is a valid trade mark registration). In the *Bonnier* case in **11.9**, it was held by the Scottish Court of Session that the intent of the infringer was a critical factor, ie were they intending to defraud the legitimate user of the trade mark?

If a domain name is a registered trade mark, the criteria used to decide if there is infringement are those under the Trade Marks Act 1994. In particular, the criteria identified the case of *British Sugar plc v James Robertson & Sons Ltd* [1996] RPC 281 concerning the use of the word 'Treat' in relation to sweet sauces and syrups.

Even if the trade mark is not in use in the UK, it may be protected in the UK as a 'well known mark' under s 56 of the 1994 Act (see **11.10**).

A2.6.2 Copyright issues

In the case of *Shetland Times v Wills* [1997] FSR 604, the Shetland News internet site had a link which enabled the reader to access pages from the *Shetland Times*, but without seeing the front page of *The Times*. Such unauthorised use of *The Times* pages was held to be breach of copyright.

The BBC has recently undertaken similar action in regard to infringement via the internet of its copyright in the Teletubbies.

A2.6.3 Intercepting communications

The Regulation of Investigatory Powers Act 2000 makes it illegal for a business to intercept communications without the consent of both the sender and recipient. Permitted interceptions may be allowed under the Telecommunications (Lawful Business Practice) (Interception of Communications) Regulations 2000, SI 2000/2699. However, even permitted interceptions may fall foul of the Human Rights Act 1998 or the Data Protection Act 1998.

See also the offences under the Computer Misuse Act 1990 at **A2.7**.

A2.7 COMPUTER CRIME

There have been attempts in the past to use the law of theft and criminal damage in relation to problems related to computers (eg problems caused by hackers, people who attempt to gain unauthorised access to computer systems). The problems in using the conventional law proved to be immense; what has been stolen, or what has been damaged? The Computer Misuse Act 1990 seeks to avoid such esoteric questions by creating offences that are specific to computers.

A2.7.1 Section 1 – unauthorised access, hacking and like activities

Section 1 of the Computer Misuse Act 1990 makes it an offence to obtain unauthorised access to a computer system as follows:

'(1)   A person is guilty of an offence if—

   (a)   he causes a computer to perform any function with intent to secure access to any program or data held in any computer;
   (b)   the access he intends to secure is unauthorised; and
   (c)   he knows at the time when he causes the computer to perform the function that that is the case.'

The punishment is a maximum of 6 months' imprisonment and/or a fine.

In *Ellis v Director of Public Prosecutions* [2001] EWHC Admin 362, (2001) unreported, 15 May the appellant had been convicted of offences under s 1 of the 1990 Act, which were upheld on appeal. He was entitled as a graduate to use computers in the library but only those designated as open access, which could not access the internet. However, he had used non-open access computers in the university library, which he had found to be already logged on to the internet. He used his unauthorised access to browse various internet sites. Lord Woolf CJ held that s 1 was wide enough to cover the actions of the appellant and upheld the convictions.

A2.7.2 Section 2 – the ulterior intent offence

This is committed by a person who secures unauthorised access to a computer system with the intent of using that access to facilitate the commission of a further serious criminal offence. Such offences are those where the sentence is fixed by law (eg murder) or where a first offender aged over 21 years could be sentenced to 5 years in jail. For example, a case has been reported in France where access was sought to medical records in order to blackmail sufferers of AIDS; if such facts arose within the UK, they would be capable of giving rise to the s 2 offence.

In *R v Delamere* [2003] EWCA Crim 424, (2003) unreported, 11 February the appellant had pleaded guilty to two counts under s 2(1)(b). He was a bank employee and had provided details of two bank accounts to two people known to him. In the end, he was not paid for the information. The two acquaintances were convicted of attempting to obtain property be deception and given community punishment orders. The appellant's sentence was reduced on appeal from 8 months in custody to 4 months.

A2.7.3 Section 3 – modification of computer material

The act must be intended to impair the operation of a computer or to prevent or hinder access to any programs or data, or to impair the operation of any program or reliability of the data. Sending out a computer virus would come within s 3, as would deleting or altering data, or indeed adding jocular comments to the Duke of Edinburgh's email *(R v Gold* [1988] 2 WLR 984, where the prosecution failed).

The offences in ss 2 and 3 are triable either way. The maximum sentence is 5 years' imprisonment.

In *R v Maxwell-King* [2000] 2 Cr App R (S) 136, the appellant had his sentence reduced to 150 hours community service from 4 months' imprisonment. His company had had to pay £10,000 costs. He had engaged in the small-scale manufacture of 'multi-mode' boards for computers, which allowed access to television channels without paying the subscription. This was apparently the first case under s 3 of the 1990 Act. Wright J described the subject area as:

> 'a field which makes up for in fascination what it loses in obscurity.'

In *R v Parr-Moore and Crumblehulme* [2003] 1 Cr App R (S), the Court of Appeal decreased the sentences of the appellants from 7 months in custody to 4 months. They had manufactured and distributed devices known as cable cubes. These allow people who subscribe to cable television services to view programmes, which they had not paid for. They had made a total profit of about £6,000 from the sale of the cubes. They had both pleaded guilty.

In *R v Lindesay* [2001] EWCA Crim 1720, [2002] 1 Cr App R (S) 86, an appeal against of a sentence of 9 months in custody was not allowed. The defendant was a computer consultant. He had been dismissed from his job with a computer company. In a fit of pique, he had accessed the internet sites of three clients of the computer company and had deleted contents and images but not done major harm. The total cost of the damage was estimated to be £9,000.

In *Zezev, Yarimaka v the Governor of HM Prison Brixton, the Government of the United States of America* [2002] EWHC 589 (Admin), [2002] Crim LR 648, it was held that the offence allegedly committed by the applicants was equivalent to the s 3 offence. They were also charged with four counts of blackmail and two of conspiracy. The applicant, Zezev, was employed by a company in Kazakstan, which used the services of Bloomberg LP. This is a business which provides news and financial information. Zezev and Yarimaka gained unauthorised access from Kazakstan to the Bloomberg system (which is located in New York). They were able to access the email accounts of Mr Bloomberg himself and his head of security. They demanded $200,000 from Mr Bloomberg or they would reveal the breach of security to Bloomberg clients. Their extradition to the United States was being sought, and was granted.

A2.7.4 Jurisdiction

The Computer Misuse Act 1990 introduces the concept of a 'significant link' with one of the UK jurisdictions. In the case of the s 1 or s 3 offences, it is enough that either the offender or victim was located within the jurisdiction. For the s 3 offence, the court only has jurisdiction if the further act would be an offence in the country where it was intended that it should occur.

A2.8 DATA PROTECTION

The Data Protection Act 1998 has revised the law in this area.

The Act, which is complex, extends the principles of the Data Protection Act 1984. Broadly, it consists of provisions for:

- notification by those who use data;
- general data protection principles; and
- a supervisory body headed by the Data Protection Commissioner.

The 1998 Act includes manual records, not just computer ones, as was the case under the 1984 Act.

Key definitions include:

- 'processing', which includes altering, retrieving, or disposing of data;
- 'data controller', who is the person who determines the purposes for which data are to be processed; and
- 'data processor', who is the person who processes data on behalf of the data controller. (Note that the data controller is responsible for the actions of the data processor.)

Common conditions that have to be met are:

- that the data subject (ie the person to whom the data relate) has given his consent to processing; or
- that processing is necessary for the performance of a contract to which he is a party.

Data subjects have the right to:

- be informed that data is being processed;
- the nature of the data;
- require that data is not processed if it causes them damage or distress; and
- object to direct marketing.

For transfers of data outside the EEA, the countries of destination have to have an equivalent level of data protection. For example, Japan and the USA do *not* meet this requirement, though an agreement with the USA looks imminent.

A2.9 THE DATABASE RIGHT

As noted in Chapter 14, this is a relatively new right relating to the keeping of information. The Copyright and Rights in Databases Regulations 1997 implement Directive 96/9/EC on the legal protection of databases by amending the Copyright Designs and Patents Act 1988.

A 'database' is defined in CDPA 1988, s 3A(1) (see **14.2**). In practice, a database could, for example, be information on the daily price of stocks and shares, a telephone directory, 'Lexis', or the CD-ROM law reports. Copyright protection is afforded to a database specifically as a literary work, although the standard is not only that of originality, but also that it is the 'author's intellectual creation'. This seems to be a higher standard than for copyright in literary works in general.

Whether or not it is protected by copyright, a database also attracts a new database right, which arises automatically. The database right runs for 15 years from the end of the year of completion. It prevents unauthorised use of the database or a substantial part of it.

As noted in **14.2**, data arrangements have the protection of database right if there is a substantial investment (including any investment, whether of financial, human or technical resources):

- in quality or quantity;
- in obtaining, verifying or presenting the data.

Further points to consider in relation to database right are as follows.

Qualifications for the database right

There are copyright-style qualification requirements (Copyright and Rights in Databases Regulations 1997, reg 18) based on nationality or corporate seat.

Ownership of the database right

The maker of a database protected by the database right is the person who takes the initiative in obtaining, verifying or presenting the contents of the database and who assumes the risk of investing in that obtaining. (See Copyright and Rights in Databases Regulations 1997, reg 14).

The maker is the first owner of the database right (reg 15).

Duration of lesser protection

The database right lasts for the longer of 15 years from the end of the calendar year:

- of completion of the database; or
- during which the database was first made available to the public (reg 17).

A 'substantial new investment' (see above) will 'top up' the right so the period starts again.

Infringement of the database right

Infringement is the extraction or re-utilisation of all or a substantial part of the contents of a database without the consent of the owner (reg 16).

'Extraction' means the permanent or temporary transfer of the contents of a database to another medium by any means or in any form.

'Re-utilisation' means making those contents available to the public by any means.

'Substantial' is in terms of quality or quantity or both.

'Substantial part' can include repeated extraction and/or re-utilisation of insubstantial parts (reg 16(2)).

Exceptions from the database right

Database rights are not infringed (regs 19 and 20):

- by fair dealing with a substantial part of a database made available to the public if:
  - such dealing is for illustration in teaching or research; and
  - sufficient acknowledgement is given;
- generally, by copying or use with the authority of the keeper of a database available for public inspection as a statutory record.

The database right can be licensed or assigned (as can the copyright in the database).

A2.10 WHAT IS E-COMMERCE?

This is a case of the existing law being applied to new facts. The term 'e-commerce' is a trendy term for doing business electronically with another party who may be located far away. The concept is hardly new, therefore, as international trade has been established for thousands of years. However, the process has speeded up with the arrival of the internet, and other electronic means of communication. Even so, the contractual process is still in many ways analogous to mail order transactions.

E-commerce encompasses both business to business transactions and business to consumer, sometimes referred to as 'B2B' and 'B2C'.

The internet also provides an excellent medium for advertising and for making contact with potential customers. This type of activity would usually be included in 'e-commerce'.

A2.10.1 Contract formation

The internet is international and without frontiers. Contracts can be entered into with ease and with little formality. There are questions as to the law of which country applies to the contract, which courts have jurisdiction and which legislation controls the contract.

In order to work out the legal consequences, it is necessary to analyse the chain of events to see if or when a contract has been formed. For example electronic messages could be classed as follows:

- the sending of mere information (eg 'I will be late for the meeting');
- the sending of unilateral messages (eg an invoice); and
- contract-forming messages (eg an offer of goods).

The basics of contract formation need to be considered. Is an advertisement on a website an offer or an invitation to treat? If it is an offer, then the consumer accepts it by keying in their credit card details. However, if it is an invitation to treat, then the consumer is making the offer which the website advertiser can accept or decline. There is an obvious analogy with goods in a shop window, which are taken to be an invitation to treat under English law. Similarly, it is likely that an advertisement on a website will be regarded as an invitation to treat.

A contract is formed under English law at the place and time that acceptance takes place. In the case of a telex transmission, it was held that the contract was formed when the acceptance was received, and was formed in the country where the acceptance was received (*Entores Ltd v Miles Far East Corporation* [1955] 2 QB 327).

The postal rule may be of application. Here, the offeror agrees that the offer has been transmitted to him when the acceptance is placed in the hands of the postal system. This would suggest by analogy that an electronic acceptance is effective when it is received by the network.

However, it is permissible to specify in a contract the acts which will constitute acceptance, and also the applicable law and jurisdiction. The Directive on Electronic Commerce, 2000/31/EC, requires the supplier to explain to the customer the steps which will give rise to a contract, and to make its terms available. It also provides that these communications are only effective when received.

A2.10.2 Evidential problems in proving there is a contract

There are prima facie problems with computer records which might render them inadmissible in evidence:

- they are not original;
- they may constitute hearsay; or
- some rule of law prevents them being admitted.

Section 1 of the Civil Evidence Act 1995 removes all of these potential problems. Under s 9, business records are admissible.

Electronic communications will be facilitated in various areas by the Electronic Communications Act 2000. There have already been amendments to the Companies Act 1985 (see Chapter 9 of the LPC Resource Book *Business Law and Practice* (Jordans)). In any event, CA 1985, s 723 permits company accounts to be kept electronically. Some forms can even be submitted electronically to Companies House.

A2.10.3 Applicable law and jurisdiction issues

E-commerce contracts are just international contracts, so if law and/or jurisdiction are not expressly dealt with in the contract, Regulation 44/2001 (Brussels II), and the Rome Convention will apply (see Chapter 7). This assumes that the other party is also resident in a state which is a member of the relevant Convention. (If they are not, then the situation is less certain and beyond the scope of this book.)

An interesting example of jurisdiction problems in an internet dispute is *Bonnier Media v Greg Lloyd Smith* [2002] ETMR 86 (see **11.9**). The first defendant was a man domiciled in Greece, who was the managing director of the second defendant, a company incorporated in Mauritius with offices in London and Greece. The pursuer (claimant) was resident in Scotland. The matter concerned the use of the pursuer's registered trade mark, and passing off. In the Court of Session, Lord Drummond Young held that the court did have jurisdiction to hear the matter as the threatened tort would have been committed in Scotland, as the alleged acts were directed at the pursuer's business. This aspect of jurisdiction is taken from Article 5(3) of Brussels II. The court granted an injunction restraining use of the potentially infringing domain name.

A2.10.4 Business to business electronic commerce

This was solely conducted on private networks until recently. It is usually referred to as Electronic Data Interchange (EDI). However, the internet is increasingly used.

The benefit to business may just be in speeding up transactions. For example, in the trade in one particular bulk chemical, there are four producers worldwide and 12 customers who use it as a raw material in their own processes. They already know each other but the benefit of e-commerce is that the customers can see at any time of the day the prices being offered by the four producers. They can then make a contract immediately with the cheapest, or possibly with the producer offering fastest delivery. The advantage is the time saved in the tendering process. This also makes 'just in time' ordering feasible so that the customer only needs to keep minimal stocks of raw material.

It is also possible with EDI to set up the system to form contracts automatically, perhaps when a certain price level is reached. In effect, many B2B systems will operate as an online auction. It is thus possible to automate the cycle of ordering, delivery and payment. It also means that a lot of paperwork is no longer needed.

Legal issues which may raise their head include that of competition law. There are two concerns. One is that commercial information can be exchanged between parties that has the effect of giving them an unfair advantage over businesses that are not participators in that B2B group. Another is the extent to which there is no free access to the market place for other parties, so that they are in effect excluded from the market place, or placed at a serious disadvantage. The more developed the B2B exchange system, the more likely it is to be essential to do business effectively in that particular market. It becomes a barrier to entry into the market. Thus, there are potential problems under Article 81, and possibly also under Article 82, of the EC Treaty (as amended by the Treaty of Amsterdam).

A2.10.5 Business to consumer electronic commerce

As well as the basic problems of contract formation (see **A2.10.1**), consumer protection legislation can impose constraints on the parties.

For example, Directive 97/7/EC on the Protection of Consumers in Respect of Distance Contracts ('the Distance Selling Directive') covers all situations where the seller and consumer are not face to face, including e-commerce. It requires the consumer to be given prior information about the contract, and gives the consumer the right to withdraw from the contract within 7 days of formation.

This area also impinges on consumer credit. For example, under s 75 of the Consumer Credit Act 1974, a consumer who pays for goods valued between £100 and £30,000 with a credit card has a claim against the credit card company if the seller does not fulfil their contractual obligations (see **A1.3.1**).

Provisions such as the Unfair Terms in Consumer Contracts Regulations 1999, SI 1999/2083 will govern the terms of consumer transactions. As these regulations derive from EC Directive 93/13/EEC, equivalent provisions will apply to consumer transactions concluded in any of the Member States.

The Directive on Electronic Signatures, 99/93/EC, requires Member States to ensure that their laws do not render electronic signatures inadmissible. The directive lays down a set of criteria for legal admissibility. 'Electronic signature' does not literally mean the computer writing out your name in handwriting. Rather, it means the provision of a means of identifying the contracting party. It could be a card with your details on it which can be swiped through an electronic reader, and identifies you to the person that you wish to contract with. In many cases, it would simply be a program on your computer that puts your email message into code before sending it. This code would be unique to you, and would enable the recipient to identify the message as a genuine one. The Directive has been implemented by the Electronic Signatures Regulations 2002, SI 2002/318. The regulations lay down the data protection requirements and provide for the supervision of certification service providers. These are the businesses which organise the encoding/decoding systems. As regards existing requirements in legislation for signature or for a matter to be in writing, the current view is that the definition of 'writing' in Sch 1 to the Interpretation Act 1978 includes electronic signatures. Extensive amendment of legislation is therefore not needed, though if it were it has been estimated that there are 40,000 provisions which would have to be changed.

The Data Protection Directive 95/46/EC will apply to information imparted during an e-commerce transaction (it is implemented in the UK as the Data Protection Act 1998). The Directive requires that personal data may only be processed with the consent of the data subject, or as is necessary for performance of the contract with them. The European Convention on Human Rights could also apply to e-commerce, notably Article 8 on the right to privacy including correspondence. Article 10 on the right to freedom of expression may also be relevant.

The Electronic Commerce (EC Directive) Regulations 2002, SI 2002/2013 apply to all businesses that trade or advertise goods or services over the internet. The regulations require such businesses to give information about themselves on their sites, including their geographical location, full contact details and a clear statement of prices, taxes charged and delivery costs. The Directive on Privacy and Electronic

Communications 2002/58/EC will control commercial email promotions sent to the public.

A2.10.6 Advertising to consumers

When a business places an advertisement on an internet site, it is in effect advertising to the world. (The situation is different in the business to business EDI site, as that is a closed network.)

Most jurisdictions will have controls on advertising. In the UK, perhaps there are two areas of most concern. The first is financial services. The Financial Services and Markets Act 2000 has been drafted to include internet usage. The Act regulates a wide variety of financial activities primarily in relation to shares and there is a prohibition on unauthorised persons promoting financial services. There is an exemption for internet advertisements which are not directed at the UK. Other regulations such as the Public Offers of Security Regulations 1995 may apply. These regulations require a prospectus to be published where securities that are not to be listed on the London Stock Exchange are offered to the public for the first time, unless the offer comes within the exemptions in reg 4. An offer of securities on the internet could fall within these regulations.

The Electronic Commerce Directive (Financial Services and Markets) Regulations 2002, SI 2002/1775 implement the Directive on Distance Selling of Financial Services.

The second area is medical advertising. In the UK, the advertising of medicines to the general public is tightly controlled by the Medicines Act 1968, and regulations thereunder. This is because medicinal products in the UK can only be used on humans after a lengthy period of testing and regulatory approval. It is also due to the fact that medical professionals are deemed to be in a better position to judge which medicine is appropriate for which patient. This control is not necessarily as tight in other jurisdictions where it is possible to advertise directly to the general public, for example the United States, and to sell medicines to them without a doctor's prescription.

A2.11 USEFUL INTERNET ADDRESSES

Readers wishing to explore these issues further may like to look at www.wipo.org and www.icann.com.

INDEX

References are to paragraph and Appendix numbers.